How to Market Your School

How to Market Your School

A guide to marketing, public relations, and communication for school administrators

Johanna M. Lockhart

iUniverse, Inc.
New York Lincoln Shanghai

How to Market Your School
A guide to marketing, public relations, and communication for school administrators

iUniverse books may be ordered through booksellers or by contacting:

iUniverse
2021 Pine Lake Road, Suite 100
Lincoln, NE 68512
www.iuniverse.com
1-800-Authors (1-800-288-4677)

ISBN-13: 978-0-595-36133-5 (pbk)
ISBN-13: 978-0-595-67337-7 (cloth)
ISBN-13: 978-0-595-80574-7 (ebk)
ISBN-10: 0-595-36133-1 (pbk)
ISBN-10: 0-595-67337-6 (cloth)
ISBN-10: 0-595-80574-4 (ebk)

Printed in the United States of America

I dedicate this book to my first grandchild, Ian John Lockhart, born July 29, 2004. The educational environment that prepares him for his role in life will include inventions and discoveries unimagined in my school days or even those of his parents. I hope that among the advantages that enhance his learning experience will be dedicated teachers and administrators who understand the power they have to shape, even change lives through high professional standards, a caring nature, and a love for giving the gift of knowledge.

Contents

Preface

The present environment for public schools is unlike any in the past. This new environment calls for public schools to do something that would have been unheard of fifteen, even ten, years ago—market themselves.

Schools are no longer dealing with students, parents, staff members, and the community in their traditional roles. These groups are now "customers" who can choose to attend, work in, and support a school or not. Their choices are dependent upon the public's perception of public education in general and their local schools in particular.

Successfully marketing a school or district involves a concerted effort that includes public relations, media relations, relationship management, and communication. However, many school administrators are not familiar with these fields. Two years ago, at the request of school administrators in the Houston Independent School district, I created a workshop, *Marketing Your School*. The administrators who attended were aware that the landscape was changing for public schools, and they wanted practical tools and skills to control the new environment rather than be controlled by it.

The success of the *Marketing Your School* workshops led to a subsequent program, *Building Beneficial Partnerships*. As I conducted these workshops, participants repeatedly expressed a desire for a user-friendly guidebook to help them as they implemented their marketing and public relations initiatives. I designed *How to Market Your School* to meet that need. Whatever your goals are, I hope *How to Market Your School* is a book in your collection that will become worn from use.

Introduction

Many district and school administrators view school marketing with the same enthusiasm as regulatory mandates. It is one more thing they are told they should do, but resources and assistance are rarely available to help them in their efforts. Even those who enthusiastically recognize the benefits of marketing may feel ill prepared for the task.

When I conduct workshops for school administrators and their staff members, most of the participants embrace the marketing concept with enthusiasm, but others struggle against it. Marketing was not part of the job description when they chose to enter public education. However, whether those in public schools view the idea of marketing as exciting or bothersome, the need to market is not going away. If anything, the need will grow.

Actually, most schools already are marketing to some degree whether they call it that or not. Anytime a school seeks to improve its products and services, reach out to the community in positive ways, or communicate more effectively with its internal and external audiences, it is marketing. What many schools lack is the ability to maximize their efforts through an organized, strategic process.

When looking for guidance, school administrators often hear advice such as, "You need to have an effective brochure," or "The first thing to do is develop a good marketing plan." Other marketing advice stresses that utilizing public relations, developing media relations, conducting research, strengthening community partnerships, and implementing effective communication strategies are equally essential to any marketing effort. However, information to help school administrators know exactly how to do these things is limited.

Of the numerous marketing books, presentations, and seminars available, few address marketing for educational institutions, especially public schools. Most educators have neither the time nor the desire to decipher how to apply private sector marketing information to their particular school situations.

The purpose of *How to Market Your School* is to help principals, assistant principals, business managers, and district administrators apply the knowledge and tools used successfully in the private sector to organize, implement, and maintain an integrated marketing program that achieves their particular goals. Success in any complex endeavor requires an understanding of the fundamentals. Likewise, successful school marketing requires an understanding of the basic principles of integrated marketing.

Integrated marketing is an approach that recognizes activities such as public relations, media relations, communication, advertising, and relationship management as integral parts of the marketing effort. Benefits include a more efficient use of resources, improved communication, and better coordination of activities.

This book presents the fundamentals of integrated marketing without jargon, theory, or debate over the merits of the latest marketing trend (although they may be mentioned). However, to implement a marketing strategy, school administrators need to know how to apply those fundamentals effectively to the specific environment of their schools. Although the focus of this book is on the marketing of public schools and school districts, the ideas and concepts provided in this book are equally applicable to the marketing needs of private, parochial, for-profit, and charter schools.

Most of the book's content is presented through succinct explanations of the many ways that administrators can develop, implement, and maintain an on-going marketing program to promote their schools internally and externally. I chose this format because administrators in my workshops indicated that they do not have time to read the traditional text format to extract ideas and activities they can use. Having the information in manageable "chunks" they could read quickly was appealing.

The book organizes the content into eight chapters. Chapter 1, *School Marketing: What It Is and Why It Matters*, provides a definition of marketing as it applies to schools, speaks to the influences that make school marketing essential, and describes the benefits of an effective marketing program. Even administrators who are convinced of the importance of marketing should find this chapter helpful if they must persuade less than enthusiastic internal staff members, board members, and community partners of the importance of making a commitment to the school's or district's marketing efforts.

Building the foundation of a marketing program is described in Chapter 2, *Getting Started*. A systematic, well-informed start is the most critical step in any marketing strategy. Marketing efforts will be disorganized and unproductive without a sound beginning. A sound beginning requires knowing exactly where you are and where you want to go and having a strategy and the resources to make the transition. Chapter 2 provides a systematic model to help administrators avoid some of the most common marketing mistakes that result from inadequate planning and lack of focus.

Conducting market research and maintaining a database are activities that can enhance marketing efforts. Without proper research, your marketing strategy may be based on faulty perceptions. Chapter 3, *Marketing Research and Database Marketing*, provides guidelines for determining when research is warranted and how to conduct various research activities. This chapter also shows the advantages of using a database to target specific audiences, personalize messages, and promote proactive communication.

Communication is the lifeblood of any marketing effort. Whether written or spoken, verbal or nonverbal, channels of communication strongly influence the impression people have of your school. Effective communication must be receiver-sensitive and reciprocal. Too often, the sender bases his communication on what he wants to say rather than what the receiver wants to know. In addition, a successful marketing strategy must create avenues for reciprocal communication with various audiences. Chapter 4, *Marketing Communication* looks at the essentials of receiver based communication, offers ways to improve two-way interaction, and provides guidelines for creating effective communication materials.

The growing importance of technology in marketing demands a chapter devoted to using electronic channels as a means to foster effective two-way communication. Chapter 5, *Electronic Communication: An effective marketing tool*, provides a detailed approach to improving communication with students, parents, teachers, and the community by integrating technology into the marketing effort. This chapter was written with the invaluable assistance of Mark Franke of the Relatrix Corporation which specializes in helping organizations improve community relations through effective electronic communication channels.

Many administrators, with some justification, do not look upon the media as an ally or even a benign necessity but rather as a propagator of negative hype. This need not be the case. A proactive approach to working with the media can generate positive stories about your school and mitigate negativity if there is a crisis. Chapter 6, *Dealing with the Media*, offers advice on creating positive relationships with the media and, if necessary, how to respond when faced with a crisis.

Decreasing resources and increasing needs require that many schools look to external sources for assistance. Chapter 7, *Building Better Partnerships*, addresses the question I hear from so many school administrators, "How can I develop and maintain successful relationships with external partners?" namely businesses and non-profit organizations. This chapter includes a mutually beneficial approach plus support materials for initiating, developing, and maintaining good external relationships that can improve the learning environment for all children.

Finally, Chapter 8, *Public Relations, Inside and Out*, describes how to build positive internal and external relationships. Included is a variety of activities to enhance the marketing effort. Incorporate these activities into your plans as time and resources permit.

To provide examples and illustrate content, I use case studies of two schools, *Riverside High School* and *Lincoln Middle School*, which are composites of schools I have worked with in the past. The *Success Stories* offer valuable insight from education administrators who have been successful in marketing-related initiatives and were willing to share their experiences and expertise. I have included their stories not only to serve as real-life examples, but also to inspire and motivate.

Acknowledgements

I extend my sincere gratitude to those who shared their time, talents, knowledge, and experiences with me.

Mark Franke, Senior Business Consultant, Relatrix Corporation

Hector Rodríguez, Principal, John Herrera Elementary School, Houston, Texas

R. Neal Wiley, Fine Arts Director, North Central District, Houston Independent School District

Joe Nuber, Administrative District Superintendent, North Central District, Houston Independent School District

Joanie Haley, Executive Director, The Robert and Janice McNair Foundation

Elaine Naleski, Director of Community Relations, Colorado Springs School District 11

Robert Farquharson and Pamela Minks for their proofreading expertise

A special thank you to my family and friends who were always there to remind me of the light at the end of the tunnel

1

School Marketing: What It Is and Why It Matters

School marketing is applying the principles of integrated marketing used successfully in the private sector to the increasingly competitive environment of public primary and secondary education. As discussed in the Introduction, integrated marketing includes activities such as public relations, communication, advertising, media relations, and any other activity that can help administrators successfully promote their schools internally and externally.

What school marketing is and what it is not

School marketing is a way of doing things that expresses to students, parents, staff members, and the community that the school or district, as a public-supported institution, is dedicated to serving the educational needs of the community to the highest degree possible. This includes activities and materials that consistently and effectively promote the school as the best education choice for students and parents, an asset within the community, and a responsible administrator of taxpayer's money.

Activities include all the things the school does to develop, implement, and maintain effective marketing, public relations, and communication strategies. Materials include the brochures, newsletters, prospectus, or school Web site that support marketing activities.

However, marketing is more than activities and materials; it is a way of thinking, a *mindset*. Mindset, especially in the early stages of the marketing effort, is a critical element for success. Some views about marketing often found among school administrators and staff members can sabotage a marketing effort.

One detrimental view is that marketing is just one more onerous task imposed upon school administrators. "In addition to all the other things we are expected to do, now people are telling us we have to spend time marketing ourselves" administrators often complain. Yes, marketing does require time and effort, but the rewards of a successful marketing effort are well worth the investment. An effective marketing program can significantly decrease the time school administrators spend on dealing with disgruntled parents, recruiting volunteers, teachers, and staff members, finding additional resources, and building community support.

A second detrimental view is that marketing public education is a distasteful activity that is not relevant to educating children. If you feel this way, consider that universities and colleges, institutes and trade schools, private and parochial schools, charter schools, and for-profit schools have been marketing themselves successfully for some time. Public and private schools in Great Britain, New Zealand, and Australia consider marketing programs essential to creating viable institutions. The truth is, every time you make improvements that enhance the learning environment, increase the attractiveness of the physical surroundings, or seek to improve community relations, you are thinking in the same way a marketing professional does when he or she develops marketing activities.

Successful school marketing is about meeting the needs, wants, and expectations of internal and external audiences and receiving value in return, an exchange that benefits both sides in increasing proportion. Determining the *needs, wants*, and *expectations* of an organization's various customers or stakeholders is an essential part of any marketing strategy. For schools, the need already exists. We need to provide our children with the means to receive an education. The law requires it. A school's marketing strategy will focus on the public's wants and expectations. The goal of the marketing effort is to create an educational organization to which parents want to send their children, in which qualified staff members want to work, and for which there is community support. This is accomplished when the school can meet or beat the expectations of these groups.

The value that the school receives in return for meeting the needs, wants, and expectations of internal and external audiences is increased enrollment, quality teachers, contented employees, greater parent participation, more volunteers, improved community support, and beneficial relationships with external organizations. The equation is mutually beneficial and sustaining.

Equally important to understanding what marketing is, is knowing what it is not. Below are some common misconceptions about marketing. These misconceptions can undermine a marketing effort, waste resources, and create ill will. Before beginning the marketing effort, it is important to ensure that everyone has an awareness of what marketing is not.

School marketing is not an *ad hoc* activity. Have you ever had an acquaintance or relative whom you heard from only when he needed help? After a while you probably avoided him. If a school continuously ignores its stakeholders until a need or crisis arises, the eventual response is likely to be negative. Marketing is not an effort initiated in response to a crisis, concern, or need, then abandoned once the issue is resolved. Marketing should be an ongoing undertaking that is incorporated into the daily actions and thinking of all school personnel. To do otherwise wastes resources, weakens future marketing efforts, and conveys the idea that the school responds to its stakeholders only when compelled to do so.

School marketing is not hype or spin. When marketing is used as an attempt to obscure the school's or district's inability or lack of willingness to meet the needs and wishes of its customers (students, parents, employees, community), the result is the loss of credibility not only for the school's marketing efforts, but also for any subsequent efforts to meet customer needs. Creditability is essential to every aspect of a marketing initiative. Once creditability is lost, it is difficult to regain.

School marketing is not sales. To many people, marketing and selling are the same. They are, however, significantly different.

Marketing activities are strategic, comprehensive, and indirect. Marketing includes multiple phases of activities such as forecasting, product development, position assessment, market research, branding, creation of communication materials, and public relations that enhance the school's long-term relationship with its "customers" or audience.

Sales is a short-term, direct, operational activity that is a part of the marketing process. In school marketing, sales-oriented activities generally include one-on-one interaction with prospective students or their parents, presentations to community groups, requests to external groups for support, and promotion of special programs or initiatives. Sales efforts are much easier when the marketing initiative is based on a thorough understanding of and a desire to meet your audience's expectations.

Peter Drucker, a recognized management expert, wrote that, the aim of marketing is to make sales superfluous.[1] The goal is to know and understand your customers so completely that your product or service fits their needs and wants perfectly. Then you need only to let them know that your product or service exists and how to get it.

An example of the truth of this viewpoint is the marketing of Cabbage Patch dolls in the 1980s. The marketing strategy for these dolls was so effective that "selling" became a matter of letting customers know where they were available. People waited in line for hours to get one. In some instances, police had to control the crowds.

Created by Xavier Roberts, each doll looked a little different from any other and had its own name, birthday, and birth certificate. The dolls were "adopted" from the maternity ward at Babyland General Hospital in Cleveland, Georgia. The idea and the resulting product and promotion were perfectly attuned to the consumer, children. Children loved the idea of adopting their own, one of a kind, doll.[2]

When a school makes an effort to understand the expectations of its audiences and meets them to the best of its ability, having to "sell" the school becomes less important than creating an awareness of what the school has to offer.

School marketing is not a department. In his excellent book, *Selling the Invisible,* Harry Beckwith emphasizes that marketing is not a department [3] The idea is that everyone in an organization is part of the marketing effort. Marketing is about perception, and everyone in an organization is responsible for how the organization is perceived.

When I was an undergraduate student, I worked my way through school as the evening manager at a luxury hotel. The hotel had a well-trained and motivated marketing department that spent significant time and money selling the hotel to companies nationwide. However, the hotel staff members who interacted with the guests on a daily basis ultimately determined how the hotel was judged. If our service had been consistently poor, even the best marketing efforts would not have produced repeat business. The loyalty of our guests was maintained in large part by the excellent customer service provided by front line employees.

Likewise, in a school, marketing efforts can be undermined by unhappy employees, apathetic students, and indifferent parents. However, when properly motivated, these groups can bring tremendous energy, expertise, and support to activities that promote a positive image of the school.

Bus drivers, office staff members, crossing guards, custodians, and cafeteria workers should be aware that they are representatives for the school as much as administrators and teachers. This is a very important concept. So important, that the phrase, *"Everyone is in Marketing,"* should be the mantra of the school's marketing effort.

As your marketing efforts succeed, there is an increased sense of pride and accomplishment within the school and the district that is concomitant with success. This pride should be felt by everyone, because each has contributed to that success and each is affected by it.

Why is marketing your school important?

The fact that you are reading this book indicates that you are open to the idea that marketing can provide benefits to your school. Colleges, universities, and vocational and private schools have been marketing to varying degrees for decades. Public schools may not yet need the kind of heavy advertising and promotion activities that these learning institutions do, but the changing environment of public education warrants a proactive approach.

Below are some important changes in the last several decades that affect the climate in which schools must survive. They provide a good argument for serious consideration of a school marketing program. If you are already convinced that marketing is important, use the information presented here to bolster your arguments to unconvinced administrators, motivate school staff members, or recruit volunteers to assist you.

Increased Competition. The number and kinds of schools competing for your students have increased dramatically. In the past, private schools, most of them parochial, were the only competition for public schools. Decisions for sending children to private schools were generally based on tradition, desire for a particular curriculum, or a preference for a specific religious environment.

Today, charter schools, home schooling, for-profit schools, voucher programs, and, in some cases, even schools within the same district may compete for students. With so many choices available, becoming the school of choice is a matter of survival for many schools. Chances are your competition already is marketing to your present and potential students. Marketing is essential to managing the competition by positioning your school as the preferable choice.

Loss of students can significantly decrease a school's funding. According to the National Center for Education Statistics, in the school year 2001–02, average expenditure per pupil was $7,734, instructional expenditure per pupil $4,755.[4] Consequently, losing just a dozen students in a school can mean a loss of revenue which is roughly equivalent to the salary of an experienced teacher.

When other schools take your students, they take not only the funds attached to those students, but also the voter and community support that is needed in advancing school initiatives. Loss of one student loses the support not only of parents, but possibly grandparents and other relatives who live, vote, and pay taxes in the community.

However, competition need not be anathema to public education. The key is to look at competition as a catalyst that creates new vigor, innovation, and higher expectations within your school.

Changing Demographics. Over the past few decades, the demographic landscape has changed significantly and the changes are having an impact on schools. Of major influence are changes in the family structure, increased diversity, and a shift in the adult/child ratio.

One-parent families and those with both parents working are the norm in many school districts. Parents may have less time and inclination to become involved in the education process and even in their own children's activities.

Handling new non-instructional responsibilities, getting working parents involved, and replacing the volunteer services stay-at-home mothers previously provided often tax the resources of schools and the dedication of school staff members. Marketing can help you assess the needs of your particular community, find additional resources, and create programs that adjust to societal changes without diminishing the educational experience of the children.

Racial and ethnic diversity among the student population is significantly greater than in the 1950s and 1960s. The U.S. Census Bureau reports that in

2000, almost 20 percent of school-age children have at least one foreign-born parent.[5] This creates special challenges within both the school and the community.

Diverse customs and languages can present obstacles to student assimilation, parent participation, and two-way communication. A sense of alienation or exclusion may cause parents to avoid contact with the school or to seek other educational opportunities for their children. Both the children and the valuable contribution of cultural diversity are lost to your school.

An important element of an effective marketing effort is a culturally sensitive and inclusive environment for students and parents that avoids alienation and fosters a sense of belonging and school loyalty. Any marketing strategy in a culturally diverse school should include outreach programs that encourage and facilitate not only parent but also community participation.

Another significant change is the shift in the child-adult ratio. Unlike the 1950s and 1960s when children outnumbered adults, today, there are considerably more adults than children in the U.S. Many of these adults do not have children in elementary and secondary schools. The school district, in which I currently live, reports that 80 percent of the residents in the district do not have children in school.

The influence of these groups is so significant that marketing and advertising groups have created acronyms for them: OINKs (one income, no kids), DINKs (double income, no kids), LINKs (low income, no kids), POOKs (parents of older kids), WOOFs (well-off older folks), and FISTs (fixed income senior taxpayers). For young adults, who plan to have children, the quality of schools is an issue. Older adults and those who do not plan to have children want to feel that their tax dollars are being spent responsibly.

Because they vote, pay taxes, and participate in civic associations, building support among these groups is important. An effective marketing plan can build and maintain positive lines of communication with these groups and create a perception that the school is a positive contributor to the community that is worthy of their tax dollars.

Public Skepticism Nearly twenty years ago, the National Commission on Excellence in Education published its now famous—some would say infamous—report on the condition of public education, entitled "A Nation at Risk."[6] The criteria and degree of objectivity the commission used to examine and assess the public education system is still a matter of debate. Whether justified or not, the findings and recommendations of the commission generated a high level of scrutiny and criticism of public schools.

Higher standards, greater accountability, teacher salaries tied to performance, and more stringent graduation requirements for students were some of the commission's recommendations. A significant portion of school administrators and the public supported these requirements. Unfortunately, schools became the scapegoat for many of society's ills. Some groups used the assault on public education to foster their own interests such as charter schools, for-profit schools, home schooling, and voucher programs. Schools now face the task of maintaining and, in some cases, rebuilding public confidence while dealing with a changing society.

However, increased examination of public school performance has had a positive side. Greater public demands have caused schools to be more aware of how the public perceives them. Marketing provides the opportunity to dispel the "myths" that have developed around public education and inform the community of public education's accomplishments and contributions.

Media Scrutiny. No news is good news to many school administrators. In a 1997 study for Public Agenda, Steve Farkas found that seventy-six percent of educators agree that negative media coverage contributed to the decline in public confidence in public schools. Ninety-one percent feel the media covers "what sells."[7]

School administrators complain that local news reporters often use exposure of inefficiencies within their school districts as major items on the evening news, but do not give the same prominence to school achievements. The negative implication of national news items such as isolated incidents of school violence spill over to the entire education system.

It should be recognized, however, that school administrators have played a part in the adversarial relationship with the news media. Administrators often are perceived by the news media as uncooperative and obstructive. Stonewalling the media has become the *modus operandi* of many school communication offices. The result is a spiraling downward of effective communication and relations on both sides.

Without proactive measures to build positive relations, interactions with the media can become negative and reinforce unfavorable opinions on both sides. Therefore, an important part of any marketing program is media relations. An effort to build and maintain constructive relations with the news media will pay off when there are both positive and negative events at your school.

Scarce Resources. There are never enough resources to do all that districts and their schools would like to do. At the same time that government mandates and public pressure are placing greater demands on schools, the resources to meet those demands are becoming increasingly difficult to find. Having stretched their budgets to the limit, school administrators spend much of their time determining how to provide more services with fewer resources.

Additional resources exist in every community. Accessing them should be a part of the school's marketing plan. Businesses and local organizations benefit when the schools in their area are good; therefore, local businesses are more willing to support schools when they see them as assets within the community. By designing marketing programs that build and maintain supportive relationships in the community, your school can generate extra funds, services, and help.

People are attracted to success. That is why attendance increases at sporting events when the home team is winning. As the achievements of your school are recognized through marketing activities, high-quality teachers, reliable staff members, and motivated students are more easily attracted and retained. As these groups are attracted to the school, they raise the level of achievement and success.

The benefits of successful school marketing are many. Effective marketing can positively affect virtually every aspect of a school. The most important result, however, of effective school marketing is that it creates an enriched learning environment for all students.

2

Getting Started

When working with schools, I constantly hear the question, "How do we get started?" Even school administrators who are solidly convinced that marketing is essential to the school's growth and improvement find the process of getting started a major obstacle. Consequently, many good intentions remain just that, intentions.

A good start is essential to a successful marketing effort not only for practical reasons but also for the motivational boost it will give the marketing team. A thorough job in gathering resources, assessing the school's present position, and developing a marketing approach will provide considerable rewards during the implementation, tracking, and future modification of the marketing strategy.

As you begin to design and implement the marketing strategy, an important thing to keep in mind is that you can do as much or as little as you and the marketing team feel comfortable attempting and still achieve some level of positive results. Indeed, a key to success is not taking on more than your resources or capabilities can handle at any one time. A small marketing project successfully completed is preferable to a huge project that fails.

Even if the school already has implemented a marketing initiative, I strongly suggest that the marketing team go through the assessment process described in this chapter. One reason why marketing efforts are not as successful as they could be is that there is no clear and valid assessment of the organization. The result can be decisions based on inaccurate information. Knowing the strengths and weaknesses of your school and the opportunities and threats that influence its success are crucial.

As success leads to greater confidence, the marketing team can attempt strategies that are more complex. If on occasion, efforts do not meet with success, just keep in mind that even the strategies of marketing experts sometimes fail. Remember the "new" Coca Cola campaign? It was a costly failure by experienced professionals with enviable resources available to them. Mistakes, especially in the beginning, are inevitable. Accept them as lessons and stay motivated.

Develop the best product/service you can

Providing a quality product or service is the single most important element in any marketing effort. Without a commitment to providing the best product or service possible, all marketing efforts are futile. None of the following ways to market a school will compensate for an inferior product or service nor should they.

As stated in the beginning of this book, marketing is not a way to divert attention from a school's deficiencies or its lack of willingness to improve. Build a commitment to excellence into your marketing goals. The information provided in the following pages is designed to help your school create products and services that are valuable to those the school serves and to promote an awareness of its efforts within the community.

Building a winning marketing team

Even though I have stated emphatically that everyone in a school has a role in promoting it, a team of motivated individuals is necessary to develop, coordinate, implement, and track the marketing effort. At the school level, the team leader should be the principal or a designated administrator who reports directly to the principal. At the district level, a logical choice for team leader is a marketing, community relations, communication, or public affairs officer who reports directly to the superintendent. It is critical to communicate that the marketing program is a high priority activity with the highest level of support.

The team leader should have the authority to make decisions. If a majority of activities are delayed because someone, not on the team, must review and approve each action, the result will be wasted time, frustration, and loss of momentum.

Initially, the team may be small, comprising a team leader and three or four individuals. Their task is to set preliminary goals and complete a school assessment. Expand the team according to the expected scope of the marketing need. If a major effort is planned, seven to ten members may be needed. To ensure diversity in talent and opinion, I recommend no fewer than five members for any program.

The marketing team will make decisions that have a dramatic impact on school success, so select members with care. Maximum marketing effectiveness calls for a marketing team whose members possess the following characteristics:

Belief in the marketing effort. This is the most important qualification. No matter what capabilities a person possesses, if he or she does not believe that the marketing program can make a significant contribution to the school or district, those capabilities will not be put to best use. True believers will have the dedication to follow through on assignments and remain motivated long-term.

Marketing can be fun and rewarding; however, the work can sometimes be time consuming and demanding enough to test the commitment of even enthusiastic team members. It is vital that team members believe what they are doing is important, be able to convey that belief to others, and stay motivated even when demands are heavy and results fall short of expectations.

Willingness to make a long-term commitment. Getting the marketing plan up and running is not something that is likely to happen in a few weeks. Team members should be willing to make a commitment for a least several months to a year. A long-term commitment conveys the importance and sincerity of the marketing effort not only to those on the team, but also to individuals or groups with whom the team interacts. If external groups constantly must familiarize themselves with new people and vice versa, the perception is that the effort lacks commitment and organization. Even one or two members dropping out and being replaced can disrupt team spirit and the momentum of activities.

Strong communication skills. Good written and oral communication skills are necessary. This cannot be stressed enough. Good communication is at the heart of your marketing effort. All your marketing activities involve communication in some form.

Some members may be more adept than others at written or oral communication; however, all members should be able to express ideas clearly and concisely, use correct grammar, and construct a logical line of reasoning. Creative people with technical skills and experience in publishing software and materials design are valuable team members.

Ability to work in a team and independently. Much of the work in the beginning will involve planning and decision-making as a team. Members should be able to develop and sustain a team energy directed at promoting a common vision and shared goals rather than individual projects and objectives. When members pool their work in a coordinated way, the team's efforts are maximized.

However, members often must complete assigned tasks on their own. It is essential that members realize that when they are working independently, they must meet deadlines and complete their assignments as defined by the team. Even one member not contributing his fair share of the work or not meeting deadlines can cause frustration and resentment.

Willingness to consider another point of view. Being able to look at a problem or issue from all sides is crucial, especially when the school's population is multi-cultural, there is socioeconomic disparity, or the community is in transition. It may be that negative situations the school now faces are a result of not being aware of other points of view in the community. By welcoming disparate points of view, the marketing team can set the standard for open communication with the school's public.

Issues have several sides and there are multiple ways to approach them. Members should be willing to look at all sides, objectively weigh the merits of various ways to proceed, and be willing to support team decisions.

Goals, objectives, and strategies

Goals are the results that the school hopes to attain with its marketing efforts. A school may have one or several goals. Goals describe a desired end state. Goals may or may not be achieved totally. Goals may change as situations change.

Goals become actionable when they have measurable objectives attached to them. Objectives are the tasks that must be accomplished collectively for each goal to be reached.

As a goal has objectives attached to it, so an objective will have strategies linked to it. Strategies are the plans that result in actions by which objectives are accomplished and goals are achieved. A strategy is what gets you from where you are to where you want to be.

Think of your marketing effort as analogous to establishing a successful garden. If you were to sow seeds and set plants without any thought as to the purpose of the garden, existing climate, soil conditions, light, and water requirements, or required maintenance, it is doubtful that you would have much to show for your efforts.

Planting a successful garden requires that you first determine your goal. Is the goal to create a pleasing environment? To provide privacy? To produce food?

The next step is to determine the objectives that will allow you to reach your goal. Objectives might include building the right kind the soil or drawing a layout of the garden.

Finally, your strategy is the overall plan that would include making all possible improvements to your environment, determining the correct time frames for planting, initiating the planting stages, and developing methods for maintaining the garden with the proper amounts of food and water.

Without sufficient attention to all these details, effort and resources are wasted. Not only will you not reap the rewards of fresh and tasty foods or beautiful flowers, you may be discouraged from any future garden projects.

Similarly, the school marketing team should go through a process involving the following steps:

Determine goals   ⎫
Assess the school's present position   ⎬   May be reversed
Develop marketing plan   ⎭
Initiate plan
Monitor progress

When conducting marketing workshops, I am often asked the question, "Shouldn't I assess my school's present situation before I determine what my goals should be?" Well, that depends.

Remember when you and your high school classmates were planning for college? Some of you knew exactly what goals you wanted to accomplish. With these goals in mind, you were able to set out objectives and develop a plan to achieve them based on an assessment of your capabilities and resources. Other students needed to assess their capabilities and resources first, and then look at the options available to them. From their set of options, they were better able to set goals.

Similarly, some schools have clear ideas of what they want to accomplish with their marketing programs. Obvious issues, needs, or problems within the school's environment may have created the motivation to initiate a particular marketing program. The marketing team's job is to translate the ideas into understandable, manageable goals and then assess the school's ability to achieve them.

If the marketing team is uncertain about what the school's goals should be, the assessment process described in this section will help them get a clearer picture of areas that need improvement. Goals should reflect those areas of needed improvement.

SMART goals

Your marketing team may develop multiple goals. One goal might relate to your volunteer program, another to developing business partners, and another to increasing communication with the community. After goals have been determined, they should be prioritized.

An often-used acronym, **SMART**, is a good tool for developing sustainable goals. **SMART** goals have the following qualities:

Specific. Goals that are not specific are subject to interpretation. Make your goals as specific as you can. Phrases such as "more effective" or "improved efficiency" have varying interpretations. An individual may consider his efficiency as "improved" if he manages to answer a couple more of his E-mails each day.

A goal to "improve our volunteer program" is too ambiguous and subjective. "Improve" has different meanings to different people; it may mean one thing to the administration and something else to volunteers. What does *improve* really mean? Does it mean more volunteers? Happier volunteers" Different kinds of volunteers? Who decides when improvement is sufficient?

If the marketing team is having difficulty forming goals, it may be that they do not understand the related issue well enough. Spend more time determining exactly what the need or problem is, and then write a specific goal to correct it.

Measurable. Goals should be quantifiable. Write goals in a way that allows the team to measure how close the school is to achieving the desired results. A school's goal to "increase interaction with the community" is stated better as "make one presentation per semester to a local civic organization". If only one presentation is made during the entire school year, you have a measure that indicates that the goal has not been met. Instead of an ambiguous goal to increase volunteer participation, a measurable goal for the volunteer program would be to recruit two volunteers to work with the new music program or to increase the number of reading volunteers from five to eight. Measurable goals eliminate any ambiguity or dispute about how effective efforts are.

Attainable—It is admirable to set high goals; however, it is not always the best approach when your marketing team is just getting started. Enthusiasm may lead to taking on more than the team can handle. The risk is that the team may fall short of the goals and lose motivation.

To set attainable goals, break big goals into smaller ones. Instead of setting a goal of 100 percent attendance at Parent's Night, figure out what your present attendance is and aim for a 20 percent or 30 percent increase or concentrate on a specific, smaller group such as new parents and aim for a 50 percent increase. Success with smaller goals will provide the school with the experience, confidence, and motivation needed to take on larger ones.

Attainable goals are also realistic goals. The definition of marketing speaks to meeting the wants and expectations of the school's various audiences. In setting goals, the team should realize that they cannot meet ALL the wants and expectations of ALL groups or even most. If group A expects one thing that is in direct opposition to what group B expects, the school cannot please both completely.

The marketing team should consider the publics' desires and expectations and make an honest effort to meet them. However, the school's central and most important responsibility is to its students. The wants and expectations of individual parents or community members are secondary when they come into conflict with what is best for the students.

Results-oriented—Achievement of the school's goals should lead to the intended results, and there should be an understanding of exactly what those results should be. Frequently goals are created without an understanding of either the desired results or a recognition of possible unintended consequences.

Sometimes administrators tell me one of their goals is to increase the number of volunteers, but when I ask them what they expect the result to be, they are not sure. It sounds like a good idea. However, remember the old adage, "Be careful what you wish for, you might get it." Achieving your goals should not result in additional responsibility that the school is not prepared to handle. If the goal is to increase the number of volunteers, what is the desired result? Is it to lessen the workload of the school staff members through volunteer help with office tasks? Will more volunteers achieve that? Or, will training, scheduling, and supervising additional volunteers add to the workload of staff members and cause resentment?

The team should ask, if we achieve this goal, what will be the result and will it be advantageous? It is worth spending time to consider the ramification of attaining goals so your success does not lead to unexpected and unwanted circumstances.

Time-related—Without limits, time like money is often wasted. Without time limits, procrastination is tempting; especially in a school environment where so many other activities are competing for staff members' time. Setting completion times for projects or activities promotes a sense of importance, holds team members accountable for completing their tasks, and builds satisfaction as projects are accomplished. Do not make timelines so short that everyone is stressed or so long that there is no sense of urgency. You might start out with quarterly, semi-annual, and annual goals and adjust as required.

After the team has developed a set of goals, categorize and prioritize them. See if there are links between them so that the team can maximize its efforts. For example, by recruiting volunteers in one area, present staff members and resources can be reallocated to work on improving another area.

At some point, discuss the top two or three goals with teachers and school staff members to solicit suggestions and foster dialogue about how they can participate in achieving them. Remember, everyone is in marketing. Teachers and staff cannot help in the marketing effort unless you inform them about what the effort is supposed to accomplish and provide them guidance about how they can contribute.

Know thyself

A lack of self-knowledge is a common marketing mistake. People generally feel confident that they are sufficiently knowledgeable about their own organizations. However, this knowledge often is based on unquestioned assumptions, false perceptions, and wishful thinking. Decisions based on inaccurate knowledge lead to mistakes that cost time and money and result in ineffectiveness.

To avoid marketing mistakes based on faulty knowledge, the marketing team should complete a self-assessment process. A systematic, comprehensive way to assess your school's marketing needs is to conduct a **SWOT** analysis. **SWOT** stands for Strengths, Weaknesses, Opportunities, and Threats.

The SWOT Matrix, shown in Fig. 1, will help the marketing team assess the school's strengths, weaknesses, opportunities, and threats in five areas known as the *5Ps* of marketing: *P*roduct, *P*rice, *P*eople, *P*lace, and *P*romotion. Explanations of each of these elements are provided in this chapter.

The purpose of the matrix is to help the marketing team identify school strengths that the school can use now in its marketing, pinpoint weaknesses that need to be addressed, determine what threats stand in the way of achieving goals, and find opportunities that can help the marketing effort succeed.

Gather the marketing team and have a chalkboard or flip chart available. Give team members a copy of the marketing matrix to help them keep focused and organize the information. If you anticipate considerable input for each area, provide a separate sheet for each "P".

As a team, examine each of the five areas looking for strengths, weaknesses, obstacles, and opportunities. Write comments on the board or chart. Some items may appear in more than one category. For example, students may appear in the people, product, and promotion categories.

After the first session, team members can spend some time reviewing the matrix, then return for a second session to share new ideas and reach an agreement on the school's present position. Depending on the level of assessment needed, the team may want to assess only one of the "Ps" at each of five weekly sessions. If so, each session should include a brief review of the last session discussion with any revisions before moving to the next category.

In the assessment, include as much information as possible about verifiable external or community perceptions of the school. External perceptions can provide valuable and often surprising information about your school's perceived strengths and weaknesses and uncover opportunities and threats.

You may be surprised to find that internal perceptions differ from external ones. Discrepancies in internal and external perceptions signal that the school's judgment of how it is perceived is inaccurate. Address discrepancies in your assessment. If, for example, the administration and staff members do not see the physical appearance of the school as a weakness, but information from external sources reveals that those living around the school find it unattractive, this difference in perception is an issue that should be indicated on the matrix.

The key to using the marketing matrix is to go through the process until the marketing team has a thorough understanding of the school's SWOT. The more information you gather, the more useful your assessment will be.

Keep in mind that as the school's marketing effort moves forward, the assessment will change. As the marketing plan is implemented successfully, strengths are reinforced, weaknesses are diminished or eliminated, opportunities appear, and obstacles are overcome. An annual review of the matrix will provide insight into the success of your marketing efforts.

Completing an assessment is part of the marketing process that often meets with resistance from school administrators. First, school administrators and staff members feel that they are sufficiently knowledgeable about their school and its place in the community. Second, the process seems too time-consuming. And, third, it is often hard to convince participants that completing this process now will save time and resources in the future.

I strongly advise not to skip this part of the process or to make a cursory attempt. Accurate self-knowledge is essential to sound marketing strategy. The following information provides an explanation of how to complete the matrix.

	Strengths	Weaknesses	Opportunities	Threats
Product				
People				
Price				
Place				
Promotion				

Fig. 1

Count your assets

Strengths are positive attributes that make a school exceptional, different, or advantageous to employees, students, parents, and the community. Some obvious strengths are above-average test scores, excellent academic programs, student and teacher awards, high graduation rates, and quality extracurricular activities. However, other, less obvious strengths may be overlooked. For example, it speaks well of a school to have dedicated, long-term employees. They are a great strength that should be acknowledged and developed as an asset.

In assessing your strengths, ask questions such as the following:

• What do we do exceptionally well?

• How are we different in a positive way from other schools?

• Why would someone want to send a child to this school?

• Why would a high school student choose this school over another?

• Why would someone want to work or volunteer at this school?

• If someone does not have children in this school, why would he support it?

• In what ways is the school considered an asset to the community?

• What are the school's/students'/teachers' achievements?

Write down every strength you can think of. Strengths are the foundation of your marketing program. They are what you have to work with *now*.

Consider a weakness as an opportunity

We all dislike admitting a weakness, but perfection is rare, so it is best to acknowledge a weakness then deal with it. In the *Weaknesses* column, be open and truthful. It is counterproductive to justify or ignore deficiencies or to cast the blame on others. If the school's relationship with its immediate neighbors is not good because the residents protest that students are throwing trash around the school, it is not helpful to label the neighbors as whining complainers. This situation signals a weakness in your community relations that needs to be addressed.

Some weaknesses can be turned into an advantage. Avis Rent-A-Car turned their market position as a weak number two to Hertz into a highly successful advertising slogan, "We're Number 2, we try harder." No car manufacturer would view having its one of it autos labeled a "bug" as a marketing strength. However, Volkswagen produced highly effective and creative ads based on the size and shape of its little car. VWs became cool, fun, and hip, in addition to being inexpensive to buy and economical to operate.

Some weaknesses, however, cannot be turned into an advantage. Inferior quality and poor performance require improvement. Part of the marketing effort should be to determine how weaknesses can be addressed.

Weaknesses may be in the form of misperceptions about the school that can be corrected. For example, the school may be having great success with an excellent new reading program, but if most people outside the school do not know about it, the program may not be considered as one of the school's assets.

After the team has completed the matrix, it should categorize the school's weaknesses. In one category, list weaknesses that the school can attend to immediately. For example, the school could address the problem of neighbors who are upset with litter around the school by organizing student clean-up days, adding extra trash receptacles, creating an anti-litter campaign, and initiating programs to boost school pride.

In another category, list weaknesses that are most detrimental to the school. Not all of these can be addressed immediately; some may be formidable. Low academic performance, high incidents of student violence, or teacher unrest are serious weaknesses that promote a negative view of the school. Determine what obstacles and opportunities exist that influence the school's ability to correct these weaknesses.

A third category should include potential weaknesses that need a proactive approach. The potential for a loss of some of the school's best teachers will lead to a weakness unless action is taken. Addressing potential weaknesses can prevent them from becoming a reality.

It may be that much of the work in the marketing program will come from the weakness column; therefore, it is important to give this area considerable attention.

Don't wait for opportunity to knock

In the *Opportunities* column, try to think of any and every opportunity that could reinforce the school's strengths, remedy its weaknesses, and overcome any threats. In my workshops, this is the column that participants find most difficult. It is sometimes hard to see where opportunities exist. This category requires some imagination.

When looking for opportunities, do not prejudge any possibilities. The tendency is to look for the big event or important person who can have a great impact and save the day. Instead, look upon each person and situation as a possible opportunity.

If you need mentors or volunteers, are there groups in the area that have been overlooked such as the residents of a retirement community? Are there civic organizations that can help with special projects? Are there parents or teachers who can provide referrals to businesses or influential individuals? Is a new residential community being built? Do staff members or teachers have untapped talents?

Think about what might be created from existing opportunities. Imagine that a high school's music program has been a source of pride for the school and the students. Teachers credit it with keeping some students in school. However, reduced revenues require that the school cut funds for the music program. A weakened music program may cause the school to lose students either by transfers to other schools or through dropouts. A staff member mentions that a retirement community has opened recently in the neighborhood. This could be an opportunity.

An effort by the marketing team to recruit volunteers from the retirement community yields a piano teacher who agrees to come one day per week to give piano lessons at a highly reduced rate and a saxophonist who volunteers to work with the students two afternoons a week. Positive interaction with the students and school staff members encourages the saxophonist to recruit two more members from the local music community to volunteer. The musicians persuade a local music store to donate some used instruments. Taking advantage of small opportunities can bring significant benefits that may not be anticipated at first.

Be aware of threats

Threats are anything that jeopardizes the school's ability to achieve its marketing goals. Competition from other schools or districts can threaten the school's ability to recruit or retain students. A higher pay scale in neighboring districts may threaten the recruitment and retention of highly qualified teachers. A loss of volunteers can threaten the effectiveness of mentoring programs.

In the threats column, list both small and large threats. Small threats may become large if not addressed. Be aware that some threats may be too great to overcome in one effort. However, they may be broken down into smaller hurdles or worn down over time. If an incidence of violence at the school threatens the community's confidence in the school's ability to provide a safe learning environment, time and a range of efforts may be required to restore confidence.

Sometimes we need to go around threats rather than confronting them directly. If the school or district is receiving slanted and unwarranted attacks from a news reporter who refuses to tell a balanced story, it may be necessary to go directly to the public with the school or district's side of the story.

One way to address threats is look in your opportunity list for solutions. One final word on opportunities and threats: opportunities can sneak past you; threats can sneak up on you.

SWOT of your school's 5Ps

To complete the assessment, assess the strengths, weaknesses, opportunities, and threats of each of the school's 5Ps: Product, People, Price, Place, and Promotion.

Product: For school marketing purposes, *product* refers to any product, service, or attribute that provides benefits for the school's internal or external constituencies. In a school environment, products and services may include students, curricula, extra-curricula activities, the school's use as a community center, or its ability to enhance the community's status as a good place to live and work.

Students are the school's most observable products. School strengths are students who meet or exceed standards for moving through successive levels of study, achieve outstanding academic, civic, and community recognition, graduate with the ability to be productive members of the community, or become alumni who contribute to society. Above-average dropout rates, poor student performance on assessment tests or high levels of truancy are weaknesses. An opportunity might be a grant for a program to decrease the dropout rate. Increasingly higher achievement standards may present a threat.

As a product, the curriculum may have appeal because it is rigorous, specialized, broad, or innovative. Weaknesses include a curriculum that fails to meet the students' needs, for example, a lack of bi-lingual, college preparatory, or vocational classes. Opportunities include grants to develop new academic programs or improve existing ones. A lack of teachers who can fully utilize a new curriculum can threaten its success.

Extra curricula activities, which enhance the learning experience, such as sports, fine arts activities, debate teams, or school publications are attractive to many students and their parents. To some parents and students these activities are as important as the courses of study. Regard them as a strength of the school. Even for students who do not participate, recognition from these activities can provide a sense of school pride. Poorly administered programs that fail to provide true opportunity for student success are a weakness. Limited resources are often a threat to extra curricular programs. Opportunities may come in the form of alliances with external professional groups that provide extra training or resources for students.

Recognition of the school as a supportive member of the community is an invaluable strength. The services the school provides to the community as a site for civic meetings, election polling, or adult education are an important consideration when assessing the school's services. Assess the quality of interaction with the community. Is the school seen as a reliable partner? Within the limits of its resources, does the school offer services to the community?

Opportunities to reach out to the community are generally plentiful; however, it is important that the school manage external relationships successfully. Detachment or indifference on the part of school administrators and staff members can threaten the perception of the school as one that provides meaningful services to the larger community. If there is a tendency in the school to overlook the general community until a need or crisis prompts greater involvement, then support from the public may be unenthusiastic.

Do not overlook the district's or school's ability to attract people and industry as a valuable service to the community. This attribute is especially important to businesses, government, and civic organizations. Generally, when new families move into a community, the entire community benefits socially and economically. If a principal reason why people move into an area is the school, then it is a valuable asset to the community.

What is your school rating compared to others in your area? Do you have indicators that show one reason people choose or choose not to move to the area is the quality of the schools? The loss of students to other schools in your area is indication of a weakness. Opportunities are occasions to publicize your positive attributes through media sources, presentations, and communication pieces. A threat may be the school's inability to communicate effectively its economic and social benefits to the community.

As the team assesses the products and services the school provides, it should ask the following questions:

- Are our products meeting the needs of our students, their parents, and the community? For example, if many of the students do not intend to go to college, is their education preparing them to compete in the workplace for well-paying jobs? If they are college bound, are students' writing and research skills what they should be?

- What services does the community need that the school could provide, but does not? Could the school provide adult language or driving classes? Is what the school provides the best it can be? Does everyone in the school believe in the school's goals? If not, why not?

- What are the tangible and intangible benefits of the school? Is the school a source of pride within the community?

Critically assess the quality of education your school provides. The marketing effort should involve activities to determine the school's deficiencies and look for ways to improve them. As stated in Chapter 1, no amount of marketing will conceal your school's inability or lack of motivation to provide the best education possible to all children.

People: The category of people includes any person who has or could have an impact on the school.

Students play an important role in the school's assessment. Student achievement, enrollment, satisfaction, and needs should be assessed. Remember, in addition to being products, students are also customers. Their level of satisfaction with courses, teachers, extra-curricula activities, and the school environment can be strengths or weaknesses.

The quality of the teachers and staff members the school attracts and retains must be considered. Certainly happy employees are an asset. If the school has productive, long-term employees, their tenure as employees is a demonstration of loyalty, continuity, and stability that speaks well of the school. Employees are also members of the community and the level of satisfaction, loyalty, and pride they communicate outside the school environment is crucial to how the school is perceived. As customers, their level of satisfaction is influenced by compensation, the work environment, administrative support, and the school's relationship with the community.

Parents and guardians with children in your school can be strengths when they are satisfied, active, and approving of the school's efforts; they can be weaknesses when they are not. Do not ignore people who do not have students enrolled in your school. Do you know who within your community is choosing to instruct their children at home? What is your relationship with them? Home-schooled children may become participants in your extra-curricula activities and distance-learning programs or join in school social activities. Their participation provides additional support from their families.

Who are the various groups in your community? Do you know them? Do you know what their needs and expectations of your school are? Is there cultural and language diversity in your community? Is diversity viewed as an obstacle or an opportunity for the school? Is the community in transition economically or demographically? What is the school's or district's relationship with school board members or other elected officials? How about civic organizations or school-related associations? Are school and district administrators active in such organizations?

A retirement village in your area may be an opportunity for volunteers. Supportive taxpayers are an asset in bond elections. Mutually beneficial relationships with the business owners are crucial in good community relations. What is the school's relationships with these groups?

It is likely that the *People* portion of your assessment will generate the most information. Virtually everyone who is in your community influences your school in some way. However, people offer tremendous opportunity and can be a great asset to the school; therefore, it is advantageous to give as much time and attention as necessary to this section.

Place: In a school environment, the *Place* category refers not only to *where* your product or service is delivered but also *how*. *Where* includes the physical environment of your school such as buildings, grounds, classrooms, equipment and other facilities, The most obvious example of place is the school structure and grounds.

In assessing place, there are several things to consider. What is the condition of the physical plant and surrounding grounds? Are buildings safe, in good repair, and aesthetically pleasing? Are the grounds attractive? Do classrooms provide sufficient space and the proper equipment for teaching? Is the facility new? Has it been updated? Is it inviting to students, employees, and visitors? What are the security measures? Is it an historic building?

In the case of one elementary school in a major city, two characteristics of place helped the school develop a beneficial relationship within the community. The unique characteristics that set it apart from other schools in the district were its place in history and its architecture. The school is the oldest continuously occupied school in the district. Its classic Spanish-style architecture embraces the playground with old world grace. A serendipitous meeting between the principal and a local resident, who stopped by one day to see the building, began a successful relationship with the local civic association that has helped form a bond between the school and the community.

The local civic association saw the classic architecture of the school as an asset that could benefit property values by helping to maintain the character of the neighborhood. Residents who wanted to preserve the old building established a nonprofit organization specifically to raise money for the school.

When the district made plans to renovate the school, administrators within the district recognized the importance of place in the school's relationship with the community. The decision was to preserve the architectural style. Later additions to the original building will be removed and replaced with new space in the original architectural style.

Because of its history and architecture, the school is on the civic association's annual home tour and many alumni return for a visit during that time. Twice each year—once right before the home tour—the school holds Gardening Day. Parents, students, and residents put in new plants, trim bushes, and pull weeds around the school. Recognition of place has provided the school with new and continued support.

The *how* aspect of *place* includes how your product is delivered. For example, teaching methodologies, whether traditional or innovative, may be an asset or a weakness. If a new approach to teaching math produces outstanding results, it is a strength. Obviously, methods that are not producing the desired results are a weakness.

The use of technology to deliver instruction and remedial support is increasingly important to parents, teachers, and the community. An aggressive plan that brings needed technology into the school is a strength. A lack of basic or up-to date technology is a weakness the school can address through opportunities provided by federal programs and relationships with external organizations.

How students access educational services is included in place. Weaknesses exist when it is difficult or time consuming for students to get to school or if parents are reluctant to put their children on a school bus because the safety record is poor, bus breakdowns are frequent, or the pick-up and drop-off places are unsafe. Threats may be a lack of funds to replace old equipment or the inability to hire and retain qualified bus drivers.

Price: Public education is not free. Virtually every adult supports public education directly or indirectly through taxes and school bonds. One of the greatest strengths of public schools is the quality education they offer for the dollars expended per student. When compared with private schools, many public schools provide a level of education excellence that is equal or greater at a much smaller cost. However, it is also true that many public schools fall short of meeting this standard. Unfortunately, these schools often receive the most attention.

When community members examine public education as taxpayers, they often use the cost/benefit approach, i.e., compared to the costs what are the benefits to the students and the community. Consideration of this comparison should be a part of any marketing effort. A major strength for a school is public recognition that the school's or district's benefit to the community is equal to or greater than the cost.

Increasingly high costs of salaries for quality teachers, technology, and maintenance and construction of buildings are challenges every district faces. These challenges are compounded by taxpayers who are opposed to increasing revenue through higher taxes and school bonds. Marketing is important in tax increases and bond referendums. Often a lack of support for additional revenue sources is based on inadequate information. If the public does not understand the issues that require additional funding, they cannot make informed decisions. For example, many taxpayers are not aware of how schools are funded.

When a bond referendum for a school district failed to pass, research after the fact showed that many people did not understand how public schools were funded and why the district needed additional revenue. It was determined that these misunderstandings were largely responsible for the failure. The district created a brochure that explained exactly how tax dollars flow to school districts and made a concerted effort to explain to the community specifically how the district would use the bond money. The next bond referendum passed.

Costs are not always monetary. Time and effort provided by volunteers, parents, business partners and civic groups have great value to the school and should be included in the price assessment. Strong community participation is one of a school's greatest strengths. Apathy, alienation, and competing demands may be threats. If so, give them special attention in your marketing plan.

Opportunities in the price section come from new people and businesses in your community, grants and financial assistance, and a growing awareness of the contribution of public schools. It should be the goal of your marketing effort to make the most of these opportunities.

Promotion: Any activities and materials the school uses to reach out to its various audiences, build a caring internal environment, and create an awareness of the school's efforts to meet the public's desires and expectations are included in this section. Promotional activities should support and enhance your marketing goals.

In assessing your promotion section, first look at what you are doing or have done that was successful. Is your newsletter generating positive feedback? Have you formed beneficial business alliances? Did your volunteer recruitment campaign succeed? Discuss all your promotional activities and review your marketing materials.

Under Strengths, list those that have met their objectives and determine why they were successful. Under Weaknesses, list those activities that have not succeeded and try to determine why they failed. Do not personalize any failures. It may be that good ideas were implemented at the wrong time or without sufficient planning or resources. Sometimes good strategies are abandoned because time frames were unrealistic. Given more time, they may have succeeded.

Threats are as varied as the activities. Does your promotional effort lack support from central administration? Your school board? Do you feel that you do not have sufficient internal staff to plan and carry out effective activities? Do you need external expertise, but feel that you cannot afford it? Are there linguistic and cultural obstacles that must be overcome?

In the beginning of your marketing effort, keep doing the things that are working and choose new activities that are within the range of the school's resources and expertise. In Chapter 8, you will find additional activities the school can use to improve relationships with internal and external groups.

Who is your competition?

After the marketing team has completed the school's assessment, they should determine who the school's competitors are and assess them using the same matrix. Competition may not come solely from another school or district but also from apathy within or separation from the community. Competition must be addressed if you are to reach your goals.

Information about competitors may be limited, but the team should gather as much data as it can. An awareness of the strengths and weaknesses of the school's competition is an essential part of developing an effective strategy to position it as a desirable choice for students and as an asset to the community.

Being different makes a difference

Why do consumers select one product over another? Because one product offers something to the consumer that the others do not. That "something" could be price, special features, ease of use, status, name recognition, or any number of things that appeal to the consumer. Parents and students select a school for a reason, even if the reason is simply that it is in the neighborhood or it is the school their friends chose. Nevertheless, the school offered something another school did not.

Because administrators and teachers tend to see themselves as doing the same kinds of things in parallel ways with similar goals, defining what makes their school different is often difficult. Use the Assessment Matrix to help determine what sets your school apart from other schools. Do you have a long-standing presence in the community? (Place). Are you in an historic building? (Place) Are you in a new, high-tech building? (Place). Do you have bilingual, arts, sciences, reading, or extracurricular programs that are above average or have gained recognition? (Product). Are your support organizations such as the PTO, booster clubs, volunteers, and businesses especially strong? (People). What are the special achievements of your students? (Product, People). Your teachers? (People). Are school employees active in community activities? (People, Promotion). The marketing team should ask the question," What makes our school special?", and then answer in as many ways as they can.

Take a position

The school's positioning statement is not the same as the school's position. The school has a position whether it markets itself or not. The school's position is how it is perceived by its various internal and external groups. The school may do things to influence its position, but it is created in the minds of its audiences. The positioning statement, however, is a one or two sentence statement that defines how the school *wants* its various audiences to perceive it. It is the core message that the school wants to send to its constituencies. It defines for internal and external audiences who you are, what you offer, to whom you offer it, and why you are different. It is the sum of the school's attributes. It articulates why the school is distinctive.

If you have completed the SWOT and objectively assessed your 5 Ps, you should have a good understanding of your position with its strengths, weaknesses, opportunities, and threats. Now the marketing team should use information from the SWOT matrix to write a positioning statement. The statement is not something that is written in a thirty-minute meeting. It takes time and thought. Seek input from internal and external groups to help develop it. Expect revisions as the team refines the statement. The positioning statement should answer the following questions with a succinct, strong statement

Who are we?
How does the school define itself? Is the school a magnet school, Montessori school, exemplary school, established neighborhood school?

What does our school offer?
Does it offer special language, technical, or college preparatory curriculum? A caring environment? An accelerated curriculum? Fine arts programs? A rigorous science and math curriculum?

What are the benefits of what we offer?
How does what the school offers benefit its various constituencies?

How is our school different?

Does the school have innovative programs, above-average test scores, a highly qualified teaching staff, a special academic ranking, extracurricular activities, an attractive campus, small class sizes, special facilities, special community involvement, or other attributes that make your school different from other schools? Differentiation is a key element in your positioning statement. It is the part of your positioning statement that says, "This is how we are different from others"

Do not fall into the trap of creating a positioning statement that the school cannot support. Be realistic. If the difference between your position and your position statement is too great, your audiences will not accept it. The ultimate goal is for the school's position to align with its positioning statement, that is, that the internal and external audiences perceive the school as it wants to be perceived. Create a statement that makes that possible.

Often positioning statements do not receive the attention they deserve. A well-written positioning statement provides the direction and focus the marketing team needs to develop and adhere to the marketing plan now and in the future.

Positioning statements relate to the present, but the school also needs a mission that relates to the future and provides motivation for continued improvement.

What's your mission?

In the early 1960s, President John Kennedy set for this country the mission of putting an American on the moon and returning him safely within the decade. A bold mission that inspired a courageous, focused, and ultimately successful effort to put the United States in the forefront of space exploration.

Frequently, I see mission statements that resemble advertising slogans more than a statement of purpose. If an airline tells me its mission is to make me a "happy repeat flyer", I am inclined to see this as promotion. A more believable statement might be, "To earn our place as a major international carrier by creating innovative incentive programs and pre -and post-flight services designed to meet the needs of international business and leisure travelers."

A mission or vision statement gives the school a future goal to target. It is the moon the school wants to shoot for. The purpose is to provide a focus for forward movement. Be bold in your mission statement. Ask, "What could we really do if we put our hearts and minds into it?" A statement without passion will provide lackluster results.

Harry Beckwith[3] states if a mission statement is well written, most employees can regularly answer the question, "What have you done this week to advance the mission?"[2] From time to time, ask administrative and office staff, teachers, and other employees what they have done recently to support the school's or district's mission. If more than a few cannot give you an answer, then the mission statement is not having the desired effect.

Words to live by

Often a positioning statement and mission are created to help get the marketing effort organized, then forgotten until the program loses focus and momentum. Do not let the school's positioning statement and mission become catchphrases that sound good but have little meaning or effort behind them. Use them to keep your marketing effort on track.

Periodically, begin marketing team meetings by reviewing the positioning and mission statements and discussing what is being done to fulfill them. Use them to guide communication and public relations activities. Create statements that reflect the school's mission and put them in places where employees can see them. If you find that the school's mission is not providing the focus and motivation for which it was created, revise it.

As you articulate the school's positioning statement and mission in your communication with internal and external groups, you are building an expectation that the school is making every effort to fulfill them. If your audiences perceive that the actions of the school do not match the words, the statements become meaningless and disingenuous. Disingenuous statements will eventually generate internal and external cynicism.

Always have a plan

As stated earlier, marketing strategy is what gets the school from where it is to where it wants to be. The assessment process has helped the marketing team determine where the school is. The positioning and mission statements provide direction. Now, the strategy is to make the most of the school's strengths, improve weaknesses, address threats, and take advantage of opportunities to take it where it wants to go.

After the marketing team has completed the assessment, written a positioning statement, and determined its mission, it is ready to articulate the marketing strategy through a plan. A marketing plan is exactly that, a plan for how to achieve marketing goals. The purpose is to keep the marketing effort focused and on schedule.

Opinions vary on what a plan should include and how long it should be. I once read an article in which a marketing guru said that a plan should fit on a cocktail napkin. Others will argue that a plan of any worth would fill a dozen pages. Of course, some marketing plans will be complex and involve considerable research. This is especially true when companies are launching a new product and the marketing plan includes market research, market-segment profiles, revenue projections and production schedules. However, the school's marketing team should be able to construct an initial marketing plan in no more than three to four pages.

Anything more than several pages should be divided into an overall marketing plan and smaller project plans. The school's initial marketing plan should provide an overview of the marketing strategy: What does the school hope to accomplish within what time frame and with what resources. As the marketing efforts progress, expand the plan to include more details. The plan should provide the marketing team with an outline of what it hopes to accomplish within a specific time frame.

The following case study is provided to give you a better understanding of the assessment process, positioning and mission statements, and the marketing plan,

A Case Study
Riverside High School

Riverside High School is located in a close-in neighborhood within a large metropolitan area. The school was built in the early 1950's when the community comprised mostly middle class working people. Over time, the neighborhood has changed to one that is more racially mixed and economically diverse with a large number of retired people. In addition to public schools, several parochial elementary and middle schools are located in the area, but there is no other high school nearby.

In the last couple of years, large tracts of land became available when some abandoned manufacturing plants were demolished and the land was cleared. Developers bought these tracts to meet the growing demand for new close-in housing and are building moderate to expensive single-family dwellings, low-rise apartments, townhouses, and some commercial construction. Plans are to complete 300 new residences within Riverside's boundaries within the next three to five years. Local realtors estimate that 40 percent of these residences will have occupants with school-age children. It is likely that the new residents will comprise middle to high-income professionals and well-off retired people.

Over the last five years, under the leadership of its principal, Mr. Johnston, Riverside High School achieved "recognized" status, the second highest ranking given by the state. The new academic rating has raised student and teacher morale and generated praise from the community. As a result of the new ranking and the work of teachers and administrative staff members, the school has received a $200,000, two-year grant from a local chemical corporation to start a "Scientists in the Making" program. However, some of the school's most experienced and popular teachers, who were instrumental in Riverside's academic improvement, may soon retire.

The PTO has gained new members and become more proactive. Recently their fund raising activities generated enough money to install new landscaping. The members have also worked closely with school administrators and parents to address school safety issues.

Riverside has a strong vocational education program that offers classes in auto mechanics, culinary arts, and technology-related subjects. Equipment for these classes is becoming obsolete. The school has dedicated money to update the equipment for vocational education, but the gymnasium is also in need of renovation.

Employee relations are good, but some teachers have begun to complain lately that too much money is spent on sports. Their complaints have caused some difficulties in gathering support for renovations to the gymnasium. The school district's Board of Education is considering allowing businesses to advertise in return for renovation funds. Some parents and teachers find the advertising option offensive and oppose the idea.

The school's relationship with the community has always been good. The local paper has been helpful in promoting the school to the community. Several established businesses, including local realtors, have actively supported the school over the years. However, the business environment is changing to meet the new demographics. New businesses are expected to move into the area to serve the expanding and more diverse population.

At the beginning of the next school year, Academy for Academic Excellence (AAE), a for-profit school, will open. Initially, the school will offer classes from pre-K through grade 8; but AAE plans to add a high school within the next two to three years. AAE has a very aggressive and well-funded marketing effort. The school is positioning itself as a forward-thinking organization that provides a classic education in a high-tech environment. In the past few months, AAE's Director of Marketing has made presentations to two of the local civic associations.

Riverside wants to develop a marketing program that will capture a substantial portion of the new residential market and position itself to face any competition from AAE, while continuing to meet the needs of the community of which it has been a part for so many years. The marketing effort is meeting with some resistance from staff members who see it as just more work.

Now look at the assessment matrix in Fig. 2. for an example of responses that a marketing team might have included in an assessment of Riverside High School. Although this is not an in-depth assessment, it will give you an idea of how the marketing team might begin a matrix. Even with the limited amount of information in the matrix, the marketing team can determine that despite the school's significant strengths, a concerted marketing effort is needed now to address the possible loss of key teachers, growing internal tension, and highly organized competition that could erode their present and future enrollment.

	Strengths	Weaknesses	Opportunities	Threats
Product	Scientists in the Making Program. Vocational Ed. AP program next year Recognized Status	Needs funds to sustain and expand curriculum	Possibility of expanding science program if more funds become available	Possible retirement of some teachers could affect the science program
People	Excellent teachers. Active PTO. Good leadership & employee relations. High student morale. Key communicators	Not all staff members support marketing effort. Need external marketing expertise	Additional students from new housing addition. More PTO members	Discontent of some employees regarding new initiatives
Price	Community support. Grant money	Need to be more proactive in pursuing additional funds.	Possibility of additional grant money and support from businesses if science program is successful	New for-profit school could take present and future students from us
Place	New science equipment & materials. PTO provided new landscaping.	Gym in need of repair	School board may approve selling advertising space to bring in funds for gym repair.	Resistance to advertising to raise money for gym
Promotion	Good relationships with local businesses. Positive media coverage of science program.	Need more, better organized promotional activities	Some business partners have agreed to help with marketing activities	New for-profit school has well organized and funded marketing campaign. They have already contacted some of our local businesses and orgs.

Fig. 2

The marketing team has decided that the high school should position itself as a school that has achieved success through attributes that benefit all the students and that the intent is to continue to maximize student potential. The team feels it is also important to recognize that the school has always enjoyed good community support, but that the community is changing and the school will respond to those changes. Below is an example of a positioning statement that would reflect this way of thinking.

Riverside High School Positioning Statement

Riverside High School is a *Recognized* school that is proud of its success in creating an environment in which every student benefits from high standards, innovative programs, a dedicated teaching staff, and a safe environment. We are dedicated to preserving the strong community support we enjoy by continuing to meet the education needs of our changing, diverse neighborhood.

Let's take a look at this statement. Riverside High School positions itself as an organization of significant accomplishment through an awareness of its new status as a recognized school and its success in providing the means for student achievement. It states what it offers to those who attend the school and recognizes that the school is there to serve *all* its students. The statement concludes by reinforcing the importance of community support and the school's intention of maintaining that support by being flexible enough to serve a changing community. Riverside is positioning itself as a school of achievement that will continue to meet the needs of the community that has supported it for decades while adapting to the community's changing demographics. It is a message of dedication, assurance, and progress.

Riverside's achievements in the past few years have raised school morale and expectations. The marketing team wants to create a mission that will motivate continued improvement.

Riverside High School Mission

Our intention is to capitalize on our present achievements and the talents and dedication within our school and community to achieve the highest school ranking of Exemplary within the next three years.

This is an unambiguous statement of a high, but achievable mission. It affirms that the school has the internal and external means to achieve its mission within a stated time frame. This is a mission that leaves no doubt about what the school wants to accomplish. This statement makes it possible for administrators, teachers, staff members, students, parents, and external audiences to ask themselves and each other at any time, "What are we doing to achieve are mission?" and from their answers be able to determine their progress.

Riverside High School Marketing Plan

After much work, the Riverside marketing team is now ready to create an initial marketing plan. The initial plan is a framework upon which to build. The team can expand and refine it as necessary. As ideas are generated and activities are initiated, the plan will include more detail. The plan begins with the positioning statement, mission, and goals and a summary of the SWOT to keep the team focused and avoid plan "creep", the tendency to move in a direction or expand the plan in a way that is not consistent with the intent of the marketing effort. The Potential Market and Competition reinforce the present opportunity and the threat. These parts of the marketing plan are not likely to change in the near future.

The remainder of the plan will undergo the most revision. A time-line for the year with activities will likely be expanded and revised after the marketing initiative in launched. Some of the activities may develop into separate plans with designated teams. The resources needed may change as activities are expanded or modified. Noting the names of the team members is recognition of each member's commitment. Finally, the benefits are stated to keep the team motivated.

Marketing Plan—Riverside High School

Positioning Statement

Riverside High School is a Recognized school that is proud of its success in creating an environment in which every student benefits from high standards, innovative programs, a dedicated teaching staff, and a safe environment. We are dedicated to preserving the strong community support we enjoy by continuing to meet the education needs of our changing, diverse neighborhood.

Mission

Our intention is to capitalize on our present achievements and the talents and dedication within our school and community to achieve the highest school ranking of Exemplary within the next five years.

Goals

To increase test scores in all core subjects

To maintain all current external partnerships

To add three new partnerships among the new businesses in our area

To have a minimum of one positive news story each month in the local paper

To make one presentation each school year to each of the civic associations in our area

To create a new marketing materials for our school

To capture 60 percent of the potential high school students among new homeowners within the next five years.

SWOT

Strengths: School achieved "Recognized" rating last two years. $200,000, two-year grant from XYZ Corporation for "Scientists in the Making" Program. Highly qualified, dedicated teachers. Good leadership. Pro-active PTA/PTO organization. Good community support

Weaknesses: Support for marketing effort is not strong enough. Gym needs renovation. Vocational classes need better equipment. Inadequate funds to implement all needed improvements.

Opportunities: New residential and commercial construction in the area. Three major realty companies have indicated a willingness to participate in our marketing effort, local newspaper very pro public schools, increasing population with greater diversity.

Threats: New K-8, for-profit school with a significant marketing campaign is opening next fall within our school boundaries. Opposition to gym renovations. Discontent among staff over new initiatives. Possible retirement of teachers.

Potential Market

Potential for additional students from new development in the area. Realtors estimate that within our school's boundaries 300 new residences will be completed within the next 3–5 years. Past sales indicate that 40 percent of these homes will have occupants with school-aged children.

Potential for increased external support from new commercial development in the area

Potential to lose present students if shift to accommodate the wants and expectations of new students is perceived as abandonment of current student body

Competition

In the fall of 2005, Academy for Academic Excellence (AAE), a for-profit school will open. AAE has a very aggressive and well-funded marketing effort. They are positioning themselves as an organization that provides a classic education in a high-tech environment.

Activities/Time-Line

Sep–Oct: Set-up marketing team schedule, add members to team, and assign tasks
Determine need for research and initiate as required
Determine marketing audiences and develop appropriate messages and activities
Hold brainstorming sessions as needed
Develop public relations ideas
Create and pre-test marketing materials
Establish contacts with external partners who have agreed to participate
Begin to build a database
Set up teams to work on "weaknesses"
Meet with fund-raising committee to coordinate efforts
Develop a presentation for external audiences

Nov: Produce marketing materials
Acquaint all internal staff, students, and external partners with marketing new marketing materials and initiatives.
Implement marketing effort

Dec: Set-up tentative presentation schedule for remainder of school year

Jan–Feb: Monitor marketing efforts and make adjustments as required
Reaffirm relations with present external partners and reach out to new ones
Initiate public relations ideas as resources permit
Evaluate efforts to improve weaknesses

Mar–Apr: Develop next year's marketing and public relations program based on analysis of present marketing efforts
Conduct periodic market research to aid marketing efforts.

May   End-of-school event, build enthusiasm for next school year
             Set up plan so that marketing efforts are maintained during the
             summer

Jun–Aug   Maintain marketing effort as time and resources allow

Required Resources

Man-   *First three months*—3–5 Hours per person per week for internal
power: team members, 1–2 hours per week for support staff, 1–2 hours
           per person per week for external members.
           Remaining months—1–2 hours per week for team members, 1–2
           hours per week for support staff. 0–2 hours per week or external
           members.

Money: $6,000–$10,000

Materials: Marketing materials and presentation

Machines: Copying equipment

Methods: Marketing—Public relations—Customer service—Advertising

Marketing Team

Robert Johnston, Principal
Ellen. Grunell, Assistant Principal
Allen Archer, Business Manager
Alicia Cooper, Teacher
Belinda Gardner, Hudson Realty

Benefits

Increase new student population
Retain present student population

Build new relationships with the external partners
Attract and retain highly qualified staff
Enhance standing in the community
Systematic plan for improved marketing and public relations

Leverage your brain power

"Two heads are better than one," is a core belief of brainstorming.

Effective brainstorming sessions can foster creative thinking and produce imaginative solutions. Thoughts produce ideas that generate discussion that stimulates thinking that leads to more ideas. If the sessions are focused, the atmosphere is motivating, and free thinking and expression are encouraged, creativity and innovation will result.

Too often, however, brainstorming sessions produce the same old ideas reconstituted or lapse into a litany of grievances and complaints. Following a few simple guidelines can make your sessions a worthwhile activity.

Create the right environment. If possible, conduct the session away from the school in a comfortable, relaxed environment that encourages inventive thinking. If a site away from school is not an option, make the session room as visually pleasant as possible with flowers, plants, or visually appealing posters (with themes or images unrelated to school). Chairs should be comfortable and arranged informally. Set aside a minimum of two hours time. If possible, schedule early in the day when minds are less likely to be overtaxed from daily activities.

Large projects, such as planning a community parade and fair, may require a full day or multiple sessions. Provide a selection of beverages and light snacks. If the session is long enough to include lunch, keep it simple. Have at least one easel with a full pad of paper, colored pens, and tape or pins to stick sheets on the wall. Provide each participant with plenty of paper, index cards, colored pens, even toys. Include idea provokers related to the purpose of the session such as sample brochures, magazines, layout or design books, news paper articles, short stories, videos, or photographs.

Start with a clear statement of purpose and stick to it. Write one clear, specific statement that defines exactly what is to be accomplished. Write it large and place it on an easel or tape it on the wall so that everyone can see it during the session.

Examples of statements of purpose:

"To generate ideas for our new fine arts program brochure that will encourage more minority students to become involved?"

"To determine the theme of our school float in the annual neighborhood parade and how we should illustrate the theme?"

"To find three ways we can increase participation of new immigrant parents in our school?"

"To generate ideas for making our new teacher luncheon motivational for both new and experienced teachers?"

"To find ways to generate greater participation from our business partners in the Back to School event?"

Do not let the session wander off track. If new issues arise, write them down for future consideration, but keep focused on your present objectives.

Select the right participants. Select people who are creative and outgoing, but also include methodical, analytical thinkers. They are the ones who figure out how to make creative ideas a reality. Avoid chronic naysayers or people who are likely to dominate the session and inhibit participants from freely expressing themselves.

Aim for diversity. It is a good idea to pick some people who are familiar with the issue or project and some who are not. Include people with different functions and different talents. If possible, include people who are representative of your target audience, such as students, volunteers, or business partners. Include enough people to achieve some diversity, but do not exceed seven or eight people.

Designate a session leader to coordinate the preparations and lead the activities. Send a notice at least a week in advance. In addition to time and place, the notice should provide participants with a brief overview that includes the purpose of the session and any background material that might help participants prepare for it. Encourage participants to think about the session topic and collect materials they think may be helpful in stimulating ideas and discussion. There are some of us who need to think quietly before we experience the great "Aha!"

Conduct the session. The session leader should start by welcoming the participants and thanking them for their time. Give a brief overview, then allow time for questions. Hand out a copy of the session rules and guidelines or post them on the wall next to the objective. Discuss each one before the session starts to reinforce them. Following are some rules and guidelines to consider:

- Turn off all cell phones and beepers.

- Take a 10 minute break every 50 minutes.

- Indulge in atypical thinking.

- Avoid negativity. Don't look for what is wrong with an idea, look for what is right.

- There is no such thing as a dumb idea.

- Remember, an idea that doesn't work today, may work tomorrow.

- Let one idea lead to another.

- Take an idea and run with it.

It is up to the leader to ensure that the session stays on task and that everyone is participating. Make an effort to include those who may be reluctant to participate and to keep in check those who try to dominate the session. If enthusiasm wanes or creative block sets in, engage in a brief physical activity, then stop for a couple of minutes of meditation or quite time or play a creative game or puzzle.

It is helpful to have an assistant to the leader (not one of the session participants) write ideas on the easel pad as they are generated and stick them on the wall, assist with any creative games, and help with lunch and refreshments.

At least once during the session, twice if the session is long, stop to review the ideas. Vote on the ones to keep. Think of ways to improve or build upon the ideas you keep. Then start on a new set of ideas.

About 45 minutes to half an hour before the session ends rank the ideas. Take the best ideas and try to improve them. Be sure to keep all the notes and flip chart pages. Some of the ideas not selected may be useful at another time. At the end of the session, assign "next steps" to the appropriate people.

In some cases, the group may not feel the session has been sufficiently productive. In this case, the participants should write down the ideas generated then leave and let their subconscious minds do the work. A week later, meet again. The chances are good that the result will be a more productive session.

Encourage ideas. Marketing thrives on creativity. Creativity requires a willingness to express ideas that others may consider controversial, silly, non-traditional, and even wacky. It is up to the team leader to establish an environment in which participants feel free to express ideas without fear of censure or ridicule.

Be aware of and give consideration to shyness or cultural traditions that may inhibit the kind of nonconforming thinking and self-expression looked for in a creative brainstorming session. To overcome participant shyness or cultural reticence, use silent brainstorming. Give each participant several large index cards at the beginning of the session. Participants can write down any ideas or comments they have. Ask every participant to write down at least one idea. The cards can be dropped into a box or collected at a break toward the end of the session. On a flip chart, write the ideas large enough for everyone to see them. Tear the sheets off and tape them on the wall. When the participants return from their break, go through the ideas one by one. Check those the team wants to pursue further.

Follow up after the session. Send each participant a thank you memo with a summary of session accomplishments and subsequent action. Follow up with any participants who were assigned tasks for progress reports.

At this point, the marketing team should have sufficient understanding of the school's strengths, weaknesses, opportunities, and threats and established goals based on that understanding. With a positioning statement, a mission, a marketing plan, and some ideas, the team is now ready to move forward with the marketing initiative. The next chapters provide guidance to help them.

Success Story
John J. Herrera Elementary
Marketing Makes a Difference

John J. Herrera Elementary School in Houston, Texas is an example of how a well-executed marketing effort can benefit a school's students, staff members, and community.

The level of excellence achieved by the students and staff of John J. Herrera Elementary contradicts the stereotypical view of its student demographics. The student population is 96 percent Hispanic (45 percent Limited English Proficiency) 95.5 percent Free/Reduced Lunch, 51 percent At-Risk, with a mobility rate of 21 percent. Yet, the school ranks as an Exemplary School, the highest rating granted by the Texas Education Agency (TEA).

In addition to teaching experience and a Masters of Education, Herrera Principal Hector Rodríguez has an M.B.A. and several years in private business. His experience in the private sector gives Mr. Rodríguez an appreciation of the power of a well-organized and focused marketing effort.

To Mr. Rodríguez, marketing is not an option. "We have a different environment from past years as we are accountable for what we are doing in our schools. We are also performing in a more competitive and sophisticated environment. To succeed in the type of environment, schools need to have a complete understanding of what they are doing and how they are doing it. Then they need to communicate, and, in some cases, educate their communities about what they are doing. Finally, every school needs to understand how similar and different their services are from those of other schools and learn how to highlight their uniqueness."

"Marketing is not something we do occasionally," stated Mr. Rodríguez, "because marketing is about product improvement, customer satisfaction, and effective communication, and these are things we are always striving toward. An effective marketing program should come naturally in everything you do within school activities. It is an understanding that the final product is student growth directly and staff and community growth indirectly. A positive culture sells itself!"

Principal Rodríguez knows that no amount of marketing can substitute for an inferior product. The highest marketing and academic priority for administration and staff is creating the best academic products possible. A good product is one that meets the needs and wants of the customer: an outstanding product is one that *exceeds* the customers' needs and wants. The administration and staff dedicate considerable thought to academic programs that not only shape the students' present and future success, but also benefit the community at large.

The marketing approach creates an atmosphere in which individuals are always thinking, "How can we create a better product?" At Herrera, the administration and staff continually strive to create a product that is excellent in quality and innovative in its approach to learning. Part of the marketing strategy is to combine the latest technology with inventive programs that continually improve the learning environment. The school is dedicated to finding creative ways for students and teachers to venture beyond the boundaries of textbooks and to search the world electronically for new ideas. This approach has made Herrera a preferred school for students and parents.

One of Herrera's outstanding products is its two-way language immersion program in grades kindergarten through second. Limited English Proficient students and monolingual English students are together in classes where they develop fluency in both languages as well as a strong foundation in academic areas. The ultimate goal is to produce bilingual and bi-literate students throughout the school. This type of program is attractive not only to parents, most of whom are Spanish speaking, but also to businesses in a state where being bilingual is a valuable asset.

The school's technology-driven curriculum transcends the standard computer-based learning. One example is the daily morning show transmitted from the school's broadcast center. The show is a means to communicate important information, recognize achievements, encourage confidence and build self-esteem. A typical morning includes comments from the principal, a weather report and the lunch menu delivered by the students, and recognition of student accomplishments and birthdays. The program always closes with the school pledge, "Today, I will respect my teacher, my peers, and my school. I will do more than is expected of me."

The daily broadcast provides more than a means to communicate information within the school. The program helps students to develop technical expertise early in their academic careers while teaching valuable lessons in organization, project management, research, design, and communication.

Students have used the school's technology to address issues important to them and the community. During the recent war in Iraq, the school wanted a way to lessen the fears and concerns of the students, many of whom had relatives in the military. Students and faculty created a video that incorporated excerpts from student essays on "Why I Like America" and pictures of relatives in the military with patriotic symbols and music. The video had a significant effect on the students' ability to cope with the uncertainty and apprehension they felt about the war.

The high-quality programs at Herrera Elementary allow the school to position itself as an organization that takes the community's needs and wants seriously and is meeting them successfully. The ultimate product of Herrera, however, is the student who is enhanced significantly by the quality programs the school provides. From the earliest grade levels, students are acquiring language and technical proficiency that will benefit their lives and the economics of the community.

Explaining his philosophy, Principal Rodríguez said, "Marketing is developing a product or service and its concept. In essence, you understand your product and create a concept around it. For example, at Herrera Elementary, we want to communicate quality education which is based on caring for children, relationships with our community, use of technology, and language development and maintenance, both Spanish and English."

Mr. Rodríguez knows that the environment where the product is delivered is important in marketing. The school's emphasis on using technology to maximize the learning experience is evident. To utilize fully the benefits of the broadcast studio, every classroom has a VideoLAN server, a CD player, a VCR, and television monitor. There is one computer for every two students.

Mr. Rodríguez also believes that schools can and must strike a balance between a safe environment and a welcoming one. Schools need to protect their children. At the same time parents, volunteers, or community partners must feel welcome or they will not participate. At Herrera, the welcome is apparent before the visitor enters the front door. The school grounds are clean and tidy and visitor parking is available at the school entrance. The school interior is immaculate. The staff implements security measures in ways that do not make visitors feel like intruders. The atmosphere is one of high energy and activity with a purpose.

An environment that represents excellence attracts top-notch people. In return, these people are motivated to sustain and cultivate the level of excellence that makes the environment so attractive. The marketing effort at Herrera is successful in attracting talented people and in utilizing their participation to promote the level of excellence.

All professional staff members are qualified for gifted and talented education. Last year, the school lost none of its quality teachers. Principal Rodríguez attributes the school's ability to recruit and retain quality staff to an internal atmosphere of respect, high standards, and professionalism. The high level of professionalism mixed with a heavy measure of enthusiasm and pride creates an environment that attracts quality people.

The level of achievement and pride exhibited by the school's staff and students also attracts parents. Parents and the community in general, are eager to be a part of the school's positive atmosphere. The school encourages participation in various ways. Herrera uses traditional methods, which include VIPS (Volunteers in Public Schools), PTA, and an "Open Door" policy for parents; however, it also uses more unconventional methods. Each year, Herrera hosts its annual Fathers' Night, where between 100–150 fathers (and some mothers) attend presentations on school and community issues during a catered dinner. This is an effort to target an important segment of the population that traditionally does not participate in such events. The school makes the evening fun for the fathers, each of whom receives a book to "autograph" and present to his child as a gift. To add special interest, fathers can win door prizes, such as tools and sports equipment.

Another such event is the "Día del Nino" celebration, during which the PTA and community members and business partners come together to celebrate childhood. This events relates to the Mexican tradition of the Día del Nino, celebrated every year on April 30.

The school holds celebrations, often featuring traditional Mexican Mariachi music, throughout the year to recognize achievements. After TAKS (the state-mandated test), the school celebrates with a carnival for the children. A Mothers' Day celebration recognizes mothers and provides certificates of appreciation to the school's VIPS.

The school conducts weekly parenting sessions that address community and family issues, as well as developmental considerations for fifth graders moving on to middle school. When needed, teachers bring parents into classrooms to sit with their children to help them establish long-term goals and evaluate their children's academic and behavioral performance.

Another annual event, which takes place after the beginning of the school year, is a field trip for parents and their children to the Museum of Health. This event involves parents in their children's learning, introduces parents and students to the museum, and increases parents' awareness of health issues concerning their children and themselves.

The after-school program at Herrera is designed to assist the working parent. Students remain in school under supervision until 5:30 PM, when parents can collect their children. The children experience enrichment activities, both academic and cultural. This has become a critical program in the development of strong relationships with those working parents.

The school creates an awareness of its presence in the community by participating in community parades and other civic events. School tours are scheduled on Friday mornings from January to May, a time when parents are most likely to be selecting a school for the next year.

Herrera has developed strong relationships with many community partners, including the City of Houston, Museum of Fine Arts, YMCA, police and fire departments, and the neighborhood Fiesta food market, who help with children's festivals and other events. Partners donate items as door prizes for the Fathers' Night, or become involved as guest speakers for career days and/or Fathers' Night.

In other situations, organizations have helped by awarding grants for special projects, such as the YES Grant ($2,000 for use in purchasing safety equipment) the Houston Rocket's $1,000 grant for field trips for kindergarten students. Herrera has enjoyed the Harris County grant, which has provided more than $200,000 for after-school program over the past several years, and the Capital Investment grant, which provides over $40,000 to spend with parents and teachers.

Many parents who have skills in the crafts have donated their time and resources to the school. Some of these relationships have resulted in donations for faculty luncheons or holiday celebrations. The participation of individuals, businesses, and organizations from the community creates an encouraging climate within the school.

Mr. Rodríguez expresses the importance of involving everyone in the marketing effort when he says, "Our teachers and our parents are our best salespeople." Their commitment and participation are powerful testimonials.

Mr. Rodríguez is aware that everything, even the smallest thing, about the school creates an impression and communicates a message. "Simply, we want everyone to know what sets Herrera Elementary apart from the crowd: what make us different and unique." The school uses a number of mediums to create an awareness of the school and its accomplishments.

The school uniform is a polo type shirt or t-shirt with the Herrera Elementary School logo and "We ♥ Our Children" on the front. On one sleeve is printed "Exemplary School 2002–2003". The uniform is a tangible, public announcement of the school's pride in its accomplishments. In addition to being an "advertisement" for the high quality of the school, the uniform creates a sense of belonging and special membership among the students. In turn, students are more likely to give extra effort toward maintaining the excellence of the school and their place in it.

The school brochure is a simple, concise, and straightforward expression of the school's achievements, programs, and mission. In addition to a photograph of the school, the cover lists the school's academic standing since 1995. The first thing the reader sees is a clear, objective affirmation of the school's commitment to excellence. The brochure text communicates the school's emphasis on excellence, technology, and foreign language development and provides information such as educational strategies and programs and a profile of teacher demographics.

The Web site reaches out to the community by going beyond supplying school information that students and parents want to know. It draws parents to the site by providing links to valuable information that can help families in their daily lives. Herrera has recently developed a school CD-ROM that highlights much of the spirit and programs at Herrera Elementary. This CD-ROM is used for special guests and visitors, or specific groups with interest in the school. The school will use this technique to target potential business partners, (in marketing terms, "selected segments" of interest to our school).

The community around Herrera Elementary is not wealthy, but Rodriguez believes that the community deserves a level of education and resulting student achievement equal to schools in more affluent neighborhoods. Principal Rodríguez and the staff members at Herrera Elementary are delivering a product that is of the highest quality. In return, the community gives value back to the school. The community pays taxes, but value does not always involve money. A high level of parental involvement and community support adds value that helps the school maintain a high level of quality. The community, in turn, believes it is receiving value for the price it pays in taxes, contributions of time and money, and support of the school's goals. A price the community pays willingly.

3

Marketing Research
And
Database marketing

For decades marketing professionals have conducted research to determine customer needs, wants, and satisfaction levels, pretest new products, and forecast trends. The benefits of "opinion" research led to its use by political and advocacy groups. Things happen. Perceptions vary. Demographics shift. Opinions evolve. Keeping abreast of change requires continual investigation.

Marketing research involves activities that provide the information needed to make informed marketing decisions. Marketing research can take a variety of forms. It can be an informal chat with members at a civic club luncheon about the upcoming bond referendum or a professionally conducted community survey concerning multiple issues. Actually, marketing research is not much different from research conducted for other purposes such as determining political or economic environments. The difference is that marketing research is focused on gathering information specifically to guide marketing activities.

A key to productive research is a genuine desire to obtain the information needed to make better decisions. Research as window dressing to imply interest in constituencies' opinions or to bolster decisions already made is a waste of resources. The research methods described in this section should help the school either conduct a useful research project itself or, if someone else is conducting the research, to know what they should be doing.

Who are your constituencies and what are they thinking?

Rarely will people call to tell you why they are not sending their children to your school. Potential businesses partners will not call to discuss the reasons why they are not working with your school. New residents will not call to tell you that they have moved into the neighborhood so you can update your demographic information. Parents will not call with their rationale for not participating in school activities. However, this is information schools need to determine their marketing goals, assess the school's present position, and make sound marketing decisions. Decisions based on assumptions and partial knowledge result in a waste of resources, poor relations with internal and external groups, and a loss of better educational opportunities for students.

Knowing why some parents or students do not select your school or district as their education choice is as important as knowing why some do. Parents who have chosen not to enroll their children in your school can provide valuable insight into how the community perceives your school in particular and public education in general. Ask high school students what influenced their choices. What did your school offer that others did not? Or, if they chose another school, why? Did they consider your school at all? Did they visit the school? What were their impressions? What, if anything, would influence a decision to reconsider your school?

Ask business and university administrators if students from the district entering the workplace or colleges have the skills and characteristics they need. What do they lack? Can these people offer suggestions that would address any deficiencies?

Today, finding out who your constituencies are and what they think are necessary activities for any school or district that wishes to build support and credibility with internal and external groups. How do schools find out these things? One of the best ways—sometimes the only way—is to ask.

School administrators often neglect marketing research because they view it as a complicated, expensive, and time-consuming endeavor. Others see marketing research as unnecessary because they feel that they truly know and understand what internal and external groups think about them. However, when persuaded to conduct a community, employee, or student survey, the data often show surprising results. The steps in any market research process are:

Determine your research objectives;

Develop a research plan;

Collect the data;

Analyze the collected data; and

Take action on the results.

Conducting some level of marketing research on a regular schedule provides valuable information that helps schools stay abreast of changes in their internal and external environments, communicate more effectively with internal and external groups, determine public perceptions, meet community expectations, increase levels of employee and student satisfaction, and build support for school or district initiatives.

Setting research objectives

Before beginning any type of research, it is important to have a clear understanding of what the school hopes to achieve by gathering information. If the survey targets parents and students to determine their needs, wants, and expectations, what does the school intend to do with the information it gathers? If the study shows that many students and parents want accelerated classes, is the school prepared to make changes to the curriculum? Or add special courses? If a survey of volunteers shows that they are leaving because of apathy and disorganization within the school, is the school willing to address their grievances with action?

To help establish marketing research objectives, think carefully about what information the school needs to move forward with its marketing efforts or even what those efforts should be. A question to ask is: What do we already know and how do we know it? The key word here is *know*, not assume. The school cannot know the level of parent approval, employee satisfaction, or community support without periodically checking the validity of its information. Having determined what the school does know, the marketing team can then determine what additional information it needs to gather.

Below are examples of school or district related research issues:

Who in the community does not send their children to our school and why?

How much does the community actually know about the school or district?

How does the public get information about the school or district?

What level of credibility does the district have within the community?

What are the perceptions held by various groups within the community relating to specific topics (school safety, communication, the school board, the administration)?

What is the status of parent/teacher relations?

Who are the school's competitors and how are they competitive?

What are the top five concerns of the students? Of parents? Of employers?

What is the level of volunteer satisfaction? Employee satisfaction? Student satisfaction?

Once you have established your objectives, the next step is to decide how to gather the information you need. The following paragraphs describe the commonly used means to gather information including literature searches, surveys, focus groups, and interviews. Each method has advantages and disadvantages.

What you need may be a click away

There is no reason to collect the information you need if someone already has. Information may be readily available from sources such as government or non-profit agencies, the Internet, universities, or published research papers. Information about the demographics of your community is available from city, county, or national census data. A local university may have conducted studies regarding local public opinion on issues related to public education. Information about businesses in your area is available through company Web sites or the archives of local newspapers.

A wealth of information is available via the Internet. Newspapers, magazines, trade publications academic journals, government data at the federal, state, and local levels, and Web sites of other districts and businesses may provide some of the information you need. One of the fastest ways to find sources of information is through Internet search engines such as Google!, Vivisimo, and EZ2WWW. When you find a particularly useful source, add the link to your "Favorites" list so you can call it up easily.

A literature search is an inexpensive way to gather information; however, bear in mind that the information may not be as up-to-date as you need.

Moreover, a literature search will not provide you with specific information regarding the opinions and perceptions of your internal and external audiences. The best way to gather that kind of information is through contact with the people in those groups. The school can accomplish that through interviews, focus groups, and surveys.

Use interviews and focus groups for depth and discovery

Companies interested in consumer research frequently use interviews and focus groups to elicit spontaneous and insightful information about attitudes and motivations. These methods are particularly helpful to schools when there is uncertainty about the concerns of various groups or when a misunderstanding of a group's sentiments has led to failed initiatives.

A primary use of interviews and focus groups is as a preliminary research method to discover what issues are important to specific groups, to identify any underlying or unknown concerns, and to reveal opinions and attitudes that can be used to develop more detailed queries.

One-on-one interviews usually involve persons who represent a larger group of people, such as executives of companies or leaders of organizations. Make it clear whether you are seeking the person's personal opinions or those of the group with which she is affiliated.

The typical interview lasts from 45 minutes to one hour. At the time the request for the interview is made, state the purpose of the interview and the topics to be discussed. It may be helpful to the person to tell her why she was selected for the interview. For example, "As a key member of the group opposing the latest bond initiative, we believe you can provide insight into why the initiative did not pass." Interviews generally are conducted at the interviewee's location. Unless the person objects, tape the interview. It is difficult to interact with the interviewee, ask follow-up questions, and take notes at the same time. Be punctual, come prepared, and do not take more time than you have asked for unless the person indicates that she has more to say.

Focus groups generally comprise 8–15 people who represent a specific group, such as parents, retired people, students, or a diverse group that represents the demographics of the community. If the purpose is to gather information from external groups, do not include employees of the school or school board members. This can inhibit a free exchange of information. A typical focus group session lasts 1 ½ to 2 hours.

Unlike interviews and surveys, the group is asked to discuss one or more general topics rather than answer specific questions. The idea is to generate spontaneous dialogue.

The moderator explains the meeting's purpose and objectives. It is important that the participants understand what the school plans to do with the information gathered. The moderator then offers topics for discussion and allows the group to express themselves on each topic. For example, "There has been much in the media lately about the new higher state standards and concerns over testing. We would like to learn what you know about the new standards and your views on how those standards are tested in our schools." To stimulate discussion, the moderator may also show pictures or a film clip or read a brief excerpt from an article.

The moderator participates in the discussion only to keep the conversation going, refocus the discussion if it drifts from the topic, and encourage shy participants to participate. The moderator is not there to debate any subject or correct any misperceptions. The purpose is to gather information. The session is recorded either on audio or video tape.

Research firms, especially those conducting product research, usually pay focus group participants; however, it is likely that the district or school can find residents who are willing to volunteer their time. I recommend providing refreshments or a light meal. The sharing of food and drink creates a relaxed atmosphere that can encourage the sharing of opinions and attitudes.

The location of the facility should be convenient and easy to find. Be sure to provide maps to participants who are not familiar with the area. The room should be pleasant and the chairs comfortable. Sitting around a large table or in a circle creates an inclusive feeling and promotes exchanges among the participants. Be sure to send thank you letters to all participants.

Interviews and focus groups offer the following advantages:

Quality and quantity of information. The greatest advantage of interviews and focus groups is the depth of information they generate. Because participants are not restricted to specific responses to predetermined questions, the amount of information generated can be significant. The probative nature of interviews and focus groups can reveal concerns, feelings, and beliefs previously unknown to the district or school. Not only can you learn how someone feels or what someone thinks, but also why. The school or district can use the information obtained to construct questionnaires that are then disseminated to a larger group.

Flexibility. The unstructured nature of interviews and focus groups allows the discussion to go in many directions. If a topic seems to be an emotional one that is generating a lot of discussion, the moderator can pursue that avenue. If the discussion stalls, the moderator can take it in another direction or introduce a new topic.

Rapid results. The gathered data is available for analysis as soon as the audio tapes are transcribed. The gathering and analysis of data can occur within a week.

The disadvantages of interviews and focus groups are:

Small sample. The major disadvantage, and it is significant, is that the sample or number and type of respondents from interviews and focus groups is very small. It is not likely that the beliefs and opinions of the participants in a few interviews and focus groups will reflect those of the general population.

Expensive. Effective interviews and focus groups depend on the quality of the questions, the effectiveness of the interviewer or group moderator, and the accuracy of the data analysis. Unless someone in the school or district has experience in arranging and conducting interviews and focus groups and evaluating the gathered data, it is best to use trained, experienced interviewers and moderators from a professional research firm. In that case, the per-person costs of interviews and focus groups may exceed those of surveys. If you are using the same research firm to conduct the school's or district's surveys, negotiate to have at least one focus group included at little or no cost.

Use surveys to reach larger groups

A survey is a systematic method of gathering data about specific topics from a selected group of people. The term *survey* may refer to both the process and the instrument or questionnaire used.

The information gathered from surveys makes significant contributions toward organizational improvement in a number of ways. For example:

Information: Surveys are one of the most effective and efficient ways to gather specific information on a wide range of topics from both internal and external audiences. Surveys are used to determine satisfaction with the organization, target areas that need improvement, evaluate programs and procedures, and reveal perceptions about the school or district. A well-designed survey can provide precisely the information the school needs to know for planning, decision-making, and improving relationships with internal and external groups.

Communication: Surveys promote communication that might not otherwise occur by providing students, employees, parents, and taxpayers an easy and anonymous way to communicate opinions, perceptions, and feelings about a variety of topics. Surveys are also a means to establish communication with people that generally are not in contact with the school. District-wide surveys are especially useful in gathering information from key groups outside the organization and for establishing communication links between internal groups such as teachers and central district administrators.

Inclusion: Asking people's opinions expresses the value that the school places on its relationship with the community. People like to feel that what they think matters and that others are willing to listen. One of the reasons taxpayers without children in schools are often critical of public education is that they feel no connection to it. Surveys are a means to express the school's and district's willingness to make a connection and confirm the notion that input from internal and external audiences is important to the organization.

Indicators: Surveys can serve as an early alert system for potential problems or for areas of opportunity. The school can detect shifts in public opinion, areas of growing concern, as well as how internal groups view changes within the organization before they have negative effects. External influences of which the school has no knowledge or control may affect opinions, perceptions, and relationships over time. Surveys conducted on a regular basis allow the school to track these changes. This kind of information is particularly helpful in improving the school's ability to be proactive rather than reactive

Perceptions: Individuals act on perceptions regardless of the reality of circumstances. Surveys offer insight into how various audiences perceive situations vis-à-vis how they really are and how correctly the school is interpreting those perceptions. This is especially true of groups with whom the school has limited contact. Surveys allow misperceptions to be uncovered and corrected before they become entrenched beliefs.

Surveys generally are conducted in three ways: written questionnaires, telephone surveys, and online surveys. Each type is discussed in the following paragraphs.

Get it in writing

Written surveys are one of the most common types of data gathering. The process involves distributing paper questionnaires to the target audiences and then collecting them.

Written surveys have several advantages that make them appealing.

Low Cost: The cost of producing written questionnaires is pennies per copy, especially if the school reproduces them on its own equipment. The cost of reproducing and distributing questionnaires allows the school to reach a large number of people.

If the school chooses to produce its own questionnaires, the quality of the copies must be high. Distributing poor quality questionnaires sends a negative message about the importance the school places on the survey process. It is better to have questionnaires printed externally if the school's photocopy equipment cannot produce high-quality copies.

Written surveys may be sent to and collected from recipients by U.S. mail. If respondents must return questionnaires by mail, a postage-paid envelope should be included to achieve a better return rate. To reduce distribution costs, students, parents, and volunteers can deliver and pick up questionnaires from community residents. Questionnaires for parents may be distributed and returned through student take-home packets.

Ease of completion: Respondents can complete a well-designed questionnaire quickly within their own time schedule; consequently, they are more likely to participate. Because respondents can complete the questionnaire privately when it is convenient, written questionnaires are not perceived to be as intrusive as personal or telephone interviews.

Greater candor: People may not answer questions about their income, education level, age, or controversial issues truthfully when speaking to an interviewer over the telephone or in person. It is not uncommon for interviewees to say what they think the interviewer wants to hear or to answer in a way that puts themselves in a good light. Respondents are more likely to answer such questions truthfully in an anonymous written questionnaire.

Ease of tabulation and analysis: Computer software can facilitate data entry, tabulation, and data analysis of written questionnaires. If the process is simple and accurate, the school or district is more likely to conduct research on a regular basis.

Written surveys are not without disadvantages. The most significant are the following:

Low Response Rate: Written questionnaires produce the lowest response rate of the commonly used survey methods. This is especially true if questionnaires are distributed and returned via the mail. Even when recipients intend to complete and return the questionnaire, they do not always follow through. It is possible to boost the return rate by delivering and picking up the questionnaires. Use the neighborhood paper to notify survey recipients about the survey and remind them about pick-up times

Inability to interact with respondent: Telephone interviewers know that some of the best information they receive is when respondents extend their answers beyond what the question asks. This kind of elaboration is rare in written surveys where few people will volunteer more information than is requested. Allowing opportunity for comments in the written questionnaire can lessen this disadvantage, but cannot compensate for the advantage of personal interaction.

Written questionnaires do not allow the respondent to ask for clarification if the wording is ambiguous or unclear. Any misunderstanding of the questions will result in inaccurate information.

Inadequate sample. The goal of a public survey is to gather information from a wide range of residents. Generally, people who are motivated to complete and return questionnaires are those who have an interest in the topic or an association with the organization collecting information. The responses to a written questionnaire may not represent the opinions of the total population.

Is it better to call?

Telephone surveys offer some advantages over written surveys.

Greater sampling: More than 95 percent of households in the United States have telephone service. A telephone survey can reach a greater sampling of people, especially if a random dialing system with callback capability is used. Individuals who will not take the time to read and fill out and return a 15–20 minute written questionnaire are frequently willing to participate in a 15–20 minute telephone survey.

Quick completion time: With good organization and sufficient staff, it is possible to complete a telephone survey in a week. A written survey could take one month or more to distribute and collect.

Produce more information: It is easier to talk than to write; therefore, people generally provide more information when they give their responses verbally. People who agree to give the interviewer a specified amount of time will often talk much longer and more openly than expected. The personal interaction allows a skilled interviewer to probe for more information. A telephone survey also allows the respondent to ask for clarification of a question he does not understand, whereas on a written survey the respondent may skip the question or worse give an answer without understanding what is being asked.

Telephone surveys also have disadvantages.

Cost may be higher than written questionnaires. This is particularly true if an external firm conducts the survey. However, the higher cost may be warranted if you are conducting a major community survey. Because professional research firms have personnel experienced in conducting surveys, multiple phones lines with random dialing capabilities, and tabulation equipment, they generally produce better results than schools and districts that do not have the requisite personnel or equipment. For some participants an external firm offers the notion of impartiality and credibility. Participants may be more willing to provide frank answers to an interviewer not associated with the school or district, and they may have more confidence in the results.

Respondents have little time to think about their answers. The quickness of completion that makes telephone surveys attractive also has a downside. Prior to the survey, participants may not have spent much time thinking about an issue yet they must provide an immediate response. If the survey deals with complex issues, the result may be a significant number of "don't know" or "no opinion" responses because respondents have neither an opportunity nor enough information to form an opinion.

Answering machines. People often use answering machines to take their calls even when they are available to answer the phone. If the call is not answered, the opportunity to participate is lost. Alerting people through the local media or notices in the school paper prior to the survey can improve participation. If possible, give specific days and times when the survey will be conducted. For example, "The community telephone survey will be conducted during the week of Feb. 2–6 from 7 p.m. to 9 p.m."

Go online

The increasing use of home personal computers has made surveying via computers an attractive option for gathering information. Computer-driven surveys take two forms: E-mail questionnaires sent directly to the target audience and Internet/intranet surveys posted on a Web page. Use E-mail messages to direct the target audience to a Web page that contains the survey. As with other methods, there are advantages and disadvantages.

Computer surveys offer the following advantages:

Cost. Computer directed surveys eliminate the cost of producing, distributing, and collecting paper surveys, the personnel and equipment necessary for telephone surveys, and substantially decrease the cost of data entry and tabulations costs. The costs are limited to labor attached to questionnaire design and construction. However, in the case of E-mail surveys, unless you possess the E-mail addresses of your audience, you may have to purchase them.

Speed. Hundreds, even thousands, of surveys can be sent and returned in a day or two via E-mail. Web-based surveys require the respondent to visit the site, but as with E-mail surveys, hundreds even thousands can be gathered in a day or two and the data are instantly input and tabulated.

Skips are automated. Skips occur when a respondent is requested to skip specific questions based on a previous answer. For example a question that states, *If you have answered Question 5 as "No", please skip the next three questions.* Web-page surveys (not E-mail surveys) can automatically guide the respondent through the questionnaire to prevent errors.

Increased response rates. The ease of completing and submitting a computer-based questionnaire, plus their newness, increases the response rate.

Disadvantages include:

Limited access. The use of computer-driven surveys requires that the target audience have E-mail and access to the Internet. Those channels may not be available to certain populations. If the respondents are limited to people who have Internet access, the results cannot be generalized to the whole community.

Skewed results. If your questionnaire is on a Web page, you do not know who is responding or how many times. People from anywhere in the world can complete the questionnaire multiple times. However, it is possible to require a sign-in process to participate and software is available that prevents people from replying multiple times.

The survey method the school chooses will depend on budget, time constraints, capabilities, and the scope of the data the school wants to collect. No matter what the method of data gathering is, asking the right questions in the right way is critical to collecting useful data. Not only will a set of well-written questions produce high quality data, but they can also serve as a model for future questions. The following pages contain ways to help the school write its own survey questions or critique those written by an external organization.

Ask the right questions in the right way

A common disappointment with survey results is the realization that the questions did not provide the needed information. Asking the right questions in the right way is critical whether the survey is written, computer driven, or person-to-person. Know exactly what kind of information you want to gather, then form questions that will solicit that information. It sounds simple, but not asking the right questions is one of the most common mistakes in surveys. The result is useless information.

In a written survey, the respondent cannot ask for help if he does not understand the questions. Therefore it is essential that written surveys contain clearly constructed questions. The chance is far greater that respondents will not complete questionnaires if they find the questions difficult to answer. Below are guidelines to help you word questions properly.

Know what you need to know. Time spent determining exactly what you need to know is time well spent. Knowing whether someone does or does not do something is helpful, even more helpful is knowing why.

If you want to know whether the community finds the school Web site useful for finding the information they want, a question such as,

Do you use the school Web site for information you need about the school?
Yes   No

will not provide sufficient information to make an informed assessment of the Web site's effectiveness. A "Yes" response does not necessarily mean that the Web site is helpful, appealing, or popular. Use does not always imply satisfaction. People may go to the site as a last resort because information they receive through other means is insufficient, not timely, or not helpful. A "No" response is not necessarily a criticism of the site. People may not have Internet access, realize what kind of information the site provides, or even know about the site. Getting the right information may require a series of specific questions such as the following:

Do you know that the school has its own Web site?
Yes   No

If you have used the Web site, please answer the following questions.

I use the school Web site to get information I need.
Always   *Frequently*   *Sometimes*   *Never*

I find the information I need
Always   *Frequently*   *Sometimes*   *Never*

The information I need is easy to find
Always   *Frequently*   *Sometimes*   *Never*

Eliminate ambiguity. Do not force people to guess what you are asking. Upon first reading, a respondent may understand the following question:

I attend my child's school events.
Yes   *No*

as referring to *any* or *some* events. On second thought, the respondent wonders if a "yes" answers requires attendance at *all* events. A better approach would be to give the respondent a choice of responses such as:

I attend my child's school events.

Always   *Sometimes*   *Seldom*   *Never*

Ensure that everyone understands the same question in the same way every time. Questionnaire reliability requires that each question be so clearly worded that all respondents will interpret it in the same way every time. Specificity is the key.

Words that have different meanings to different people produce questions that are subject to multiple interpretations. In the question, *Do you communicate often with your child's teacher?* the respondent might interpret the word *often* as anywhere from weekly to once every couple of months. A better question is,

How often do you communicate with your child's teacher during the school year?

More than once a month   Several times a year   Once or twice a year

Not at all

Ask questions people can answer. This may sound like an obvious statement, but often survey questions are written with an assumption that the respondents have certain knowledge, awareness, or understanding that they may not have. A parent may not be able to answer the question, *Has your child experienced bullying at school?* Unless a child chooses to confide in his parents, they may not know whether he has been bullied at school. A possible approach might be to describe signs of emotional distress caused by bullying and ask the parent if the child exhibits any of these signs.

Respondents cannot answer if they do not understand the language that is used. Like many professional groups, educators tend to use jargon, technical terms, or acronyms that are unfamiliar to the community. If you must use such language, clearly explain what it means.

A respondent cannot answer two issues in the same question. It is impossible to give an accurate answer to the question, *Do you find the school staff members courteous and knowledgeable?*, if the respondent finds the staff members to have one attribute, but not the other. A better approach is to provide a question that offers specific answers.

In your experiences with school staff members, do you find them to be (please check all that apply)

Courteous   Knowledgeable   Helpful   Friendly

Avoid using absolute words such as *everyone, everything, always,* and *never.* It is difficult to answer a question such as, *Do you believe that the state should do everything it can to provide needed technology to our school children?* A "Yes" response to the phrase "everything it can" suggests the respondent is agreeable to anything the state chooses to do, including raising taxes. A "No" response suggests the respondent does not believe it is important for the state to help provide technology to schoolchildren.

A question that is too broad, such as *Rate the overall quality of your child's teachers,* is impossible to answer if the respondent considers some teachers as excellent and others as poor. A better question is,

The number of my child's teachers I would rate good to excellent is

All   Most   Some   None

"Yes" or "No" answers may not offer the full range of choices a respondent needs to answer a question precisely. Instead of a yes or no response to the question,

Are you satisfied with the food served in the school cafeteria?

ask the question,

How satisfied are you with the food served in the cafeteria?

Very satisfied   Somewhat satisfied   Not satisfied

People who take the time to answer a questionnaire want to answer the questions accurately. Questions that are difficult to answer or confusing will produce a negative reaction that may result in non-completion of the survey.

Avoid leading questions. Do not construct questions with language that leads the respondent to a predetermined answer. Your data will be manipulated and worthless. Special interest groups that want to use their "results" to prove a point use this type of questioning. Their interest is not in finding accurate data, but rather answers that will support a predetermined point of view. Questions such as, *Do you believe that the person who educates your children should be paid less than the person who collects your garbage?* or *Do you think tax dollars should be used to teach easily influenced children about all types of sexual behavior?* leave little doubt as to the "correct" answer.

Even subtle phrasing can create leading and confusing questions. Consider the following two questions:

Do you agree with the city council's decision to oppose limiting construction of new early learning centers?

Do you agree with the city council's decision to support construction of new early learning centers?

Although the questions ask the same thing, they are likely to produce different reactions. It can be difficult to write a neutral question, especially if the issue is a controversial one. It is helpful to have people of differing viewpoints pre-test problematic questions.

Provide range questions for demographic information. When giving personal information such as income, age, education levels, people generally feel more comfortable with range questions. For a question regarding income, for example, offer a range such as *Under $20,000, $20,000–$34,999 $35,000–$ 44,999*, etc. Choose ranges that reflect the income range of the community. Asking questions with specific ranges can avoid ambiguous answers. If you ask, *How long have you lived in the district?* some people may answer, "A long time". Instead, ask *How many years have you lived in the district?* or give ranges such as *Under five years–six to ten years, eleven to fifteen year, etc.* To avoid confusion, be certain that your ranges do not overlap. If the choices for age are 18–25, 25–35, 35–45, etc. the respondent will fall into two categories.

Give respondents an opportunity to express themselves. Close-ended questions provide a selection of answers from which the respondent can choose. Open-ended questions require respondents to come up with their own answers. Because open-ended questions do not limit responses to pre-set answers, respondents have the opportunity to express themselves in their own words. Open-ended questions can provide some of your most valuable information.

Questions should be easy to understand and answer. Asking people to, "List the three things you like best about our school" or "List the three things you like least about our school" is preferable to asking them to write a short essay on their likes and dislikes concerning the school. In addition, short answers or lists are easier to categorize and analyze.

Take care not to include too many open-ended questions; two or three should be sufficient. Too many open-ended questions may discourage the respondent and complicate processing results.

Accommodate language differences: If your community has a significant number of non-English speaking residents, questionnaires should be translated to ensure inclusivity. The translation must be precise. There are dozens of funny and not-so-funny examples of what inexact translations actually communicated. With written questionnaires, the respondent does not have the opportunity to ask the meaning of a poorly translated question or phrase. In addition, a poor translation shows a lack of respect for the group's participation

You need good instruments

The quality of the instrument used in a survey has a significant influence on its success in providing meaningful data.

KISS—Keep it Short and Simple. A 15-page questionnaire will discourage participation. Low participation will result in data that are of little value. It is better to use a few shorter surveys spread out over time than one huge survey.

Keep the length of the questionnaire to no more than four double-sided pages, shorter if it addresses a single issue such as school safety or volunteer satisfaction. Respondents are more likely to complete a questionnaire that appears to take no more than 10–15 minutes.

Look at each question and ask yourself why you need this information and what you will do with it. If you cannot find sufficient reason to keep it, take it out.

Make the questionnaire appealing. The overall look of the questionnaire can influence the response rate. Create a cover sheet that contains the school logo or an attractive, professional looking graphic design along with the school name, survey date (Spring 2004), and survey title. Use a heavier weight of paper in a pale color such as gray or cream for the cover page and add some color to the text or artwork. You want the respondent to take your survey seriously; so, avoid comic or cute clip art.

The first time the respondent looks at the questionnaire, he sees it as a whole. Use enough white space in the margins and keep the questions well spaced to prevent an overcrowded, mind-numbing look.

The type should be 11 or 12 point in an easy-to-read font. Use a high quality paper and have the questionnaire photocopied at a professional copy center if the school's copy equipment does not product crisp, clear copies. Fuzzy, faded type on poor quality paper creates a poor impression of the school and the survey.

Begin the questionnaire with clear instructions on how to complete it. Use short sentences and basic words. If the instructions are too complicated, the respondent may become discouraged even before he gets started. The first few questions should be simple to answer and non-controversial.

Once the respondent is engaged in completing the questionnaire, it is likely that he will finish it even if the questions become more complex. However, avoid putting the most important questions at the end of the questionnaire in the event that the respondent fails to finish.

Group questions together that have the same response options (yes/no, multiple choice, ranking, fill-in-the-blank). Changing the response format frequently is tiring to the respondent.

Group items into logically coherent sections. Jumping from one issue to another can make the questionnaire seem confusing and unfocused. Keeping all questions related to a specific topic or issue together help the respondent understand the rationale behind the questions.

Number the questions and number the pages (include the total number of pages, e.g. page 2 of 4) in case the questionnaire pages become detached. Printing on both sides will hold down costs and give the respondent fewer pages to keep track of.

Include an introduction letter. To introduce the questionnaire, insert a cover letter that states the purpose of the survey, how the school intends to use the data, the importance of participation, and appreciation of the respondent's participation. For example, a letter accompanying a communication survey might read as follows:

Dear Parent or Guardian,

We at Lincoln Middle School know it is important to communicate with the parents and guardians of our students. It is also important that you are able to communicate with us. You can help us determine how well we are communicating and how we can improve by answering the questions on the enclosed Communication Survey.

Your answers will be used to help us determine the best way to create and maintain good two-way communication with you. It is important that you answer all questions including the demographic information. The questionnaires are anonymous to ensure the confidentiality of your responses.

Please return the questionnaire in the enclosed envelope before October 25, 2004. We will report the results of the survey on the school Web site and in our school newsletter.

The administration and staff at Lincoln Middle School appreciate the time you give to complete this questionnaire and we thank you for your participation. If you have any questions, please contact the survey coordinator, Cindy Butler, at 713.555.5535 or at her school E-mail address <u>cbutler@lincolnms.edu</u>.

Sincerely,

Amelia Flores, Principal

If the survey is conducted by telephone, have a statement containing the same elements as the introduction letter that the interviewer reads to the participant.

Guarantee confidentially. Even when the survey does not involve controversial or emotional issues, people should feel confident that the information and opinions they provide cannot be linked to them. This is particularly important if school personnel conduct the survey. Understandably, school staff members, students, even parents, may be reluctant to express honest opinions if they feel that administrators have access to their individual responses. State, in the cover letter or in the questionnaire, that participation is anonymous.

Always pre-test questionnaires

The best way to ensure that the questions meet the necessary requirements is to have questions pre-tested by individuals who are similar to the ones you want to survey. Gather a small group and go through each question to ensure that the questions are worded correctly, the response choices are appropriate, and the instructions are clear. If the respondents speak languages other than

English, ensure that the translations are of the highest quality and that the questions are culturally acceptable.

Let them know what is coming

Alerting the target audience that the school or district will conduct a survey can boost participation significantly. If the survey audience is limited to the school's community, a pre-survey post card or flyer explaining the purpose of the survey and the importance of participation should be mailed a week to 10 days before the survey is conducted. To encourage people to return written questionnaires, send out follow-up post cards two weeks after the initial survey distribution. A PDF copy of the questionnaire posted on the school or district Web site allows respondents who have lost or misplaced the questionnaire to print copies.

An article or news spot in local media channels before a community survey can stress the importance of involvement and increase the participation rate. Provide information on the purpose of the survey and how and when it will be conducted. After the survey, issue a press release reviewing the results and explain how the district or school intends to use the information.

Timing may not be everything, but it is important

When and how often to conduct surveys depends largely on the type of survey. An annual survey to determine parents' or students' satisfaction will be more fruitful when conducted at the end of the school year. The school is likely to have greater participation and receive answers that are more reflective if it conducts teacher surveys during holiday and vacation periods when teachers have more time.

Consider how recent events might skew data. The best time to conduct a survey regarding new policies and procedures is not immediately after implementation. Allow people time to adjust to the changes and experience the benefits. A survey a few months after the changes will give a better view of how the changes are being accepted.

It is not necessary to conduct research before each marketing decision. A few well-constructed surveys should provide the school with the information it needs to make sound decisions for some time. If the marketing team has completed the school assessment, it should know what areas require more decision-making information.

Conduct shorter surveys related to single issues such as volunteer satisfaction once a year. A major survey of the community every four or five years should be sufficient unless major issues or changes have occurred. Conducting surveys more frequently will not be worth the money and effort and can cause survey burnout in your target audiences.

Is it legal?

Before conducting student surveys, check your state's regulations. Some states require parental consent for student questionnaires. Recently, parents filed and won a suit against a Texas school district to stop surveys that they considered intrusive. The parents felt that the surveys invaded not only the privacy of the student but the student's family as well. Students whose parents complained suffered retaliation. No information is so valuable that it justifies forcing students to participate in surveys that create divisiveness in the community. Besides the school or district may find itself facing legal action.

In addition to obtaining parental consent, districts can reduce objections by creating a committee of parents and school staff to review potentially sensitive questionnaires and allow parents the option to review questionnaires prior to giving consent.

Survey warnings

When conducting research, consider some pitfalls common to information gathering.

Hidden agendas will foster cynicism. If motives other than the stated ones exist, they jeopardize the credibility of future research. If a school district's stated goal for gathering public opinion is to gather information can help them make informed decisions, but the hidden motive is to use the information to create manipulative messages, the district endangers future initiatives. In the same way that voters have become distrustful of political groups that use information from opinion polls to construct messages to play on voters' emotions, hidden agendas can create a public that is cynical of the district. Clearly state objectives and adhere to them.

A project that tries to satisfy everyone will satisfy no one. Research becomes unwieldy when it attempts to meet everyone's needs. To provide useful information, a survey should explore a few important issues thoroughly rather than many superficially. It is better to prioritize objectives and conduct multiple research projects over time.

The goal is not to produce pre-determined results. Circumstances sometimes make it tempting to use tactics designed to provide the desired research results. We have already discussed how the wording of questions can lead respondents to the desired answer.

Another way to sway results is to select a survey sample that is likely to produce the preferred outcome. If a district wishes to substantiate the claim that its teachers feel safe in the classroom, a survey that limits its sample primarily to elementary school teachers or teachers in schools with no reports of teacher intimidation is likely to support that claim.

The survey results, however, are useless and deceptive. A critical analysis of the survey instrument and the methodology will reveal the intent to manipulate results. Research conducted in this manner damages credibility.

Research results should lead to action. If a colleague continually asks for your advice and opinion about how he could improve his performance, but he never makes any change for the better, eventually you would come to view his requests as a waste of your time and his. When school or district administrators ask for opinions and perceptions, the assumption is that they will use the information to facilitate planning, initiate improvements, and make informed decisions. Gathering information does not mean you are letting other people make your decision, it means you are allowing them to have input into how decisions are made.

If the information gathered is never used, participants will see the effort as a waste of time and resources. They will be less likely to participate in the future. This is particularly true of audiences such as school staff members, parents, and students who are mostly closely affected by school or district decisions.

When to get help

The school should be able to handle most small surveys related to single issues or specific audiences such as volunteer satisfaction or effective communication channels. However, conducting a major research project such as a large community-wide survey or teacher and student surveys can seem like an overwhelming task. That is one reason why administrators avoid them. If uncertainty about the school's or district's ability to conduct a survey is an obstacle to gathering needed information, consider getting help from a research company.

Another reason to consider external help is to convey a sense of impartiality and anonymity. Some survey audiences are more likely to participate and to respond frankly if a third party, not affiliated with the school or district, conducts the survey. Teachers, for example, may not be forthcoming regarding satisfaction with their work environment if district personnel conduct the survey. As tempting as it may be, you really do not want respondents to tell you what they think you want to hear.

Larger towns and cities have marketing research firms that can provide consulting services or handle the entire project. You can find companies that specialize in school research on the Internet. In addition to questionnaires for a variety of audiences, these companies provide assistance with focus groups and in-depth interviews, evaluations and needs assessment and other consultation services.

If the school decides to use an external firm, pick three or four and interview them to evaluate their level of relevant experience, ability to carry out the project, understanding of education issues, and price. A good firm will appreciate the school's limited resources and suggest ways to get the most for the dollars spent.

If the school decides to conduct its own surveys, the Internet is also an excellent resource for locating both districts that have conducted community, student, and parent surveys and companies that specialize in school-based surveys. Questionnaires specific to school issues are available for purchase and can be modified to meet your school's specific requirements.

Data-driven marketing

Data can be used in two ways to market your school. One way involves the collection, analysis, and dissemination of statistical school related data. The other way involves the organization of data related to external groups within the district or school environment.

Individuals make decisions based on information. But, people in the community are not all looking for the same kind of information. Parents who are deciding where their child will attend elementary school want information that is different from a student deciding where she will attend high school.

Parents may want data on students' performance on state accountability tests, teacher-student ratios, percentage of teachers with advanced degrees, or special programs. The high school student may want to know about advanced placement or honors classes, extracurricular activities, or the amount of technology in the school. Even among parents, the criteria for school selection may vary. The demographic make-up of the student and teachers, availability of bilingual programs, or incidents of violence may be of concern. Companies considering relocation want specific kinds of information about the local schools or district such as the district's rating, graduation rates, student performance on exit exams, and collaborative programs between businesses and schools. Teachers looking for positions may want to know about class sizes, staff turnover, professional development programs, or the percentage of staff with advanced degrees.

All school districts collect and maintain statistical data for their own internal use. In marketing your school, knowing what kinds of information the various external groups want to obtain and being able to provide it readily is critical. Establishing a source of appropriate data will allow the district and its schools to respond quickly to requests for information. When the district or school makes frequently requested data available, in paper form or on the district's or school's Web site, the message is that the district and its schools consider this information valuable to the district and the community.

A second kind of database allows the school to assemble information about the various groups within the school's environment, sort and store the information, and retrieve specific segments quickly. Several database software programs are available that make the process of inputting and retrieving data uncomplicated. The software consolidates the input data in a file and allows for quick retrieval of specific segments as required. A typical process might be as follows:

• Build a list of everyone the school may want to contact at some time.

• Input basic contact information such as names and addresses. For some groups, such as parents, volunteers, and key communicators, include telephone and fax numbers and E-mail addresses.

• Determine the categories you want to establish. Examples of categories are:

> Parents
>
> Parents of children in your school's feeder pattern
>
> Parents with children not in your school
>
> Contacts in the business community
>
> Volunteers
>
> PTO members
>
> Retired people
>
> Registered voters

There are marketing benefits attached to using a database. Being able to retrieve particular segments of the database allows the school to send specific messages to a small group or general information to a larger group or groups. Communication can be personalized. The speed of data retrieval allows for rapid distribution of information in a crisis. It is advantageous to have "crisis communication" indicators attached to names of parents, local agencies, hospitals, key communicators, even the media so their information can be retrieved and information can be disseminated to them quickly.

The ease of data retrieval promotes pro-active communication. Consider the following example of how database information could help in the marketing process by targeting specific groups with a specific message.

Riverside High School is holding an open house. The school would like to use this occasion to begin recruiting middle school students for its new *Scientists in the Making* program. The school obtains from its central administration the names and addresses of middle school students who have scored at or above a particular level on the science portion of the state accountability test.

The district can provide this data because it collects and stores this information in its own database.

Selected students and their parents are invited to Riverside High School's open house to meet with school representatives and receive an introduction to the *Scientists in the Making* program. The school asks students and parents who attend to register. Their names and addresses are put into the school's database. During the year, these students and their families are sent updates on what is happening in the *Scientists in the Making* program and invitations to science related activities.

Good information is essential to all aspects of school marketing. Marketing research can ensure that the information used is accurate and current. Database marketing then allows the school to use the information in a systematic way to maximizes the effectiveness of the school's message.

4

Marketing Communication

We cannot *not* communicate. Everything we do or say communicates something, including absolute silence. Even space and time send messages. A spacious office with a bank of windows overlooking a city skyline communicates something about the status of the occupant. How much time we are willing to give to a meeting communicates the importance we place on the subject and the participants. International diplomacy is rife with non-verbal indicators that communicate the significance of events. Who meets with whom, where, and for how long can have global implications.

Neither can we *uncommunicate*. Once we have communicated something, we can apologize, rephrase, or deny, but we cannot undo the communication act. As a result, all communication has consequences attached to it. Situations may exist when no explicit communication is the best course of action until the situation changes. However, an avoidance of communication carries its own message. Just ask someone who has received the "silent treatment".

Communication is at the heart of marketing. It is not overstating the importance of communication to say that if the school is not communicating well, it is not marketing well. Your school may have valuable benefits to offer students, parents, and the community, but if the audience is not willing to read or listen to the message, those attributes may remain unknown. Communication takes many forms: verbal and non-verbal, written and spoken, images and symbols, interpersonal, group, and mass communication. All forms are important and should be given consideration when constructing communication.

Understanding the communication process

Communication is both a simple and a complex process. It is simple in that the process includes few steps. Harold Laswell, a social scientist, suggested that the entire process could be summarized by answering the following questions:[5]

> Who
> Says what
> Using what channel
> To whom
> With what result?

In the communication model below, the sender or source constructs a message then sends it via a channel to a receiver who interprets it. The receiver then provides feedback in some form to the sender. The feedback could be a response to the message or no response, which also communicates something.

Communication is a never-ending process. The arrow before the sender or source indicates that communication received by him prior to sending his message influences how he encodes or constructs his message. The arrow after the message is decoded indicates that how the receiver interprets or decodes the message will influence messages she sends to others. The complex nature of communication derives from the variables at each stage that affect the quality of the communication.

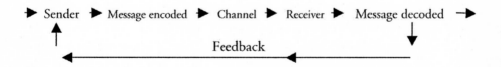

The principal, Mr. Jenkins, has received a message from a concerned parent regarding a serious emotional issue with her child. Based on the information contained in this prior message, Mr. Jenkins (sender) constructs a message (message encoded) that he sends via E-mail (channel) to the Ms. Chatham, the school counselor, (receiver) who then interprets the message (message decoded) and responds to Mr. Jenkins (feedback). The information received in the message from Mr. Jenkins will influence how Ms. Chatham constructs her message when she communicates with the concerned parent.

Variables at each stage of the communication process can affect the effectiveness of the communication process. For example, if Mr. Jenkins does not construct his message in a way that conveys the seriousness of the situation, Ms. Chatham may not respond in a timely manner, thereby exacerbating the situation.

The sender may be an individual, group, or even an organization that has a message to communicate. Sender variables are characteristics that influence what symbols (words, gestures, signs) the sender uses to encode the message. Sender variables include age, gender, education level, nationality, profession, race, even an emotional state in the case of individuals and structural characteristics and specific agendas in the case of groups or organizations. An experienced school administrator would likely use different language than a middle-school student to communicate the same idea.

Communication will be more effective, when the sender constructs or encodes the message with symbols that are meaningful and persuasive to the receiver. If the district is communicating with the community to persuade them of the merits of a bond issue, how the message sent to senior taxpayers is encoded might differ from how the one sent to parents with children in the school is encoded. In bond elections, encoding may have legal restrictions. It is, however, sometimes difficult for the sender not to be overly influenced by his own characteristics and specific circumstances as he constructs a message. When constructing a message, it is essential to consider how the receiver will interpret it. For this reason, it is important to know as much as possible about your audiences.

The channel is the method used to deliver the message. Some channels are more effective in delivering a particular kind of message than others. Information of interest to the general public is delivered best via channels (television, radio, newspapers) where people generally look for news. In addition, traditional news sources provide a level of credibility. Communication to specific groups can be delivered effectively using computer generated presentations or teleconferencing. Personal messages are generally best communicated one-to-one, although the novelty of proposing marriage via a billboard has sometimes resulted in the desired response.

When choosing a channel consider the variables that may determine how effective it will be. A public relations campaign I worked on required that we get a message concerning an event to the parents of schoolchildren. Despite our reservations, the district insisted that information concerning the event be sent home with the children. Their main consideration regarding the delivery channel was cost; ours was reliability. The event was only partially successful, because only about 30 percent of the parents received the message. Students forgot to give their parents the information or lost it. By the time the district realized the inefficiency of the delivery system, it was too late to take corrective action. The variable, in the this case, was the degree of student reliability.

To ensure channel reliability, it is best to use multiple channels. For example, if the school wants to convey information concerning a critical health issue, the situation may require that, in addition to messages sent home with children, channels include E-mails or telephone calls to parents, news stories in the media, announcements made through health or local religious organizations, and bulletins on the school Web site.

When selecting channels for school communications evaluate their effectiveness by asking these questions: Is the channel available to the intended receiver? Is the channel one that the intended receiver is likely to use? Is the channel one considered credible by the receiver? Is the channel technically reliable? In the example above, using only E-mail to convey critical health information is not effective if few in your audience have access to it.

If you choose personal interaction, such as a presentation to a group or a one-on-one conversation, as your channel, you are communicating non-verbally as well as verbally. Non-verbal communication, such as facial expressions, body movements and gestures, tone of voice, emphasis on certain words, and pauses, sends a message that parallels the verbal one. If the non-verbal communication is inconsistent with the verbal, your message will be mixed and ineffective. An administrator who professes interest in a community member's concerns, but continues to take telephone calls and fiddle with paperwork during the meeting is sending a mixed message that communicates insincerity and lack of interest.

The next step in the communication process is decoding by the receiver. The most important truism to remember in creating effective communication is that all communication is receiver based. The message you send is not necessarily the message that is received. Message interpretation is subject to the receiver's mental filters. These mental filters are influenced by the same factors, such as language, culture, level of education, emotional state, age, gender, or economic status, that influence the sender. To communicate effectively, it is necessary to have an awareness of filters that might influence the receiver's interpretation of the message. Some filters, such as an emotion, may be temporary. Other filters, such as language or education level may change slowly over time.

Feedback is always sent to the sender by the receiver. Even if the receiver says nothing and walks away from the sender, feedback has occurred. A sender can be so focused on his own message that he ignores feedback. However, feedback provides important clues regarding the interest, understanding, and receptivity of the sender's message. If a sender is attentive to the feedback, he can determine if the intended message was conveyed, and if not, take corrective action.

Choose your words carefully

Words are powerful. Words have instigated some of humans' most noble and ignoble deeds. Words can change, shape, even create reality. Remember the children's defiant rhyme, "Stick and stones, can break my bones, but words can never hurt me." Even as children, we knew it was not true. Words can hurt. Words have denigrated entire groups of people, but they also have inspired others to rise above oppression.

Choose your words carefully. Words the school uses in its messages set a tone that affects how its audiences view it. Most schools I visit have a sign at the entrance that requests that visitors go to the school office to sign in and receive a visitor badge. In some instances, the language in these signs is so inhospitable that I feel like an intruder. The language of the sign creates a negative emotional response that influences my perception of how welcome visitors are. If such language is pervasive, it can dissuade an already hesitant parent from visiting the school.

How are school communications to parents, staff members, and students worded? Do requests or directions have a positive or negative tone? *Locker doors should be kept closed and locked* is preferable to *Do not leave lockers open or unlocked.* A message that tells parents, *We can accept only checks or money orders for activities fees* is preferable to *We will not accept cash or credit cards for activities fees.*

It may seem like a small thing; but, the words the school chooses creates an effect that influences how the receiver reacts to current and future messages. How the receiver reacts influences how the receiver responds.

It's all about the receiver

Effective communication is receiver-focused. A message may describe all the school's attributes and benefits; but, the message will not be effective if it does not communicate the attributes and benefits in a way that the audience finds logical, emotionally appealing, and credible. This is one reason why it is so important to know and understand the various audiences in the community.

Always keep the receiver in mind when creating messages. Too often the sender concentrates on what he wants the audience to know rather than what the audience wants or needs to know. If the communication piece is an invitation to a school event, the sender may consider the time, place, and type of activity to be the most important items to communicate. If the receivers are new immigrants, their concerns may be whether they will be able to communicate with other attendees, if they will feel comfortable, and why attending is important for their children.

Use words, ideas, and images to which your audience can relate. Do not use jargon or technical words. Appeal to the values of your audience. For schools, pictures of children are always appealing, especially if the pictures are of children from the school. Include not only photographs of students, but also staff members, volunteers, and parents of various national and ethnic groups. If you feel that you do not have sufficient knowledge about a particular group to create an effective message, request assistance from business people, cultural organizations, religious leaders, or agency workers who are familiar with the targeted audience.

Let us say that your school has a significant number of Spanish-speaking students. Past attendance of their parents at school events has been low. You want a communication piece that will encourage these parents to come to an open house. Certainly, your invitation should be in Spanish as well as English. Use Spanish that is slang and idiom free. Slang and idioms used in Mexico may have different meanings to people from Central or South America.

Send the invitation from the students as well as the administration and staff members. Include Spanish-speaking administrators, teachers, or staff members as part of the welcoming team. If you use photographs in your communication piece, use pictures of school activities that would be of particular interest to the families and include Hispanic students, parents, and teachers.

Stress the family aspect of the open house and the importance of the child's family in his/her school life. The goal is for the parents to feel that if they attend they will feel welcome and be able to communicate their expectations and concerns to people who not only understand their language, but also their values. Most of all parents should feel that their participation will benefit their children.

It is also important that students understand that their parents are welcome. Children may experience anxiety if there is doubt about how their parents will be received by the staff members and other parents. Use students as one of your channels of communication by sending invitations home with them, positively promote the event in their classes, and encourage them to prepare work to show to their parents.

In some cases, special attention may be needed for groups who have recently suffered great personal loss and displacement from war and political or religious persecution. The school staff members may feel ill-equipped to create messages that will communicate effectively with these groups. Help can come from social clubs, religious organizations, or assistance agencies that have close interaction with the groups.

When developing communication, do not think in terms of large groups of people. Even though you may be communicating with a large group, imagine one person, the kind of person you want to reach, seeing or listening to your communication; then try to put yourself in his or her place. If necessary, get input from someone who matches the "profile" of the audience you are trying to reach. When the message is part of a major district initiative, use surveys or focus groups composed of members of your target audience such as students or senior taxpayers to gain an understanding of what the groups think.

We often create messages based on how we would view or understand them. This is like giving someone a gift because it is something that you want without consideration for the receiver's desires. The key is always construct your message with the recipient in mind.

Effective communication is a two-way street

Imagine that you and I are having a conversation; however, I do virtually all the talking. I speak about the subjects that are important to me, interrupt you frequently, and when you speak, my actions and responses indicate that I am not paying attention to what you are saying. Are we communicating effectively? I may think so; however, I doubt that you would. How would this type of interaction make you feel? Would you be inclined to repeat the experience if you had a choice?

This is how many organizations communicate. The organization believes it is communicating when it sends lots of information about itself to various groups with great regularity. School communications involve sending a steady stream of notices, bulletins, reports, and announcements about the school and its students. That is as it should be. However, if opportunities for incoming communication are limited primarily to parent/teacher conferences or the annual open house, the school is denying itself valuable, even essential, information.

The importance of acquiring comments, reactions, evaluations, inquiries, and data from internal and external audiences warrants an assessment of the school's ability and desire to seek such information and a plan to correct any deficiencies.

Below are some suggested questions for conducting an assessment.

- What channels for incoming communication does the school currently have in place?

- How do most people choose to communicate with the school? Telephone? Web site? Visits?

- Are communication channels easy to access?

- Does the school actively solicit or encourage incoming communication? How?

- What is the response time for inquires by telephone? Web site? In writing?

- Does the school have communication goals and policies? Are staff members aware of the goals and policies?

- What initiatives are there for personal interaction? How frequent are they?

- Does the school know the satisfaction level of people who communicate with the school? How does the school gather this information?

After the evaluation is complete, ask your audiences for their assessment. This can be done through informal channels such as conversations and meetings or through a formal survey. Then compare results. How well do they match? Are there major inconsistencies? A school may view its Web site as an excellent channel of communication, but external audiences may not know about it, find it difficult to navigate, or not have the ability to access it. The administration may advocate open communication with employees, but provide few secure opportunities for input.

Employees can be one of the most effective channels for collecting information. As members of social, religious, and special-interest groups within the community, employees can be eyes and ears for the school. Employees' spouses who work within the school's community have access to larger, more varied groups of people. The kinds of comments and questions they receive can provide insight about the concerns, opinions, and perceptions the public holds about issues related to the school.

Getting out of the school and into the community offers administrators excellent opportunities to solicit input. Whether you are making a formal presentation before a homeowners association or having a casual conversation at a civic club luncheon, use the occasion to ask for input.

Channels for incoming communication should offer positive experiences for the user. Invite communication only through channels that you feel confident will provide constructive interaction. If people are encouraged to submit questions or comments via an *Inquiry Line* on the school Web site, but the site is difficult to navigate and messages are not acknowledged, the channel is counterproductive. Not only will people not use it, but they will have doubts about the school's sincerity to serve their needs.

Within this chapter and Chapter 5 several avenues for creating two-way communication are described. Even with limited resources, a beneficial level of reciprocal communication is achievable.

The ostrich syndrome

I once faced stiff opposition to conducting employee and community satisfaction surveys for an organization from their public information officer. There was concern that public confidence had declined and the organization felt a survey was warranted. The public information officer, however, was afraid that any disapproving results would make it into the news and result in negative publicity. Fortunately, the organization understood that sticking one's head in the sand, and hoping problems will just disappear, is neither good marketing nor good policy.

One benefit of two-way communication is that it allows organizations to be proactive rather than reactive. When information flows in through formal and informal channels, the district or school can become aware of situations before they become issues or problems. It is preferable to find out about and address a problem or issue before it is an item presented to the school board or a story in the local paper. Parents, employees, students, and the community can provide insight about community perceptions and issues that the school might not be aware of otherwise. However, these groups will provide that information only if they feel that the school encourages and is honestly interested in gathering information from their constituencies.

Consider the following situation. A principal, who encourages input from school employees, hears that bullying in the school is becoming more than just the occasional flexing of adolescent egos. She gets with her marketing team to work out a proactive communication strategy to address the potential problem on multiple levels. The school calls upon police, district security, and mental health professionals for their expertise. Policies are established regarding bullying in the school and these are communicated to all employees, students, and parents in a variety of mediums. Confidential communication channels are set up for individuals to report incidents of bullying. School employees and parents receive guidelines for detecting the behavior patterns of the perpetrators or the recipients of bullying. Teachers, with the guidance of counselors, are requested to address bullying in their classrooms. Incidents of bullying are investigated and dealt with quickly.

Through a proactive approach, situations with the potential to harm students and the school were diffused. Does this approach guarantee that no incidents will ever occur? No, but the likelihood is diminished.

Many of us have a tendency to ignore unpleasant issues until forced to address them. Consider the lines of stressed-out people at post offices on April 15th. However, if I file my taxes late, I am the one who suffers the consequences. In a school environment, not acting in advance of problems can adversely affect a multitude of people. Being proactive can lessen the chances of an occurrence becoming a crisis.

Mixed messages, mixed results

Talk is cheap. Actions speak louder than words. If you talk the talk, you should walk the walk. Pick your favorite truism. If the school does not back up its "talk" with action, it could prove costly.

A school that says it welcomes visitors, but offers no place for them to park, has staff members that are rude or indifferent, and provides no visitor information is sending conflicting messages. A school that encourages people to volunteer but does not provide meaningful work or offer recognition for their efforts demonstrates insincerity. Inconsistency between message and action results in a loss of credibility.

Once credibility is lost, it is difficult to reestablish. Loss of credibility in one area can spill over onto others. Think about the messages sent internally and externally and honestly determine if the school can and will back them up with action. Following through with action sends a powerful message that your messages have merit.

Message consistency also provides credibility. Audiences feel they can rely on what is being communicated when there is no deviation from the message. The importance of consistency is evident in political campaigns. Staying "on message" is a major goal. Candidates frequently try to catch their opponents making conflicting statements so they can assail each other for being inconsistent. The implication being that what the candidate is saying now cannot trusted because last month he said something different. That may or may not be the case, but public perception may be swayed nevertheless.

Mixed messages generally result from a lack of focus. Having clear goals is essential to message consistency. If school safety is an issue in the community and the message is that one of the district's goal is to make safety a priority, then that message should be reinforced throughout the district in multiple ways until it is no longer an issue or concern.

If you have been on the receiving end of mixed messages, you know how confusing, frustrating and counterproductive they are. When people say one thing and do another or when messages are constantly changing, they come to have little meaning or importance. Staying "on message" is possible for the school or district when goals are clear and consistently articulated. The marketing team should monitor messages and activities to ensure that they are consistent with stated objectives.

You just can't beat one-on-one communication

Nothing is as effective as personal, one-on-one communication. Chances are a principal reason you continue to patronize a particular dry cleaners, auto mechanic, bank, financial planner, or florist is that you have come to know and trust them through personal contact and service. Would you take your business elsewhere just because you received a glossy, attractive brochure in the mail? Probably not. Flyers, brochures, and newsletters can be effective communication pieces, but they are not a replacement for personal communication. People form their strongest opinions through one-on-one contact.

When a principal found that some of her students' parents were considering a nearby private school, she did not send them a letter or brochure. The principal invited the parents to come for individual meetings. Through these meetings, the principal found out that the private school was marketing heavily to all the parents.

The private school's marketing concentrated on their special character-education program that appealed to these parents. Personal meetings gave the principal the opportunity to tell the parents about the character-education program that her school had initiated and to show them the curriculum and supporting materials. As a result of the meetings, all of the parents left their children in the school.

An additional benefit of the personal meetings was the information gathered from the parents. From parents' comments, the principal realized the school needed to communicate better regarding school initiatives and programs and that research on the school's competition would be beneficial.

Teachers and school staff have many opportunities at school functions, teacher conferences, sporting events, and holiday parties to form positive impressions of the school through one-on-one communication. It is to the school's benefit to provide training in customer service, public relations, and effective communication to teachers and staff members and encourage them to become good-will ambassadors for the school.

Clearing the hurdles to effective communication

All forms of communication face obstacles in attracting and holding someone's attention. Competition from other sources is the most obvious obstacle. Individuals are bombarded daily with messages from every medium, direct mail, radio, television, billboards, magazines, and now, the Internet. The school's message is like one in a group of children all jumping up and down, waving their hands shouting "Me! Me! Pick me!"

Not only must the school compete with the barrage of other messages, but it must also compete with the other activities in the audience's lives. The activity-filled lives people lead leave little time to give any message much attention. Think of yourself going through the pieces of mail you receive every day. How much time are you willing to give to each piece before you discard it or keep it to read? It is likely that initially each piece will receive fewer than 10 seconds of your time. Unless someone is particularly interested in the subject matter, she is not likely to give much time to processing the message. It is important to convey your message quickly and in a way that will attract and hold the receiver's interest.

In order to secure the receiver's attention, the message must stand out. Again, think about the pieces of mail that come to you each day or the multitude of commercials on television. Why do you notice one of these above the many? People are attracted to a message for any of several reasons. The message is relevant to something that is of interest to them, it creates a strong emotional feeling, it is striking or unconventional, it is humorous, or it is simply too clever to be ignored. The school's communication must be one that will stand out and hold the receiver's attention long enough to convey the message.

When a large urban district was facing a teacher shortage, the critical nature of the situation required more than the usual recruitment activities. A local advertising agency agreed to conduct a recruitment campaign at a reduced fee for the district. The results exceeded expectations.

Although many factors contributed to the campaign's success, including a generous sign-on bonus, an effective communication piece was a critical instrument in developing an awareness of the recruitment effort. Rather than rely on traditional ads in the usual recruitment venues such as classified ads and Internet sites where competition was heavy, the agency chose eye-catching billboards along major freeways and signage on mass transit vehicles where competition was less likely. By using billboards and bus signage, the agency put the message in front of people on their way to and from work who might be considering new career opportunities.

The billboard and signs comprised a black background with white and yellow text. One third of the sign displayed a photograph of an engaging child looking out at the viewer. On the remaining two-thirds in white text were the words, "Will **You** Be My **Teacher**?" The words "You" and "Teacher" were emphasized with larger, yellow text. The only other text on the sign provided the name of the district and a telephone number.

The simple layout and text of the advertisements allowed the reader to scan the message and understand the requested action quickly, a requirement for an appeal to people, in this case literally, on the move. Asymmetrical design attracted the eye to the main message. The eye then moved from the message to the sender of the message (district name), and the request for action (telephone number) in a matter of seconds.

The ads were visually and emotionally appealing in an unconventional way. The message was not the typical employment ad from a school district requesting the audience to consider teaching, but rather an array of attractive children of different races and ages asking simply and directly, "Will **you** be my **teacher**?" The face of an engaging child with a clear and touching request was sure to stand out from the usual employment ads. Atypical colors of black and yellow created a dramatic visual effect that distinguished the ads from their surroundings even in the clutter of competing signage.

In summary, the message was effective because it stood out from the competition in both form and placement, it took only seconds to read, understand, and solicit a response, and the design was dramatic, touching, and personal. It cleared the three hurdles of competition, time, and sameness.

Logos–Pathos–Ethos

Rhetoric, the art of effective expression and the use of persuasive language, goes back centuries. In *Rhetoric*, his first major work on the subject written in the 4th century B.C.E., Aristotle noted three components of persuasive communication, logos (logic), pathos (emotion), and ethos (credibility). Like much of what we inherited from the ancient Greeks, these ideas are still sound today. To be persuasive, a message, whether written or spoken, should be substantively sound, emotionally appealing, and from a source the audience considers credible.

The importance of these elements in creating persuasive communication requires that we spend some time examining each of them.

Logic. Logic requires that persuasive communication be reasonable, make the connection between ideas, define problems and offer solutions, show cause and effect, and provide information to validate the argument. In short, logic demands that the message make sense to the sender and the receiver. There may be cases when your relationship with the receiver or your level of authority is such that you can persuade someone by saying "Just trust me on this," but these instances are rare.

Logical messages reflect relationships such as cause and effect that are objective in nature. Generally, people expect these relationships to be substantiated by some kind of evidence. If the school is commending its mathematics program in its marketing materials, people are more likely to be persuaded of its excellence if the message is supported by data (evidence of higher student achievement in math).

When constructing logical messages, use language and connections that people will understand. A good approach is to state the problem, describe the solution, and show the results in a descriptive way. If you can do this by telling a story, the message is even more appealing.

In a presentation to show the effectiveness of a high school's program to decrease dropout rates, the narrator tells the story of one 16-year old student. He describes the boy's problems in school, his feelings of alienation, poor grades, and his inability to find any reason to stay in school. Then the narrator explains how the high school's program of intervention through counseling, after-school activities, and mentoring kept the boy in school until he graduated. The story ends with the boy's enrollment in a 2-year associate degree program. The personal tone of the story combined with facts about the emotional, social, and economic costs of dropouts for the individual and the community makes a compelling argument for the high school's program.

Emotion. Emotion is a powerful persuader. Even though we believe it is unwise to make decisions when we are emotional, and we are critical of arguments that play on our emotions, as feeling human beings, we are nevertheless susceptible to emotional appeals. Individuals, even entire nations, have allowed emotion to prevail over logic. History is replete with heroic and villainous deeds spawned by the ability to manipulate people through emotional arguments. The lucrative nature of motivational seminars is an indication of the appeal of emotional public speaking.

Because emotional arguments are generally more persuasive than logical ones, advertisers spend much time and money determining the types of messages that will tap their audience's emotions. It is virtually impossible to develop a persuasive message that contains no emotional appeal. Even if I try to sell you toothpaste with a logical argument about how regular brushing with my product will protect against tooth decay and loss, I still am capitalizing on your fear of potentially painful, expensive dental treatments and loss of teeth if you do not practice regular dental hygiene.

We often defend our emotional decisions with logic. If my ego and vanity influence me to spend a great sum of money for a luxury car, I may try to justify my action with a logical argument that the car is a better investment, will last longer, or is safer.

Generating positive emotions is more persuasive than producing negative ones. Often it is simply phrasing that makes one message more effective than another. Saying, "Our students will be safer with new security systems and policies", is more effective than a negative, more frightening statement, "Without the implementation of new security systems and policies, students are in jeopardy."

Because emotional appeals are subjective, the persuasiveness of the message depends on the receiver more so than a logical argument. Gender, age, race, educational level, and other characteristics play a significant role in message reception. Knowing your audience is essential to creating effective emotional messages.

Use emotional appeals with a heavy dose of caution. Highly emotional arguments may work in the short run, but if they are baseless or heavy-handed, the result is a loss of credibility. There is a difference between creating legitimate concern and scaring people.

Credibility. Many people argue that the most important element in persuasive communication is the credibility of the source. The idea is that no matter how persuasively logical or emotional an argument is, if the receiver does not hold the source as credible, he will not be persuaded. Often messages that may have been ignored are given credence if the sender is perceived as trustworthy.

The receiver determines the credibility of the source. That is why someone listening to a politician from the party she supports is likely to find the argument highly persuasive while another person from an opposing side finds the same argument incredulous. Advertisers pay entertainers and sports figures large sums of money to promote their products because much of the public finds these figures credible whether they have reason to or not.

Years ago, the actor, Robert Young, extolled the "benefits" of drinking Sanka decaffeinated coffee in television commercials. Young had no reason to be more credible about the benefits of coffee than any other actor or person. His credibility came from his years as Dr. Marcus Welby on a television series. Many people saw him as the caring, responsible doctor they knew from television. If Dr. Welby said Sanka was beneficial, it must be true.

The source of your school's communication should be appropriate to the message. Generally, we think of the principal as the appropriate source for communication, but in some cases teachers, counselors, or the school nurse may be more suitable.

In other situations, someone outside the school environment may have more credibility because she is seen as impartial. In some cases, alumni, parents, civic leaders, elected officials, volunteers, and business people may be perceived as more objective sources for communication than the school, which may be perceived as self-serving. This is particularly true for issues involving public action or approval such as bond issues or tax increases. Often religious, racial, national, or cultural groups find someone who reflects the characteristics of their particular group more credible than someone outside the group. A poor student from the inner city who regularly deals with poverty, drugs, and violence may not be persuaded by advice from an older, affluent person from the suburbs.

Other factors that influence how credible a person is perceived are appearance, status, background, age, and context. Certain audiences may find a person in professional dress more credible than the one in casual dress. Unfair as it is, studies show that many people are more easily persuaded by someone who is very attractive than one who is not. An article about the school or district in a nationally recognized newspaper may have more credibility than one in the neighborhood paper. Even the appeal of the person who introduces you before a speech may color the audience's perception of your credibility before you say a word.

Logic, emotion, and credibility should all be considered when constructing your messages. A good way to understand how these elements are used effectively is to analyze advertisements in magazines and on television. When an advertisement attracts or repels you, consider how logic, emotion, and credibility are used and why they were effective or ineffective in appealing to you. The marketing team can use this type of analysis as an exercise to help develop persuasive communication pieces.

Let your audience fill in the blanks

Messages are particularly effective when they engage the audience in the reasoning process. This is accomplished by having the audience fill in the blanks, make connections, and come to the desired conclusions without explicit direction. The most effective way to accomplish this is through an interactive reasoning device known as an enthymeme. This may sound like a big, complicated word, but enthymemes are simply truncated or shortened syllogisms. Remember the syllogism

All men are mortal
Socrates is a man
Therefore, Socrates is mortal

Enthymemes are similar to syllogisms except that the sender of the message omits either a premise or the conclusion with the expectation that the receiver will supply the appropriate missing phrase. If we take the Socrates syllogism mentioned above and omit either one of the premises or the conclusion, the expectation is that the receiver will complete the thought process in her own mind. Therefore, if I say, "All men are mortal and Socrates is a man", my expectation is that the receiver will conclude, "Oh, then Socrates must be mortal". Or, if I say, "Socrates is a man; therefore, he must be mortal," my expectation is that you will conclude, "All men must be mortal." The goal is to generate the most powerful kind of persuasion, self-persuasion.

One of the most extreme, famous, and controversial examples of the power of enthymemes was a political television advertisement created by Tony Schwartz. The advertisement known as the "Daisy" spot ran during the 1964 presidential race between Lyndon Johnson and Barry Goldwater.

The ad shows a little girl in a field trying to count as she pulls petals off a daisy. The audience hears her innocent voice saying, "1, 2, 3, 4, 5, 7, 6, 8, 9, 9" As she reaches "10" a strong male voice reverses the count, "10, 9, 8, 7, 6, 5, 4, 3, 2, 1." At zero, the freeze-frame on her face dissolves into deafening roar and the mushroom cloud of an atomic blast. The audience then hears the voice of

Lyndon Johnson, "These are the stakes—to make a world in which all God's children can live, or to go into the darkness. We must either love each other, or we must die." As the advertisement fades, a authoritative voice says, "Vote for President Johnson on November 3. The stakes are too high to stay at home."

The advertisement neither mentions Johnson's Republican opponent, Barry Goldwater, nor connects him in any way with using a nuclear bomb. However, Senator Goldwater was considered to be a "hawk" and he had made imprudent statements regarding using "nukes". Many who saw the commercial connected Goldwater's hawkish views with the chance that he might actually use the bomb thereby obliterating millions of innocents like the little girl. However, the negative association of nuclear bombs and Goldwater was made *not* in the content of the commercial but in the minds of the people who viewed it. Individuals came to a conclusion that was not stated. The audience, in effect self-persuaded.

The advertisement was so controversial it aired only once. However, the major networks reporting on the controversy showed the commercial on the evening news giving it free airtime and exposure to millions who had not seen it. The advertisement was devastating to Goldwater's election campaign.

Although the "Daisy" commercial used the enthymeme to make a negative association, they are just as powerful in making positive ones. During World War II, the government raised millions of dollars through war bonds by constructing messages built around the following premises:

Our country needs money to sustain the war effort.
War Bonds provide money.

The unspoken conclusion reached by those who read the messages and bought bonds was that by buying bonds they could help the country continue the war.

As simplistic as enthymemes may seem they are powerful because receivers construct them in their own minds based on their own beliefs, attitudes, and values. For that same reason, they can backfire when the intended message of the omitted premise or conclusion is not one with which the receiver would agree. In the example of the war bonds above, the message was effective because most people in the United States believed that continuing the war was a right and necessary action. However, if the majority of people had been against the war, the message would have had an opposite effect.

In using enthymemes, consider the audience. Will they fill in the blanks and make the conclusions that you want them to? *Remember, enthymemes are persuasive only when the message contains values, beliefs, and attitudes that are generally held by the audience.*

The following examples show how enthymemes might be used in a school environment:

The text of the message is constructed around the following two premises:

Reading by the third grade is essential to success in later years
Our school's goal is for all students to read by the third grade

(conclusion)
Our school is working to ensure that our students will succeed in later years.

Or, the text might be constructed around these two premises:

Being able to read by the third grade is essential to student achievement in later years.
95 percent of our students can read by the third grade.

(conclusion)
95 percent of the school's students have an essential element for success in later years

When school administrators of a rural district became aware that a significant number of its students were not receiving proper dental care and that the lack of care was affecting the students' academic performance and social development, they initiated a project to improve dental health care for all children. Project participants included the dental community in a nearby town, PTO members, and county health care professionals. The campaign to acquire donated goods and services wove the following premises into their messages:

Children in pain cannot learn.
Many children in the district are in pain from untreated tooth and gum disease.

(conclusion)
Many children are not learning because of they lack dental care.

The project was successful in part because the premises upon which the appeal was based are generally held beliefs and attitudes. People abhor the idea of children being in pain, they know proper dental care is important, and they believe that all children should have the opportunity to learn.

With care and practice, the marketing team can begin to use enthymemes to create persuasive messages. It is always advisable to test the efficacy of your messages by asking individuals similar to your target audiences for their reactions and interpretations.

Making an impression

Sometimes we have only one opportunity to make a good impression. Have you ever "bombed" on a job interview? You cannot call the next day and say, "I think I really made a mess of my interview. May I come back for another one?" People often form lasting impressions with minimal contact. The impression may be wrong, but an opportunity to correct it may not occur.

People in the community whether they are prospective parents, retired people, potential business partners, or community groups may form impressions of your school based solely on its communication materials. If the school newsletter is the only contact that an individual in the community has with the school, the quality of the writing, the content, and the appearance of the newsletter affects their impression of your school. If the brochure you send to prospective students and their parents is not persuasive, they may choose not to visit the school. If the proposal to potential business partners is not professional looking and well organized, they may not participate.

When I ask school administrators participating in my marketing workshops what they would most like to learn more about, creating effective marketing materials is in the top three (business partnerships and promotion activities are the other two). School administrators understand the need for well-designed materials, but are often dissatisfied with the results of their attempts.

You may be fortunate enough to have a staff person already familiar with desktop publishing. If not, a number of excellent, user-friendly desktop publishing programs will allow you to produce quality brochures, newsletters, flyers, business cards, even posters with a minimum of learning time. I find

Microsoft Publisher, Pro Publisher, and Corel Draw easy to use and I am not a techno-wizard.

Available publishing software should meet most of the school's needs. When the school wants a more complicated communication piece such as an annual report, a local print shop or graphics firm can help with layout, construction, graphics, and printing. Even if you use a professional firm to produce your communication pieces, you should have an idea of the overall look that you want and be able to provide the printer with the content.

Much of the content that follows deals with creating effective communication materials. Take the time to consider *all* elements of your communication pieces. A common mistake is not devoting enough time to the development of materials. Projects created in haste to meet a deadline are likely to prove disappointing. Always dedicate time to testing your communication pieces to avoid wasting resources on ineffective materials.

Something is not always better than nothing

A well-designed school brochure can be an effective part of your marketing effort. However, schools often create brochures in haste because the feeling is, "We need to get something out there for people to see." It is better to have no brochure than to have one that is ineffective or creates negative reactions.

Use the suggestions that follow to help your team design a brochure, then solicit honest criticism from others including individuals outside your school environment. Especially important are members of any group that the brochure is targeting. This is not a time to let egos get in the way of effective communication. Consider suggestions and criticisms as useful information.

Avoid two common brochure mistakes. The first mistake is thinking that the brochure should focus on your school, your programs, your students, your achievements. The brochure should focus on *how what your school offers can benefit your audience*. Always keep your audience in mind as you create the brochure. Consider their needs, desires, language requirements, social values, economic and social status, and perceptions of your school.

The second mistake is thinking that a brochure is a silver bullet that will meet all marketing needs. I frequently encounter the notion that marketing consists mainly of creating and distributing brochures. Brochures are an important piece in your marketing effort. A well-designed brochure is an excellent introduction piece to persuade the reader to take further action in relation to your school. However, it is impossible for a brochure to carry the entire marketing effort.

Brochures reach a limited number of people who often read them a single time. Other methods of communication can provide greater range and frequency. Brochures are best used to create interest and give the readers a brief, but tempting message that makes them want to know more.

Below are suggestions for creating an effective brochure. *These suggestions also apply to other communication materials which are covered in detail in other parts in this chapter:*

- Create an interesting cover

- Keep the reader moving through the brochure with headings, bullets, and graphics

- Use appropriate colors

- Concentrate on the benefits to the reader

- Tell the reader what you want him to do (call for details, visit our school, contact us) and how to do it (provide telephone numbers, list visiting days)

- Avoid excessive clip art

- Limit the number of fonts

- Keep imagery sharp and clear

- Group and set apart like kinds of information

- Reinforce your message with repetition

Tempt readers to look inside

Imagine yourself standing in line at the grocery store. While you wait, a dozen magazines vie for your attention. Why do you pick out one over the others? Certainly, an interest in the focus of the magazine is a primary factor. But, generally there are several magazines with the same focus (current events, sports, food, celebrities). Chances are you selected one because the photographs and the titles of the articles suggested something of interest to you was inside. Have you ever bought a bottle of wine because you found the label appealing? Or, chosen a restaurant simply because of the way it looked? Something about the outside enticed you to try what was inside.

For the same reason, the cover of the school's communications pieces greatly influences the decision to look inside. Indeed, the principal purpose of the cover is to create enough interest for someone to pick up the piece and read more. Picture your communication piece lying on a table surrounded by others that are competing for attention. Is there anything about it that would entice someone to select it over the others?

Color, images, and text contribute to an appealing cover. The colors should be appropriate (see the topic on color in this chapter) and of good quality. Images should be relevant to the message and the reader. Text should have a succinct, inviting message that leads the reader to the next page.

Keep the text on the cover to a minimum. A brochure cover with too much text tires the reader before she gets to the first page. The lead-in text or headline on the cover can engage the reader by:

- Saying something unexpected

- Communicating a benefit

- Reinforcing the school name

- Creating curiosity

- Asking a question

- Stating a problem and giving a solution

- Giving a command

- Making a connection to the reader

Accompanying images can dramatically increase the appeal of your message but they should be relevant to the message and the reader. If you are creating a brochure for Spanish-speaking parents, most of the images should represent the group's ethnicity. Images should reinforce not detract from the message.

Too much clutter detracts from the message. Stay away from ornate images unless their ornate quality is relative to the message. If you want to use clip art of typical school images such as apples, books, schoolhouses, crayons, etc, use them in an innovative or imaginative fashion to make your cover stand out from the many others that have school-related objects. Fig. 3 is an example of typical school objects used in a different way.

Grab a
pencil
and
Sign up for
Summer School
June 7 - July 16, 2004
Riverside High School
Contact Mr. Jackson or call 999-123-4568 for information

Fig 3

What's In It For Me?

A common mistake in creating marketing materials is thinking that the focus should be on the school or district. Like other aspects of marketing, promotional materials should focus on the target audience.

Often I see school brochures that visually make a good impression with excellent photographs, nice layout, good colors, and informative text about the school's performance, standards, and programs. Everything assures me of the school's dedication. However, the one thing that would create an interest in the school is missing. Nothing in the brochure communicated how what the school offered would benefit me, a reader. *The WIFM (What's In It For Me) element was missing.*

There is a saying in marketing, "People don't buy ¼ inch drill bits, people buy ¼ inch holes." The buyer is not interested in the product; he is interested in what the product can do for him. If a person has no interest in making ¼-inch holes, he will not be interested in ¼-inch drill bits no matter how great the advertising or the product is. When people are presented with brochures, advertisements, or any other type of promotional material, there is one question going through their minds, "What's in it for me?" That is human nature.

I might become interested in ¼-inch drill bits if I feel that being able to make ¼-inch holes offers me benefits. The benefits may be logical or emotional, tangible or intangible. I might be convinced that being able to make ¼" holes would make my book shelf project faster and easier to complete (logical). I would feel self-reliant (emotional), because I could assemble a new book case myself (tangible). My friends would see me as a capable and clever person (intangible).

Do not assume that the reader will inevitability make the connection between what the school offers and the benefits. The benefit to the reader must clear. One effective way to answer the WIFM question is to make the connection between the features of your product and the derived benefits or rewards. To be most effective, the benefits should be specific and stated at the beginning to peak the reader's interest.

Below are examples of feature-based statements

Last year our school introduced an innovative reading program for all students. (With no benefit attached, the likely response is, "So what?")

Good

Our school provides all students with an innovative reading program to improve their reading skills.
(This is better, but what is the specific benefit?)

Better

Our innovative reading program is helping students improve their reading skills as much as one grade level in six months.
(Now, a specific benefit is attached that clarifies the WIFM. But, to catch the reader's attention, state the benefit first.)

Best

Our students are improving their reading skills as much as one grade level in six months with our innovative reading program.
(Now, the first thing the reader sees is the benefit which will prompt him to continue reading)

Here is another example:

This year our school has a new earth sciences program

> **Good**
>
> *Our new earth sciences program encourages children to see the world in new ways.*
>
> **Better**
>
> *Your child will see the earth in new ways with our new earth sciences program.*
>
> **Best**
>
> *Learning becomes exciting when your child sees the earth in new ways with our new earth sciences program.*

A good way to write benefit focused text is to imagine yourself as the recipient. What features would attract and hold your interest? What kind of benefits would be appealing? Does the text match your interests? Then ask someone who is typical of the intended receiver to critique your piece using those same questions.

Keep the reader moving

The layout of your document can make it visually inviting or uninviting. No matter how interesting your copy is, if the document looks too wordy or cluttered, the reader may not even attempt to read it.

It is tempting to put as much information into the piece as possible. You want to tell the reader *everything*. The reader is not interested in everything at this point. In fact, the reader may not be interested in anything at this point. The goal is to create interest and persuade the reader to want to know more. Long lines of text in the document in Fig. 4 create the impression that there is a lot of information to read. And, there is nothing other than text to draw the reader's attention.

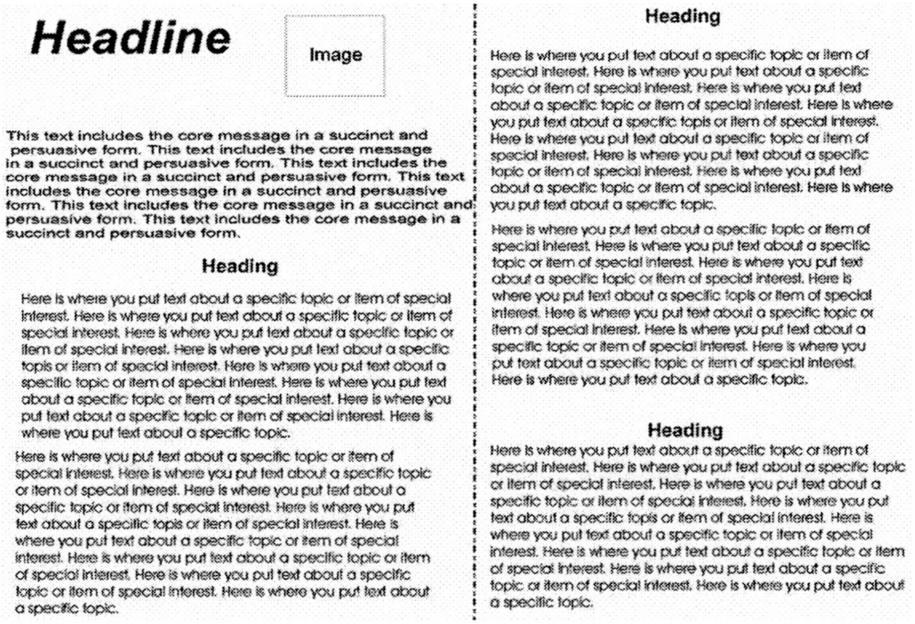

Fig 4

The text is more interesting and readable when it is broken up with images, color, headings, and space.

- Keep the reader's eyes moving forward with headings, bullets, color, images, white space, and columns. Break text into manageable chunks and use bold headings to alert the reader to the content.

- A good ratio of text to white space is 60 percent text, 40 percent white space. Take care not create large gaps of white space between chunks of text or other elements in your design. This interrupts the movement of the reader's eyes through the document.

- Use lists, such as,

  10 Reasons why…
  4 things that most…,
  5 steps to….

- Use bullets and short lines of text to list items.

The layout in Fig. 5 is a more inviting design.

Put an interesting lead in or quote here

This text includes the core message in a succinct and persuasive form. This text includes the core message in a succinct and persuasive form. This text includes the core message in a succinct and persuasive form. This text includes the core message in a succinct and persuasive form. This text includes the core message in a succinct and persuasive form.

Image

Heading

In this section, put some summary information or text that ties the following items together. In this section put some summary information

| Put an image or a topic headline here | Here is where you put text about a specific topic or item of special interest. Here is where you put text about a specific topic or item of special interest. Here is where you put text about a specific topic or item of special interest. Here is where you put text about a specific topic or item of special interest. Here is where you put text about a specific topic or item of special interest. Here is where you put text about a specific topic. |

| Put an image or a topic headline here | Here is where you put text about a specific topic or item of special interest. Here is where you put text about a specific topic or item of special interest. Here is where you put text about a specific topic or item of special interest. Here is where you put text about a specific topic or item of special interest. Here is where you put text about a specific topic. |

Image   Image   Image

Heading

Put more text here. Put more text here. Put more text here. Put more text here. Put more text here. Put more text here. Put more text here. Put more text here. Put more text here.

| Put an image or a topic headline here | Here is where you put text about a specific topic or item of special interest. Here is where you put text about a specific topic or item of special interest. Here is where you put text about a specific topic or item of special interest. Here is where you put text about a specific topic or item of special interest. Here is where you put text about a specific topic. |

| Put an image or a topic headline here | Here is where you put text about a specific topic or item of special interest. Here is where you put text about a specific topic or item of special interest. Here is where you put text about a specific topic or item of special interest. Here is where you put text about a specific topic or item of special interest. Here is where you put text about a |

Fig. 5

Give audiences a reason to take action, then tell them how

Even though people find your message persuasive, they may need encouragement to follow through on it.

The typical text below may generate some action

Register before May 15ᵗʰ by completing and returning the enclosed form or visiting our Web site.

However, more reader-oriented text with specific information will get a better response.

To ensure your child has an exciting range of fine arts programs this summer, complete the enclosed registration form and return it to your child's teacher or register on-line at arts@lincolnms.org *before May 15th.*

If you want readers to do something such as visit the school, call for more information, check your Web site, or register early, it is important to tell them exactly how. If you want people to visit the school, you need to tell them when they can visit (dates or days and hours). If they need to arrange the visit in advance, tell them with whom and how. Give directions to the school and tell them where to go when they get there.

It is human nature to find an excuse not to do something even when we think we should. Motivate your audience to take action by giving them a reason why they should, then make it easy for them to follow through.

Imagery creates interest

Photographs are as important as headlines and text. People like to look at pictures. An interesting photograph is often the reason someone chooses to read an article, newsletter, or a brochure. A photograph will draw attention to an item and a good photograph will draw the reader into the text.

Digital photography and the high quality reproductions from affordable photocopiers and printers make including photographs in your communication pieces easy and cost-effective. However, the best cameras, copiers, and printers cannot improve a photograph that is technically inferior. A photograph that is out of focus, blurred, or over or under-exposed is unacceptable no matter how interesting the subject or composition. High quality requires good equipment. Good equipment does not have to be the best or the most expensive. Quality equipment is available at reasonable costs.

Composition, the arrangement of people and objects in the picture, creates visual appeal. For many people, composition is the most difficult aspect of photography because it requires changing many of our old habits such as taking full body shots of everyone facing forward and looking at the camera.

Photographs should be relevant and interesting. They should provide visible support or explanation for the main message of your communication piece. If you are writing an article for the local paper about the new buses that can carry disabled students, a picture of a student being lifted into the bus is more interesting than a picture of the bus.

Below are some ways to create interesting photographs.

Use contrast. A photograph with shadows or silhouettes against a light background or light figures against a dark background is better than one in which nothing stands out. Contrast also draws the eye to the photograph. If you have a camera with a viewfinder that allows you to bring the background or foreground into sharper focus you can concentrate attention on a specific element by blurring the surrounding area.

Use action. I am amazed at the constancy with which people are lined up like bowling pins for photographs. My first reaction is that the related story will probably be as boring as the picture. People *do things* when they are at meetings, events, or school functions. Capture people doing something in your photographs even if it is just standing and talking with each other. A typical graduation photo is the valedictorian giving her speech. It is understandable that you want to give the valedictorian recognition, but also include photographs of students hugging each other or a family weeping with pride. A good photograph captures the essence of what is happening.

Use different angles. You can improve the most mundane photograph with different camera angles. Rather than shooting your picture head on, kneel and shoot up, stand at a higher elevation and shoot down, or shoot a side shot to create a different perspective. Consider the traditional groundbreaking photograph of dignitaries lined up with their shovels. A more interesting picture would be one taken from a kneeling position that shows the dirt flying with the dignitaries in the background. An interesting photographic angle conveys the idea the related story may also have an interesting angle.

Use imagination. Come up with interesting ways to get your message across. by indulging in atypical thinking. A typical way to photograph the new pottery-making equipment for the creative arts class would be to show the students and teacher in a group gazing proudly at the new equipment. A more interesting photograph would be a close-up shot of a student's hands as he spins a mound of clay on the potter's wheel. The mixed emotions that many students and parents feel on a child's first day of school might be captured by a close-up of parent and child saying good-by. Do not be afraid to try new and different approaches. No one has to see the ideas that did not work, but you can learn from them.

Use fewer not more. Unless there is a specific reason for having a large number of people in a picture, avoid large groups. A close-up picture of one band member pounding on his large drum is more interesting than the whole band marching down the street. The general rule is no more than five people in a picture. Also keep in mind that odd numbers of objects or people are always more visually interesting than even numbers. One, three, or five people create a more interesting picture than two, four, or six.

Use lots of film. One way to get good pictures is to take many of them. I once attended a photography course taught by a freelance photographer who had worked on *National Geographic* assignments. For an article that included seven or eight photographs he would shoot around 100 rolls of film! He did not suggest that we, as amateur photographers, do the same; his point was that getting a good photograph requires taking more than two or three pictures. Taking more than just a few shots also encourages you to be more creative and adventuresome. An advantage of digital cameras is that they allow you to take many pictures and see them instantly.

Use new technology. New software now allows you to do many things with your computer that before required expertise in a darkroom. You can improve photographs by cropping, increasing the contrast, correcting lighting, and using other enhancing capabilities. Even if you use a 35 mm camera, negatives and transparencies can be scanned and downloaded into your computer for improvement.

Use naturalness. One way to achieve naturalness in your photos is to take pictures without your subjects being aware. People have an inclination to stop and stare at the camera when they realize they are being photographed. If people stop to "pose", simply put down your camera and ask them to continue with their activities or, at least, not to stare at the camera.

Use children. Too many school-related photographs are of school officials or other adults. Children are natural attention getters. The uninhibited, spontaneous nature of children will produce far more interesting pictures than a group of administrators. In a ground-breaking event, why not take a picture of a few children with hard hats and shovels instead of administrators? The education of children is why schools exist; it is only natural that they be the focus of your photographs. One caveat, be sure to get signed permission from parents or guardians to reproduce and use photographs.

The language of color

First impressions are often lasting impressions. According to the Institute for Color Research, the average person forms an impression within 90 seconds and between 63 percent and 90 percent of their impression is based on color.[6]

Male birds are brightly colored for a reason. They need to stand out from the competition and catch the attention of females. Humans, too, are attracted by color, but as thinking beings, we attach meaning to color.

We are attracted to color from the moment we begin to distinguish objects. Babies and young children are attracted to bright colors before they are attracted to specific objects. Our color preferences may change as we grow older, but we remain influenced by color. Color becomes a way to make a statement about ourselves. I am fun. I am traditional. I am rebellious.

Colors can change from being "in" to being "out". Red is in this year, gray is out. Remember avocado appliances? Even the "always appropriate" little black dress occasionally falls from favor. Avoid trendy colors when designing logos or promotional materials that you intend to keep for a time; otherwise, you may be "out" next year.

Colors can send messages that are stronger than the words used. Black balloons with the words *"Happy Birthday"* send a message that this is a birthday the recipient may not be "happy" to celebrate. A color that is not appropriate for the message generates a sense of irony.

Much of our reaction to color is subconscious; therefore, we are often unaware of how colors affect us. But, corporations have been using color for decades in their advertising, packaging, corporate logos, and communication pieces to attract and persuade consumers.

To be effective, colors must be in harmony with the product and the message. Red and black packaging is as inappropriate for a bath product that claims to sooth and calm as are pastel colors for a gasoline additive that claims to add power to your engine. Expensive products call for colors that indicate the worth of the contents. A bargain calls attention to its low price with showy colors.

Although many reactions to colors are universal, (red always attracts attention) some are culturally specific. The traditional Chinese bride wears red, a color symbolizing great luck. White, the color traditionally worn by western brides is a color of mourning for the Chinese. A look at the arts and crafts of a culture can give clues to which colors are significant and what they symbolize. For example, Native Americans favor earth tones indicative of nature, a dominate force in their culture. It is always wise to be aware of the feelings toward specific colors of cultural groups within your schools or district.

Below are traditional Western meanings associated with colors to consider when creating communication pieces.

Red conveys excitement, passion, and activity. It is virtually impossible to ignore red. Because it grabs our attention, bright red is good for accents and important words or statements. STOP signs are red for a reason. Dark red, like most dark, intense colors, suggests richness and expense. We refer to dark, intense colors by the expensive jewels we associate with them; ruby red, emerald green, sapphire blue. However, be careful when using red for it is also associated with debt, anger, and danger.

Pink suggests femininity, innocence, and youth. Pale pink conjures up a feeling of softness and sweetness. Good health is associated with pink. We say, *in the pink*, to mean being in a healthy state. Tones of pink might be used in a communication piece for a program on health issues for girls or a woman's exercise class offered after-hours at the school.

Orange suggests fun, energy, and exuberance. It is a loud color better used in small measure to highlight or create a sense of liveliness. Avoid using bright shades of orange in situations where you want to be serious such as the school's annual report. Lighter shades, such as peach, apricot, or coral, are warm and appealing and can be used to offset more somber tones.

Yellow is associated with the sun, warmth, and energy in almost every culture. Like red, yellow is hard to ignore. The most visible car on the road is a yellow one. That is why a Yellow Cab is easier to see than a blue, white, even a red one. Pale shades of yellow appeal to our intellectual side. Pale cream colors are more elegant than white. High contrast and associated meanings make black and yellow one of the most powerful color combinations. Although a wonderful accent color, too much yellow can be harsh and annoying.

Green offers a wide array of choices with a variety of meanings. The abundance of green in nature creates an association with freshness and tranquility. Vibrant, eye-catching lime green colors are good as accents. Bright green symbolizes the new life and the sense of renewal that appears in the spring in the form of buds and grass. Pale tones of green are soothing. Dark green suggests status and money. There are also negative associations with green, being "green" with envy or turning "green" when sick.

Blue is a universally popular color that symbolizes authority, dignity, trustworthiness, and dependability. No wonder it is popular for designing corporate logos, especially those of financial institutions. Whereas bright, electric blue is dramatic and energizing, pale blue is a restful color that humans find calming; something to keep in mind if you have news that could agitate people. Dark blue connotes power and authority. That is why it is a popular color for uniforms. Teal blue is a sophisticated, distinctive, chic color that is equally appealing to men and women.

Purple is often overlooked as a color choice. Associated with royalty, (we even call it royal purple) deep purple connotes a sense of gentility, tradition, and sensitivity. Purple also evokes feelings of spiritualism and sensuality that create strong reactions. Purple is good for sophisticated, artistic messages.

Brown is the ultimate earth tone. Brown gives the sense that something is solid, steady, dependable. Depending on the context, brown can be drab or rich. Out of favor for some time, the use of brown is now more widespread with the popularity of coffee bars, upscale brown leather furniture, and vans that come with packages for us. Such trends have an influence on how we react to colors. Using brown with an array of medium and lighter earth colors produces a look that is sophisticated without being pretentious and practical without being dull.

Gray is a serious, but sophisticated color with a wide variety of shades from deep charcoal to soft pale tones. Grey can be warm or cool. Grey tones down bright colors when the desire is to have brightness without being gaudy. Conversely, touches of bright colors and pastels lessen the drabness when grey is a predominate color. A grey suit with a dark red or yellow tie is a popular combination among executives; the message is, I am serious without being dull.

Black has evolved from its traditional association with death and darkness to become a color that creates a powerful, mysterious, dramatic, elegant, and expensive aura. Who would have thought thirty years ago that black kitchen appliances would be chic. Black tie, little black dress, black limousine, black leather, and black granite represent high style and success. Black in combination with other colors is especially powerful, but take care to ensure that the effect is not harsh and excessive.

White is associated with purity and cleanliness; however, white can also represent coldness and sterility. Creamy or off-white tones moderate the starkness of pure white. But, if you want to create a sense of freshness, crispness and clarity, white is the color. White is the perfect background color, especially in contrast with more dramatic, bold colors. Black and white, the ultimate contrast, can produce dramatic results.

When choosing colors, consider how the colors work with each other to produce an effect. Combinations of colors can produce an instantaneous meaning, trigger a response, or set a mood for your message. Select colors in harmony with your message. Studies have shown that using colors inconsistent with your message generally generate negative responses. Black and orange for Christmas or red and green for Halloween will get attention, but not the kind you want.

Earthy colors such as orange, gold, dark green, brown, black, and deep red represent autumn, the rural countryside, and abundance associated with harvest. Use them in seasonal messages or messages that speak of down-to-earth values.

Festive colors such as bright pink, yellow, red, orange, bright green, and sky blue represent fun and gaiety. Use them to announce parties and events or energize people into action.

Serene or tranquil colors such as tones of deep blue, aqua, pale green, and lavender represent the sea and sky. Use them in messages to suggest tranquility, unity, or where a calming influence is required.

Combining black with colors such as yellow, purple, red, or gold creates dramatic, powerful combinations that should be used sparingly. If you constantly speak in a loud voice, you lose the impact of a shout. Use dramatic combinations only for your most important messages.

Experiment with color. Go to a paint store that provides large, single paint samples and ask if you can collect some for use at your school. Arrange the colors in various combinations and ask for people's reactions. Most publishing software allows you to change colors easily, even on clip art, so you can test various combinations.

Color makes things come alive. Remember how exciting it was to exchange the old back and white television for a color one. Color is an important factor in how people act and react. Use it to your advantage.

Repetition creates unity

Repetition of visual elements, such as colors, fonts, shapes, space, and other design elements, creates unity and consistency within your communication piece. Consistency is important if the piece is a prospectus or presentation booklet that comprises several pages. If each page has a different look, the message appears disjointed. If each page has a different design layout, the harmony is broken as the pages compete with each other. If you use a repetitive design or graphic throughout the piece, be sure that it is always in the same size, in the same place, same color, etc., unless there is a reason to deviate.

A common error is using too many fonts. Any variation in a font is considered a different font. Therefore, these fonts, **fonts,** *fonts,* <u>fonts</u>, fonts, are different even though they are all Century. Limit the number of fonts to no more than two or three.

Even seemingly small items such as inconsistent margins and indents can create a disorganized impression. You want the reader to concentrate on the message, not be distracted by inconsistencies.

Contrast creates interest

Contrast gets attention and creates interest. The same elements such as color, fonts, and space that create consistency can also produce contrast. White on black, light against dark, contrasting fonts, tight text in a large amount of white space, and an extra-large capital letter before smaller text will attract the eye to the message.

Excellence is *cool*

Don't Be a Bully

is a beautiful grade

Some documents, such as policy statements, call for a minimalist look; but, even pages filled mostly with text can be more interesting when the font sizes of titles and sub-titles are larger than the text in the body.

As with repetition, contrasts can be overdone. Whereas the overuse of repetition can be boring, overuse of contrast can be annoying.

Repeat your message in multiple ways

You want your readers to remember the key points of your message. Repetition of your message with photographs, graphs, quotes, and words can improve the chances the reader will retain key points. If the message is that a new curriculum is improving test scores, show a graph representing the improved scores over time, a quote from a teacher, or a photograph of a student proudly holding a paper with an "A". Elements, such as a picture, graph, or quote, often stay with the reader longer than lines of text.

You can reinforce your message by saying the same thing in different ways. To reinforce the message of better test results, you might refer to "improved test scores", "increased performance", and "we watched our test scores rise", throughout your piece. Take care, however, not to overdo it.

Collect the good, the bad, and the ugly

Creative people get their ideas and inspiration from the world around them including other people's work. When you see an advertisement, poster, book cover, menu, newsletter, Web site, or anything that makes a strong impression on you, good or bad, keep a copy of it and attach a note describing how you responded to it and why.

Ask each marketing team member to keep a file of samples they have gathered with notes on why they found them appealing or unappealing. Review the pieces periodically with the marketing team. Dissect the elements to decide why they were effective or ineffective. Were the colors annoying? Did the lead-in catch team members' attention and entice them to read further? Was the overall tone of the piece sophisticated, whimsical, impressive, irritating, or boring? What elements created specific impressions? When the marketing team is ready to design a new communication piece, review the samples to look for ideas.

Taglines and slogans

Have you ever found yourself using an advertising slogan as part of your everyday speech? "Where's the beef?", "When it rains, it pours", and "Just do it!" are examples of slogans that became a part of our conversation. Some slogans last for years, others for a few months.

The purpose of a slogan is to create a conscious or unconscious connection to and awareness of a product or service. To attract attention and help with retention, advertisers use devices such as rhyme, alliteration, puns, and metaphors. Slogans may ask a question, give a command, or make a promise. If the slogan creates a positive feeling toward the product or organization then it has served its purpose.

Schools and districts can use slogans to create an identity, promote a campaign, advertise a program, recruit teachers, or establish a position. Below are examples of school related slogans.

Command
Watch us achieve

Personification
A learning environment that embraces all students

Hyperbole
Our science program knows no earthly bounds

Inversion
Common sense. Uncommon results

Question
Will **You** be my teacher?

Alliteration
Creating creative classrooms

Metaphor
A bridge between thinking and doing

Puns
We attract talent (a fine arts magnet school)
A magnet for inquisitive minds (a science magnet school)

School or Mascot name
Teaching our *Eagles* to soar

If you decide a slogan or tag line is appropriate for your school, district, or program, below are some tips for creating one:

• Use one or more brainstorming sessions to generate ideas.

- Before your brainstorming session, ask the participants to collect slogans and tag lines they like.

- Ask for ideas from school staff members and students.

- In your session, review the collected slogans and discuss why they are appealing.

- Write down as many words or phrases as you can that explain exactly what the school does. What are its attributes? How is the school different? What are its goals?

- Look for words or phrases that come to mind most often.

- Try to make your tag line as specific to your school or district as possible.

- Avoid worn-out phrases (committed to excellence, standard of quality)

- Unless you can be extraordinarily clever, avoid tying your slogan to current, trendy advertising slogans. When the slogan is no longer trendy, yours will sound dated. Moreover, there could be legal consequences if copyrights exist.

After you have come up with several possibilities, try them out on people inside and outside the school. Take a poll among students and staff members. Strive for a slogan that people feel proud to use and follow.

Creating a logo

One of the charming attractions of medieval cities in Europe is the array of symbols and images hanging over the doorways of commercial establishments to designate the various trades and merchants. Many of these icons came to represent a standard of excellence that has been treasured and protected over centuries. These symbols were precursors to our present day logos.

A logo is an image that represents an organization and the product or service it provides. A logo may be an image, like the Mercedes emblem or the Nike swoop, distinctive lettering such Coca Cola's red script, or a combination of both such as the image of Colonel Saunders combined with Kentucky Fried Chicken. Some logos, such as Coca Cola's distinctive red lettering and

McDonalds' golden arches, are so well known worldwide they symbolize American culture as well as the products they represent. Logos are powerful reminders of the attributes of an organization. Like companies, schools can benefit from a well-designed logo.

To be effective, your logo should be attractive, distinctive, and memorable. Being attractive does not mean just looking good; it means attracting attention in a positive way. An attractive image draws the eye to it and holds attention even if for a second or two. Being distinctive requires that it stand out from other similar types of logos. If your logo looks like every other school logo, the message is that your school is like every other school. When people see it, you want them to think of *your* school, not *a* school. A memorable logo is one that leaves an impression so that the next time the viewer sees it, there is recognition.

Most logos comprise three elements: a graphic, lettering or wording, and color. The McDonald's logo consists of two arches, the name McDonald's, and the predominant color, yellow. There are exceptions. Some logos are so recognizable, no wording is needed, the Red Cross for example. Some logos are simply the organization's name in a consistent design, for example, Coca Cola.

The school logo should be simple, attractive, and compatible with the school's purpose. If the school is creating a completely new logo, start with the three elements of graphic, color and font, then refine the design. If the school has designated colors, use them or use the color guide (discussed earlier) to select colors in keeping with the image and message the school wants to communicate.

Think about how your logo will look in all sizes, small on a shirt pocket or large on a 10 foot banner. Use a font that is readable even when the logo is reduced in size. Some fonts become illegible in smaller sizes. Create a graphic that is clean and distinctive. All three elements should blend well. An ornate graphic with stark, ultra-sleek lettering is likely to create a conflict that is disagreeable to the viewer. However, there are no hard and fast rules. Doing something out of the ordinary sometimes results in a truly distinctive design.

A contest to design a school logo could generate excellent designs. Moreover, a logo is more meaningful if it is created from within the school. Write a brief history of logo design with well-known examples (information is available on the Internet), establish guidelines for the design, and then hold a contest. Encourage everyone, staff members, teachers, and students, to participate. Create a selection committee to pick the best one or select four or five of the best designs and hold a school-wide selection. After a design has been selected or voted on, hold an official "unveiling".

Once the school has gone to the effort to create a logo, use it. Put the logo on all school communications, decals for notebooks, school banners, uniforms, give-away items, and any other promotional materials. The logo should be a recognizable, positive symbol of the school.

Remember to copyright the logo. If the school comes up with an outstanding design that is getting attention, you do not want some other organization or school to copy it. Information on the process and requirements of copyrights is available on the Internet.

Annual reports

A school's annual report is most effective when it tells the audience clearly and concisely what *they* want to know about the school. Because a school's annual report can also serve as a prospectus to recruit students and teachers, solicit funds and community support, and report the state of the school or district to its constituents, it should be professional in appearance and content. The cover should be simple and appealing and communicate that the contents are important. If the school has specific colors, use them; otherwise, select colors that reflect a desired image of the school.

Some of the items to include in an annual report are:

- A letter from the superintendent or principal providing a summary of the year

- The district's or school's position and vision statements

- A history including important events, awards, special achievements and distinctions, and distinguished alumni

- A directory of administrators and contact information

- Description of special programs including extracurricular activities

- Student/teacher ratios

- Numerical and graphical account of student performance

- Graduation rates

- Percentage of students pursuing higher education after graduation

- Student demographic information

- School physical environment (condition of school, level of technology, special facilities)

- Safety record

- PTO activities

- Parental support

- Educational levels of teaching and administrative staff

- Grants awarded to the school

- Community involvement including external partnerships and volunteer programs

The first annual report will require the most work. Spend sufficient time and money to create layout and design features that the school will want to replicate year after year. It may be worth the money to hire a graphic designer to help with the design. After the first year, the work will involve revising data in the existing report. I suggest that the school change the cover design in some way each year. It differentiates the reports and coveys the idea that the contents are current. To cut down on printing costs, make the report available in a pdf format on the school or district Web site.

Testimonials are marketing gold

An advertisement for a new restaurant in your neighborhood may or may not persuade you to try it. However, if your neighbor tells you she tried the restaurant and the food, service, and atmosphere were superb and the prices were reasonable, then the chances are high that you will try it. Why? Because your neighbor has nothing to gain from her praise of the restaurant. Her recommendation is unbiased; therefore, it is more credible than an advertisement.

Furthermore, you now feel assured that if you try the restaurant you will not be disappointed. Her recommendation reduced the risk.

Testimonials are powerful persuaders and should be included in your marketing communication. People expect the school to sing its own praises; it is different when someone without a vested interest sings them. The marketing strategy of the infomercial is to break down the resistance people have toward a sales person by having product users tell the audience how great the product is.

Testimonials are most effective when they are specific and personal such as a parent explaining how a school program specifically met his child's needs or a high school student relating how a program is preparing her for college. Alumni can provide persuasive testimonials when they describe how a teacher or the school environment was a factor in their achievements later in life. Keep the testimonials brief, no more than three or four lines unless you are using a story as a testimonial. Do not limit testimonials to written statements. Being able to hear and see someone on a video is particularly effective.

Once you have testimonials, use them. Include testimonials in distributed materials such as brochures and the annual report, post them on the school Web site, or put them on a poster. Include taped testimonials in a school or district video. An ambitious, but meaningful project would be to create a testimonial calendar. Each month include a picture of students, teachers, parents, or alumni involved in a school-related activity with an accompanying testimonial. For instance, a picture of children involved in a science project would include a testimonial from an alumna about how Mr. Simon's science class was the beginning of her path to becoming a doctor.

Testimonials add credibility to your message. They also generate loyalty. When people really believe in a product, they want to help it succeed. A testimonial is a way for supporters to feel they are playing a part in the school's success.

More than just a cover sheet

Your school's fax cover sheet can be more than just a transmittal form. Use the cover sheet as a vehicle to market your school by communicating positive information to everyone who receives a fax. Include text boxes and photographs to share good news items; acknowledge students; employees, volunteers, and business partners; publicize your achievements; issue reminders; and promote upcoming events. See Fig. 6 for an example. Update it monthly to keep recipients interested in its content.

Back to School Open House
August 21, 2004

TO:

FROM:

FAX #

NO. OF PAGES

Space for school news such as
- Upcoming Events
- Goals for the coming school year
- Changes in the coming year
- Welcome to new teachers
- Thanks for donations
- Special awards, grants, etc.
- End of school thanks and acknowledgements
- Holiday reminders
- New community partnerships
- Special achievements

Fig. 6

Newsletters should be newsy

Everyone in your community should be aware of your school's or district's accomplishments, its value to the community, and the important issues related to education. Within the first few months of moving into a new house, I received a district newsletter from the school district where I live, and I continue to receive one each semester. Even though I no longer have children in public schools, I am a taxpayer and the school district believes I should be informed about the value received for my tax dollars.

Newsletters sent to your community are a way to maintain an awareness of your existence and to keep open a positive line of communication. To be effective, a newsletter should be:

- **Informative.** If the reader does not find any "new" news, why should he read it? The purpose of the newsletter is to provide information that the reader is not likely to have, but would like to have.

- **Current.** A notice of an event that happened days before the newsletter arrives is of no use.

- **Inclusive.** Include news that covers the interests of a wide range of readers. News about the upcoming bond referendum or school board meeting may be of interest even to those without children in school.

- **Interesting.** Use photographs and headlines that will pique the reader's interest, then write text that will hold it.

- **Visually attractive.** Use layout, color, white space, and fonts to create an overall effect that looks appealing.

- **Readable.** Avoid jargon, acronyms, educational theories, and complicated statistics unless there is a reason for them and you explain them simply and thoroughly.

Put newsletters in the waiting areas of businesses. Doctor's or dentist's offices, tire or auto repair services, banks, or veterinarians provide an opportunity to get positive news about what the school is doing to people in the community who may not otherwise know. You never know who might pick up one of your newsletters and become interested in volunteering, enrolling a child, or becoming a business partner.

Your publications reflect the standards of your school so be sure that they are well done and interesting. Have article titles that are likely to catch someone's interest. Include "thank you's" to the school's partners, recognize volunteers, and give readers an easy way to contact the school and learn more about special programs and activities.

Are you sure they are reading it?

When I was in public relations in the private sector, our firm conducted a special member promotion for a new client, a large credit union. To save money, the credit union asked us to enclose the promotion announcement in the monthly member newsletter. When we asked our clients if they were certain that most of the members read the newsletter, they exclaimed, "Of course! Our members love our newsletter". The promotion announcement was sent to approximately 7,000 members. The newsletter requested that the members call my firm's office to indicate their interest in participating in the promotion. We had extra staff ready to handle the calls.

The first week we received a small number of calls. The next week, a few more calls came in. We could not understand why response was so low. The client was very disappointed. The third week, we began to get calls that sounded something like this, "A friend of mine told me that he had heard from a friend of his about a great promotion that was available to credit union members. He gave me this number to call. What is the promotion and why were we not told about it?" When we explained that a promotion announcement had been included in the member newsletter, the usual response was, "Oh, I never read the newsletter".

The credit union had never asked its members if the newsletter was meeting their needs and wants. They assumed members were reading it, because members never complained about it.

To ensure that the newsletter is meeting the recipients' needs, conduct an annual reader survey. The school newsletter is an opportunity to communicate with individuals with whom the school has no other direct contact. A brief annual newsletter survey can keep your school in touch with the needs and wants of your community. Fig. 7 is a sample of a newsletter survey you can modify to meet your school's needs. Print the school's address on the reverse side so that other respondents can fold the survey and mail it.

Lincoln Middle School

3478 Elm Avenue
Houston, Texas 77019

We believe it is important to keep our community informed about what is happening in their school. One way we do this is through our Lincoln Middle School Newsletter. You can tell us how well we are meeting your information needs by completing this brief newsletter survey. We thank you for your time and look forward to seeing you at the next school event.

1. The newsletter is sent monthly. How often do you receive it?
   Every time Occasionally   Never

2. How often do you read the newsletter?
   Always Often Occasionally   Never

3. How much of the newsletter do you read?
   All of it   Most of it   Some of it

4. How would you describe the overall look of the newsletter?
   Very good Good Fair   Poor

5. How would you describe the content of the newsletter?
   Very good Good Fair   Poor

6. Please list any kind of information you would like to see in the newsletter that is not presently in it.

7. Please list any suggestions you have for improving the newsletter

Fig 7

Be "presentable" in the community

One of the best ways to promote your school effectively is to get out into the community and talk about it. Having a speakers' bureau of individuals who are willing and prepared to make presentation about school achievements and issues promotes proactive communication and builds community relationships. Presentations can be used to provide general information or address specific issues of interest to people. Administrators and other school personnel often avoid this effective communication tool due to a lack of confidence in how to create and deliver a successful presentation. Following are a few rules which will improve presentation skills.

Be organized. Outline your presentation in a logical sequence that will help the audience follow the material and remember it. Follow the old format of tell them what you are going to say, say it, then tell them what you said. That gets your point across three times.

Begin with something that will grab the audience's attention. It does not have to be a joke. It could be a story, a question, a quotation, an unusual statement or statistic, or a bit of history. "Last week a student came to my office with a story that I found shocking and I think you will too." "How would you feel if...?" "Would you be surprised to know that...?"

To illustrate your central points, you can start with a general statement or idea and then provide details to support your thesis or you can use details to build to a general conclusion. You might begin with a brief history of an issue and end with what you see in the future. However you structure your presentation, the audience should be able to see the logic of it

Be brief. The old saying, 'Leave them laughing," has merit. It is better to end your presentation while your audience still finds it interesting than talk so long that they wish you would stop. Even those who are interested will find themselves tuning out if your presentation is too long. Generally twenty minutes is a good length.

Stories are a great way to illustrate a point, create emotion, or inject some humor, but keep them short. A general rule is to keep them under two minutes. Too many details and extraneous descriptions can detract from the point. In addition, the story should have a point. To ensure brevity, limit the story to describing *who, what, when, where, how, and why.*

Leave some time for question and answers. This is an opportunity to provide specific information and to gain insight into what is of interest to the audience. Offer interested individuals ways to find out more about your subject such as the school Web site, a brochure or pamphlet, a call or visit to the school.

Do not read to your audience. A big part of being a successful speaker is personal interaction with the audience. When a speaker hunches over a lectern to read from a sheaf of papers, interaction is virtually nil and the result is audience boredom.

Generally, people read to their audiences because they are afraid they will forget what to say, stray off the message, or stumble over words. One of the best confidence builders is practice. Record your presentation on a cassette and practice in your car. Stand in front of a mirror and practice looking relaxed and confident as you speak. Practice in front of your cat. Keep practicing until you feel confident. Practicing will reinforce the content and help you with your tempo.

It is okay to use notes or an outline to keep yourself on track and jog your memory. Another way to give yourself prompts and provide visuals for the audience is with presentation software such as PowerPoint. Do not give into the temptation, however, to fill your presentation slides with text and read from them.

Of course, the best practice is speaking before an audience. The more public speaking you do, the easier and more enjoyable it becomes. When you have exciting and important things to say about your school and feel confident in your ability to communicate with your audience, you will look for opportunities to speak.

Expect the unexpected. Do not assume that everything you need for your presentation will be available for you even if you have been told it will be. Experience has taught me to carry my own equipment. Laptops, lightweight projectors, and portable, freestanding flipcharts that can sit on a table make being prepared easy.

Be prepared to give a shorter version of your presentation. If there is a speaker before you who runs over into your time space, ask if the group would prefer a shorter version of your presentation. Having a shorter version is better than trying to rush through your presentation. If the group is on a strict time schedule, they will appreciate your consideration and your adaptability.

Assume that there will questions about points in your presentation. Be prepared to back up your line of reasoning. Have sources for any quotations, statistics, or data that you provide, think of questions that could arise, and anticipate challenges to your argument. Being able to meet objections and answer questions gives credibility to your presentation.

Include internal experts. School administrators are the obvious choice to make presentations, but do not overlook individuals with special knowledge or experience. Teachers, students, parents, and volunteers can be effective speakers for the school.

School staff members who have first-hand knowledge of the subject are particularly convincing to audiences. Students demonstrating the science project that won an award or a counselor explaining what the school is doing to address the causes of violent student behavior can be more compelling than hearing it from the principal. Curriculum experts can help with presentations on new state testing standards or a new curriculum. The district health professional can bring credibility to a presentation on how the schools are working with local agencies to handle an unexpected flu epidemic.

Presentations can include more than one person. Trying to carry the entire presentation on a subject about which you feel apprehensive can elevate your anxiety level and affect your performance. The audience will understand and appreciate the inclusion of additional speakers who have special knowledge and experience.

Use visuals sparingly. I recently saw a cartoon in the New Yorker magazine in which Satan is sitting at his desk in his office in Hell interviewing a devilish looking job applicant. Satan is saying to the character, "I need someone who is an expert in torture. Do you know PowerPoint?" The cartoon illustrates the misuse and overuse of PowerPoint that has made this excellent presentation medium a torture for many people.

PowerPoint made it easy for those of us who cannot write a straight line on a flip chart, have a tendency to wander off the topic, or need memory prompts when speaking. It also relieved us of the need to make and keep track of transparencies and charts. However, many succumbed to the temptation of letting it carry the weight of the presentation.

Power Point is so visually appealing and easy to use that instead of being a visual enhancement for a presentation, Power Point slides often become a substitute for the presentation. Slides are filled with text. Now, instead of watching the presenter read from pages of text, the audience is subjected to watching him read from dozens of slides. Avoid turning your PowerPoint presentation into wall size note cards.

Charts, pictures, or other visuals can help the audience "see" the points you are making; however too many can be distracting. Use visuals only when they help you reinforce important points or simplify data.

Watch your language. The idea is to communicate your message persuasively, not to impress the audience with your extensive vocabulary or mastery of educational jargon. Use simple words and keep your sentences short. Avoid education jargon and acronyms unless they are essential to your presentation. If you use acronyms, be sure to explain them in your speech and your handouts.

Speak clearly, but do not be afraid to use contractions. Unless your daily speech is normally contraction-free, trying to avoid using any contractions will make your speech sound stilted.

We are all guilty of peppering our speech, formal or informal, with those little fillers such as "You know", "In other words", "Am I making myself clear", and the old standby, "To make a long story short" which, of course, never does. Try to make every word count and leave out the ones that do not.

Watch your body language. Nonverbal communication such as facial expressions and body language can contradict what the presenter is saying. Avoid body language that sends negative messages such as folding your arms in front of your chest or pointing your finger at the audience, or facial expressions such as smirking and frowning when speaking or listening to the audience's questions and comments.

Practice in front of a mirror or, if possible, set up a video camera and tape yourself. Ask a colleague to sit in on one of your presentations then you give feedback on your nonverbal communication.

Select public speakers carefully. Just because an individual likes to talk does not necessarily mean that he is a good presenter. I once worked with a man who was attractive, personable, and always eager to make presentations. There was one problem. When he felt intellectually threatened, he would make up words that he thought made him sound more eloquent. The result was embarrassing. Speakers dealing with controversial subjects should be able to handle a critical or demanding audience without losing their composure or confidence. Watch out for people who crave being in the spotlight. They can turn a twenty-minute presentation into forty-minutes of self-admiration.

Publicize your Speakers Bureau with a list of presentation topics through your Web site, press releases, or letters to the program organizers of local organizations. If an issue is, or is likely to be, of public interest, prepare a brief presentation and let local organizations know that the school has someone who is available to speak about the subject.

The opportunity to speak before a group is also an opportunity to listen. Allow ample time for questions after the presentation. If the function includes a reception or meal, allow time for the speaker to socialize with attendees. Use a sign-in sheet to create a list of those who attended and put them in the school's database. After the presentation, the presenter should write down any ideas and comments about the presentation while they are still fresh in her mind. Writing down impressions or special details on the back of business cards can help to personalize future communication. Periodically, meet with members of the Speakers Bureau to exchange ideas, share experiences, and discuss improvements to current presentations or thoughts for new ones.

Dispelling public school "myths"

At a dinner party, a man who did not know that I worked for a public school district began complaining vociferously about how school districts waste the "huge" amounts of tax money they receive. I asked him if he knew how school districts were funded in our state, how those funds were allocated to districts, and what percentage of district funds was spent on administration. He did not. And, he was quite surprised to learn how misinformed he was. I was able to give him the facts because I work in a school district; but, I once had the same misperceptions as he.

Myths about public education based on misinformation exist and there are groups eager to use such myths to advance their own agendas. Be proactive in addressing the misperceptions about public education. Information is available on the Internet to help you. Use a meta-search engine such as Google! and type in search words such as "myths+public+education" to find sites that provide list of myths with the facts to dispel them. Use them, as appropriate, in newsletters, presentations, on your fax sheet, and in brochures.

Determine what myths exist within your community. If you find mistaken beliefs that are pervasive and detrimental, create a brochure or presentation that provides the facts necessary to correct them. Ensure that your information is clear and concise. A lengthy, complicated explanation of school funding formulas is not likely to be read or understood, and, therefore, unlikely to change the public view.

Pass out information to staff members. It is possible that even school employees assume the myths to be true because they have heard them so often.

All points of contact should be positive

Make a list of every point of contact with the school and honestly assess if each is customer friendly. Enlist individuals from outside the school to help you in your assessment.

Are telephones answered promptly and politely? Are employees who routinely answer telephones informed about what is going on in the school or district? Is information related to frequently asked questions readily available?

Automated telephone systems are great for finding out your bank balance. However, automated systems do not convey personal attention and are particularly annoying when you really do want to speak to someone. Use automated systems only if your call level is so high that having "real" people answer the phone is disruptive to work flow. If you must use automation, make it user friendly and periodically test the system for its usefulness.

Check the school's system for effectiveness by calling into the school as if you were a first-time caller. I have had my call to a school answered by an automated system that asks me to enter the extension of the person I am calling. When I cannot supply the correct extension, the system instructs me to put in the first three or four letters of the person's last name. When I enter the name of the school principal, the system tells me that the name is not in the directory! If I redial to contact the school operator, the system sends me through the same dead end routine. In this situation, a system intended to provide efficiency is counterproductive. An ineffective system suggests that customer friendly communication is not a priority at the school.

Is the school Web site easy to navigate? Does the site provide information that users want? Does it provide a way for external viewers to communicate with individuals within the school? (See the information on Web sites in Chapter 5)

Is the school office easy to find? Is the school office inviting? Is the staff friendly and helpful? Is printed information readily available? Are requests for information filled promptly?

The goal is to increase the flow of communication in and out. When points of communication are positive and productive, people will use them more frequently.

Key communicators are key channels

Building a core of key communicators is a pro-active approach to effective two-way communication. Key communicators can help the school disseminate positive, accurate information and dispel rumors and exaggerated hearsay.

Select representatives from many groups within your community: minority groups, retired community, businesses, and organizations. Include individuals who have contact with large groups of people such as hair stylists and barbers, people who have influence such as civic and business leaders, people who are active in school related issues such as PTO and teacher organizations, and people in local activist groups.

Include people who have been critical of the school. Critics often become vocal when they feel that their views are not considered or because they are misinformed. Inclusion of school or district critics can help mitigate future attacks.

Keep key communicators abreast of what is happening in the school through mail-outs, E-mails, telephone calls, or meetings. In a critical situation, notify them immediately with an honest assessment of the problem or circumstances. As community leaders, they can help you diffuse negative repercussions. For example, if an investigative reporter manipulates the facts about an issue at the school in order to create a sensational story, your key communicators can help the school combat the misinformation. By writing letters to the editor, contacting other local business people, talking with their customers, and speaking with local groups, key communicators get the school's side of the story told.

Key communicators can also serve as a channel for incoming information. Because they are interacting with people in the community on a daily basis, key communicators can inform the school about community perceptions and potential issues. Such information allows the school to be proactive in its community relations.

How many key communicators should the school have? The answer is, as many as the school can comfortably manage. Some districts may have more than a hundred. A school may have dozens. Keep the database of key communicators current. Replace people who are no longer interested or have moved away.

A key to a successful key communicator program is trust. Ensure that information you provide to key communicators is accurate and never use them to create hype and do not provide them with slanted information to put the school in a better light. Just one incident of a breach of trust can wreck valuable relationships and deprive the school or district of an indispensable resource.

The importance of effective communication cannot be overly stressed. However, effective communication takes effort in thought and action. It is sometimes better to say nothing than to say it badly. Spend time carefully crafting your communication whether it is verbal or non-verbal, written or spoken, interpersonal, group, or mass communication.

Communication is so important to your marketing effort, it is essential that sufficient time and resources be spent ensuring that your messages are effective. The key is knowing your audiences and structuring your message in a way that they find appealing, credible, and persuasive.

5

Electronic Communication: An effective marketing tool

(Co-author: Mark Franke, Relatrix Corporation)

When considering your communication strategy, it is critical that you not forget the single biggest development in information technology in most people's lives today—the Internet. The Internet affects most of us on a daily basis, whether as a source of information when we are seeking answers through search engines like Google!; as a channel to exchange ideas at an almost real-time pace through such tools as E-mail, chat rooms, or instant messaging; or as a means to perform electronic transactions with a bank, credit card company, employer, or other person or business. These are all examples of electronic communications.

This chapter will focus on two of the most common tools in electronic communications: the school's or district's Web site and E-mail. While other types of tools, such as electronic chat and instant messaging, are growing in usage, they rely on a more "synchronous" connection between the person creating the message and the recipient or audience. Although they may be useful for one-to-one or small group communication, Web sites and E-mail still have the broadest impact when dealing with a large group of stakeholders.

Internet benefits to communication strategy

There are important reasons why your school should incorporate the Internet into its communication strategy. First, latest research shows that over 135 million people in the U.S. are Internet users and the growth trend continues with wider availability and lower costs of computing systems and bandwidth to access the Internet. Second, with the Internet, you have a communications channel that is "ON" seven days a week, 24 hours a day. Compare this with your phone system or mail service which only "connects" during office hours. Third, the Internet is a cost effective means of getting your message to stakeholders. Consider the cost of printing and mailing out a newsletter or school announcement. If you decide to send notes home with students, what percentage actually makes it to the parents? Taking into account the cost of software, computer systems, and network bandwidth, Internet communication is still around 20 percent of the cost of print communications. Finally, remember that communication is a two-way street that requires that you receive as well as send messages to your audience. With the Internet, it is far easier to let your stakeholders give their opinions through E-mail, online surveys, web polls, and other electronic tools.

Using the Internet in the communication process

Like any other channel of communication, the Internet is more about the message you send than the technology you use. Therefore, it is important that you understand the characteristics of this channel. Below are essentials to consider as you incorporate the Internet into your overall communication strategy.

Align objectives and responsibilities. Often the Web site at a school or district is managed by the IT department, as a technology issue, rather than by the communications department or marketing team which has the responsibility for crafting the district's or school's image. Consequently, the process of updating the Web site often must go through too many approvals to keep it current and relevant. The result is a Web site that is stale and out-of-date. Either put the responsibility for the Web site with the marketing team or ensure that there is a strong cooperative relationship between marketing and Web site teams.

Commit to relevance. One of the first commitments that must be made is to keep the content on the Web site relevant and timely. These authors have seen too many examples of school Web sites that have details of events that occurred in the previous school year months after the new school year has started. If parents or community members see this, what impression will they have? The impression that the school's Web site is not a reliable source of up-to-date information. They will stop visiting it.

Build integrated campaigns. When the school decides to pursue a marketing campaign, utilize all communication channels effectively, including the Internet. For example, if the school is generating a printed piece of material, then take the key message from the printed materials and incorporate it into your Web site and electronic newsletter. With this approach, the school is sending a consistent message through each channel of communication. By repeating the message, the school is ensuring that the idea sticks in the minds of the audience. If you are clever in how you present the message online, you can test the reaction of your reader with one or more forms of feedback.

Invest in electronic communication. Because many schools and districts do not operate on the premise that the Internet is part of their overall marketing strategy, they make a single, limited expenditure to built a web site, then stop. Electronic communication requires a continuing, dedicated portion of the school budget, and the more interactive and broader you want that channel to be, the larger that percentage of the budget needs to be.

Building a Web site to improve two-way communication

Web sites are an effective and cost-efficient way to promote your school. The school's site does not have to be extraordinary with every bell and whistle, but it should meet the needs of the community. Even a simple Web site can provide significant benefits if it is well designed. A Web site offers a multitude of uses and communicates that your school is progressive. Only imagination and budget limit the ways you can use it.

Through its Web site, the school can distribute information quickly, efficiently, and economically. When the media are covering a story about the school or district, a Web site is an excellent tool for alerting parents and employees before they see or hear it in the news. If the story is a negative one, a Web site is one more channel to get the school's side of the story told.

Parents can check on important dates, events, student projects, or the subjects their children are studying in school, or they can sign up to receive E-mail bulletins at the office or home. Achievements can be recognized. Events can be promoted. Use the site to inform people about public education in general such as how schools receive funds, new issues in education, legislative action related to educational issues at the state and local levels, or the criteria by which the state rates schools and districts.

The site can promote communication with other external audiences. The school can notify its key communicators about key issues or a crisis affecting the school. It is one more way to recognize business partners, volunteers, and community associations for their contributions. Realtors and the Chamber of Commerce can put your web address or hyperlink on their Web sites.

A Web site can provide a channel for incoming communication. The school can administer surveys and take polls via the Web site. The community can request information or express concerns. Parents can communicate with teachers, counselors, or other staff.

If the school does not have a technical person familiar with Web design among the staff members, offer to send someone for training. New software makes it easier to construct and maintain a site, but a certain level of technical expertise is required. If resources permit, have the site professionally designed, and then provide training to a staff person interested in maintaining it. The benefits of a Web site far outweigh the initial investment in time and money.

There are different levels of Web site "sophistication" that the school can build. You do not have to start at the most sophisticated level. However, if the school plans to use the site effectively and anticipates that the audience for it will increase, the level of sophistication should rise to incorporate new communication opportunities.

Level 1—The Shingle. As the name suggests, a shingle site's exclusive purpose is to let users know the school exists, give them a core message, and direct them to other forms of communication such as E-mail or telephone. Most small businesses start with a shingle site, and many stay there because they have not committed to the most effective use of the internet. Generally, the shingle contains no more than about ten pages and the content does not change often.

Level 2—Broad and Deep. This level expands on the shingle concept with more content explaining specific areas of operation, background on people and often addresses policy related issues. This type of site is often geared toward media personnel and those individuals looking for information on a range of commonly addressed areas of interest. This level standardizes the organization's message about such issues as a school board policy or school dress code. The content is updated periodically by a Web Master who is familiar with using web design tools.

The commitment level is higher than with the shingle site because of the additional content; however, organizations that use this level are generally not looking at their Web site as a strategic communication tool. The number of pages can vary from a dozen to even a hundred pages.

Level 3—Interactive. Interactive sites have different meanings depending on whom you ask. However, they have common characteristics. They include dynamic content (content that may change each time the user accesses the site). They have one or more mechanisms for users to subscribe or join notification groups. And, they provide users with a mechanism to give feedback.

Interactive sites generally entail two major steps for an organization. First, to get to a level of interactivity with the user will require an investment in a software program that has a database as part of its system. This is so a user list with E-mail addresses and profile information can be stored and retrieved dynamically. Software programs are available either to purchase or to lease as a hosted solution.

The second major step requires that more people become involved with the process of managing the content on your Web site. This is because with interactive sites, the user's expectation for timely information is higher and typically processes where all information is passed through a Web Master or other editor take too long.

Level 4—Personalized. These incorporate all the features of an interactive site plus the ability for users to customize the view of information they receive. Sometimes the personalization takes the form of a simple "profile", where the user can update contact details and information preferences. In other instances, as in the case of sites like Yahoo!, the entire look, feel, and content of the Web page or group of pages can be selected and edited.

Level 5—Learning Sites. The percentage of all Web sites on the Internet that would be classified as Learning Sites is small. Not surprisingly, they belong to very high-end commerce sites such as Amazon and eBay. A Learning Site differs from a personalized site in that it seeks to deliver personalized and relevant content to a user through a combination of profile details and historical interaction with the site. This often means that when the user accesses the site, he sees content that he may not have requested or knew he wanted. Based on the user's previous selections, the site has made a choice in anticipation of his desire to see more of the same or similar content. Amazon.com is effective at marketing by recommending books you might be interested in reading, based on books that you purchased in the past.

Steps to Building a Web site

In many ways, building a Web site is like a construction project. Before construction starts, you need to make certain strategic decisions, then lay out a blueprint of what you want to achieve. However, what makes a Web site more complex is that, unlike a building, you will continually modify and restructure it over time. While this section speaks in terms of building a Web site from scratch, it is equally relevant if the school decides to redesign or add any major section or capability of its site. There should be a flexible, but structured, process that the school goes through to complete the project.

STEP 1—Undertake a requirements analysis.

Do the school want or need a Web site? This seems like a strange question in a chapter on Web site development. However, it is relevant. If the school's community has limited Internet access or if the organization is not willing to commit to a long-term process of evolving the site and updating the content, it may be better to postpone the investment of resources.

If the school decides to proceed, then the first task is to define a team. Whether you use an internal or external team to develop the site, the school is responsible for the end result. The school needs to take the lead in setting priorities and making key decisions about the site.

Next gather input on requirements from each of the different audiences or groups that the school wishes to serve with its site. Ask the question, "What do we want to accomplish with this site?" Do not assume you already know. Chances are if you asked five different groups, say parents, staff members, students, central administration, and the external community, you might get five different answers.

Certainly you want to provide information, but to whom? What kind? How? How often? Parents are the principal audience. Other than giving basic information to parents, do you want to provide additional information that can help them participate in their children's education or links to sites with information on parenting skills?

It is important, however, to look not only at the groups who obviously will visit the site, but also at the ones the school would like to attract such as parents who are looking for a school or potential external business partners. What kind of information might they be looking for? Consider the demographics of the school's audiences. Do you need to provide information in languages other than English? Try to incorporate the desires from each of these group into the planning process.

Determine how much the school wants to spend. The budget for a Web site can be as little as a few hundred dollars if you buy a Web site development tool like Microsoft FrontPage and have someone in the school do the work. Alternatively, you can spend tens of thousands on a site if you use an outside firm and have a long list of requirements. Remember, you will need to update your site over time, so plan on a portion of the school budget going to Web site updates.

Finally, develop short-term and long-term objectives for your site. You will probably get more requests than you can handle with your first release, so set priorities for the content and level of interactivity to make available first then set objectives for the next year. Let stakeholders know what you plan to do and in what order so they won't be surprised by what is on the site initially.

If the school does not already have a Web site domain, you will need to check on the availability of the domain you want and reserve it for your use. There are numerous online domain registration services that will help you search for available Web domains and reserve the domain for your use. (Google! word search: domain registration),

STEP 2—Decide on a technical framework.

The technical framework is different from all content, layout, and navigation issues that come with the site design. Technical framework involves making some decisions about the development tools and deployment environment you wish to use. Not all Web sites are built on the same foundation. If you already have a Web site, some of these decisions may already have been made. Tasks include:

Determine the deployment environment. Will the school put this site on its own computers or at a third-party hosting center? Will Windows, Unix, or Linux be the operating system for the Web server and database? What Web server will you use? While the answers to these questions do not impact the content, they do impact who and how the school will maintain the Web site over time.

Determine the development tools. Whether the school develops internally or uses an external Web site development company, staff members will want to be involved in this decision because it will have a big impact on site maintenance later. If the development environment and/or tools are either too complicated or too expensive, the school may be stuck having to contract site maintenance over the long term. Note: One option here is to consider using a Content Management System (CMS). A CMS requires far less understanding of Web site coding by staff members. Much of the site development and maintenance can be managed through a CMS.

Buy or lease. Another decision is whether to buy any of the tools or systems that provide the new capabilities the school wants. Generally, buying requires a larger upfront investment; however, it gives the school more control over changes. Leasing stretches the cost out over time, but limits what the school is able to modify outside the tools being leased.

At this point, unless the school has a staff person experienced in Web design, a Web designer should be engaged to help with the process. It is also helpful for the marketing team to have a basic understanding of Web design even if the school is using an external firm to design and construct the Web site. Knowing the fundamentals of good site design will save time and money as the team works with the Web designer. A number of books and Internet sites provide guidance for non-technical people to gain a basic understanding of how Web sites work and basic design considerations. Ask the marketing team to look at other Web sites, especially those of other schools and districts, to get ideas on appealing design and function. Members should note what they like and do not like, then compare notes in a team meeting.

STEP 3—Design the site

In the design phase, there are three major points to consider: content, layout, and navigation. While addressed separately, there are strong interdependencies between each of these points. The design process tends to be a repetitive refining process that moves towards a proto-type or mock-up of the site which allows you to collaborate and make changes before final approval.

Content. Most school Web sites provide similar kinds of basic information. Content generally recognized as desirable includes names of school administrators (and possibly contact details), upcoming events, special awards and acknowledgements, the school calendar, school location and map, test scores and testing dates, a greeting from the principal, and connection to other sites such as the district site.

Part of the content should relate to information the school wants its stakeholders to have and part should provide information the stakeholders want to know. These may not always be the same. The authors have visited district and school sites where they could not find any information about how to contact administrators or even who they were. The message conveyed was that these administrators did not want to be contacted.

Think about the different groups that may access your site. What kind of information do they want? Think beyond the obvious groups such as parents. Businesses as well as home buyers outside your community may access district and school sites as part of their research when looking for a place to relocate. Teachers considering employment opportunities will use your site as part of their decision-making process.

Some information such as school calendars, event schedules, menus, and test results will be purely factual, but the site is also an opportunity to promote your school. Apply the same guidelines for effective communication as carefully as you would for any major communication piece.

Ensure that the content complies with district policy. If the school uses copyrighted material such as photographs and clip art, follow guidelines set forth by the company or individual who owns the rights. If the school has created or paid to have created any special design work, copyright the work.

If you use photographs, use ones of people, places, and events within your school or district, rather then stock photos. If you do not feel that school staff members can produce the quality of photographs you desire, hire a photographer for a day. Make a list of the kinds of photographs the school is likely to use, now and in the future, and create an inventory. Be sure to get use authorization from individuals and permission forms signed by parents for student photographs.

Remember the more graphics the school puts on its site, the longer it will take to load. As tempting as it is to "jazz up" the Web site, use bells and whistles sparingly. If the Web site does include animations or video, use standard "plugins" such as Windows Media Player, Quicktime, or Flash Player or provide links so users can download the plugins. Animations and video that make the content inaccessible or that cause the user's computer to crash are not an asset.

Layout. Now that the team knows the purpose of the Web site and what content can help meet that purpose, it is time to decide how to organize that content. The layout of the Web site is similar to an organization chart. At the top the Home Page from which the viewer can reach various Sub pages each of which may contain additional pages. Your site should have a plan that helps the viewer get through the layers to find the information she needs. The team should consider each of the following elements:

Standardization. If this is a district site, do you want to have standardization across all district departments or promote individualization? Consider content management systems that can create/use Web page templates to standardize. This can be as simple as using Microsoft FrontPage or similar tools that require training or more sophisticated Web-based content management systems.

As a matter of district policy, it is useful to impose at least a minimum set of standards on the look, organization, and navigation of "sub-webs' or web sites that are connected and subordinate to the district site. Such standards might include:

- Displaying the district logo on the homepage with a link to the district homepage.

- The basic content that should appear on the sub-web homepage.

- The minimum page layout and content that should be included

- A basic color scheme and font style to use on the sub-web.

The authors have seen department and school Web sites developed by very creative people and yet, as viewers, we had no idea what school district we were in. In some cases, details such as the school's location, the principal's name, or how to contact the school were missing.

Home Page. The home page is the front cover of your site. It serves two main purposes: First, it sets the tone and style for the remaining pages in the site. The home page creates the first impression viewers have of the site. Second, it gives an overview of the information that is available on the site and provides viewers access to the main content sections.

Main Content Pages. These pages contain the main content areas of your Web site plus additional sub pages of information. On a district site, main content pages might be *About the District, Employment Opportunities, Departments, Schools, etc.* Under these categories are subcategories containing additional information. A sub page *About the District,* might contain the history, demographics, mission, and other general information. Main content areas for the school may be *Letter from the Principal, School Information, Parents Page, Library, Faculty/Staff, School News.*

If you have trouble deciding how to set up your main content pages, draw an organizational chart to determine the content pages and how to arrange them on the site. Do not make your main content areas so thin that you end up with numerous pages with little information in them. It is equally important not to make the content areas so content laden that viewers have to drill down several pages to get to the information they want. Try to organize the content into five to seven main content areas with two to three layers of subcategories.

Resource Pages. You will likely find a benefit in creating one or more "resource" pages which do not naturally fit into the structure of the site.

Resource pages contain information of a more general nature (than say a description of a district department or a school). They often contain links to other documents (such as Word or PDF documents), to other internal Web sites or those across the Internet.

There are two types of resource pages: internal and external. Internal pages might include a "Recent News About the District", employment application forms, or FAQ (Frequently Asked/Answered Questions)pages. As the name implies, they describe and connect to resources that are within your Web site. External resource pages include lists or links to other Web sites for information that your school or district does not supply internally. For example, samples of the state assessment tests or information about pending legislation affecting public schools.

Why include resource pages? Because they help users find the information they need more quickly and efficiently, thereby, establishing your Web site as a valuable information resource. Think of a search engine like Google! where you can find information about any subject in the universe. A school or district is an obvious place to find resources related to education of children.

Although the pages will vary depending on the content, there should be a consistency in the layout that gives the site a unified look and helps the user move through the site quickly. Colors and fonts should be consistent and navigation elements should look the same and be in the same place on every page.

Users may not always scroll down the page; therefore, the most important information should be at the top of the page. Construct your text similar to that of a press release where all the important information is in the first paragraph. Use the rest of the page to expand upon what you have in the first paragraph.

Use less text (about 50 percent less) than you would in other types of communication. Many people find reading text from a computer screen tiresome. Most viewers would find a page full of text, unappealing. Present the text in short paragraphs and use bullets to break down subcategories of information. Bulleted items can also be hyperlinks that allow the user to click for more detailed information.

Navigational. Navigation elements give the user access to the pages in the site and allow him to move through the pages quickly. Some cross-navigation elements such as the home page and search function appear on every page.

Other cross-navigation elements might include employment information, the district calendar, or directories with contact information.

Viewers should be able to recognize which elements to use for navigating. Group the navigation elements together in one area and giving them the look of navigational "buttons". Using shadows, bevels, and glowing edges makes them look "clickable". If you use special effects on items to indicate that they are navigation elements, do not confuse viewers by using them on items that are not for navigation.

Use words rather than icons to indicate function and content. A stack of books could refer to the library, a reading list, homework, or textbooks. If you want to use icons to liven up the page, add text to the button to avoid misinterpretation.

Consistency is important in the navigation system. Once you have designed the navigation system, give it the same look and keep it in the same place everywhere in the site. The district or school logo should appear at the top of each page and should have a hyperlink to the homepage.

Within a given content area, you may want to provide internal navigation between various sub-pages so the users do not have to click the "Back" button. When you add new content, put a link to it on the homepage. Do not rely on users clicking their way to it. Ensure that it is easy for people to contact the district or school by E-mail or phone by including a "Contact Us" link on every page.

STEP 4—Develop the site.

This phase combines the design and content with the technology that will make the site function. Depending on how complex and large a site the school wants to create, it may not be feasible to create the entire site at once. If not, decide what parts of the site should go "live" first, then determine phases for subsequent pages.

Different technical teams have different methods of deployment. You should request that there be several phases of development so that the team can determine if the pages are meeting expectations. The following phases generally are included in development.

Mock-up. A mock-up contains the major layout and navigation elements but little or no real content. The purpose is to give the team a preview of where different parts of the content will appear and how it will be formatted.

You should have mock-ups for your Homepage, a Main Content Page, and possibly a Sub-page.

Draft. This phase should have the content and any interactivity (or links to it) incorporated for the site. It may be desirable to have multiple draft deliveries for different sections of your site so the team can review and make change requests without having to review the whole site at once.

Internal (Test) release. While the technical test should test the site to ensure that it works properly, it is up to the team to test every feature and link on every page. Just because something worked on one page does not guarantee it will work on other pages. Buttons and links that do not work or take the viewer in a non-ending cycle are particularly detrimental to your site.

Final review. A final review should be completed by individuals not involved in the design and construction such as teachers, students, and parents. In addition to the usability of the site, ask for opinions on features or information that would make the site more appealing. Take their comments seriously. This is the time to make changes. If you have incorporated the requirements of your different user groups into the Web site, you should be close to the mark on what you deliver for final review. If you are not close and there are more requests for major changes, a decision must be made. Do you make the changes before deploying or hold the requests for a later version of the site?

In the private sector, most Web sites have a life span of six to twelve months before undergoing either a facelift or a major renovation. While you may not want to change the school site that often, at least plan and budget to make changes every couple of years. Web site "look and feel", like fashion, is constantly changing.

STEP 5—Deploy the site.

Once you have completed the testing and review of the site, it is time to "go live". This is one of the easier steps to accomplish, but one that often has problems. If the school or district is hosting the site on its own server then you will need to transfer all of the Web pages, graphics, documents and associated files from your development area up to your Web server. If the site was developed with "relative" addressing, that is if all the hyperlinks between different pages point to each other by their relative location in the site (this is standard development practice), then everything should work fine. However, it is worth checking all of the navigational elements on the site to make sure that the move did not break anything.

If you are hosting through an Internet Service Provider (ISP) or other hosting service, you will need, in addition to moving your Web files, to make sure that your Web domain has been registered with your ISP. This will ensure that when people type in the school or district Web address, they reach the homepage.

STEP 6—Reassess and update.

In many ways, the school's Web site is like the daily or weekly newspaper. It needs to have new content that is time sensitive to refresh it. Continue to seek feedback about the site. Ask users what they would like to see added. Evolve the site from a static to an interactive site over time by adding various Web functions such as surveys, polls, and notification groups. As content is added to the site you will find opportunities to reorganize it to simplify and streamline content and navigation.

Useful Web site tools

If the school or district is starting from scratch, just getting something simple up and running may seem like a formidable task. After the site is up and the benefits become apparent it is natural to want to improve the site. If the school already has a site, it may not be providing the maximum benefits. Whether building a new site or improving an existing one, listed below are several useful elements or services that you may want to incorporate into the school site.

Web site search. As the site grows, there may be more pages and content than can easily be navigated by a user in a few minutes. To simplify how users get to the right page with minimal effort consider adding a Web site search capability. Google!, and several other online services offer free Web site search tools that can be easily added to your site by your Web Master.

FAQ (Frequently Asked Questions) page. It is common to have the same questions asked several times by different people. In fact, statistically speaking, about 80 percent of the questions that your staff members answer by phone or E-mail have been asked and answered before. Adding a FAQ page to incorporate these questions can reduce the number of E-mails and phone calls and save staff members' time.

Location map. Lots of people are interested in visiting district or school offices. Make it easy for them to do so. Several online services, including MapQuest, will allow you to create a page or link on the school Web site that has a map showing the location of your facility.

Web site tracking. Most ISPs provide basic Web site statistics tools that will help the school better understand how many people are accessing its site and when and where people are coming from to reach the site, what pages they most frequently view, and in some cases, details about the Web browser and where they are geographically (on a macro scale). If the school or district is hosting its own Web site, Web site tracking software is available off the Internet. Alternatively, you can "rent" software so you do not have to install and maintain it on your own.

Promoting the school Web site

Once the school has created and deployed its Web site, it should then promote it as a resource for the community. This is especially true if the site has been created as or upgraded to an interactive site. You want users to access information or provide feedback before picking up the phone or firing school staff members an E-mail.

One of the best ways to encourage Web site use is to put the school's site address on *all* printed materials including business cards, stationery, FAX cover sheets, newsletters, and brochures. This provides an ongoing reminder to people that an electronic resource for the school exists.

The school should also incorporate a reference to its Web site in its audio communication. That may involve a mention on voicemail or call holding or providing the information during phone or face-to-face conversations or presentations. Ask staff members to remind people calling in about the Web site.

If the school has addresses, notify people by E-mail of changes or new major additions to the site. Different communities have different levels of Internet access and E-mail usage. However, as you will see in the next section,

E-mail is a cost-effective channel. You should attempt to expand its use in concert with the growth of your Web site.

Using E-mail to inform and respond

There are several important reasons to consider expanding the use of E-mail as a communications channel to the school's stakeholders. First, E-mail is cost effective. The school can eliminate much of its cost for printing and postage. E-mail lets you get messages out to a broad audience, as opposed to using the telephone to reach them.

E-mail has a shorter contact period versus conventional mail. Even with large broadcast E-mail services, a message can reach 10,000 users on the same day the message is created. With many E-mail programs, the school can track who has looked at the message and whether they have clicked on any links in the E-mail that take them back to the school's Web site. With conventional mail, you are never sure if the recipient received your message, opened it, or simply threw it unread into the trash with the junk mail.

With E-mail, it is also possible to personalize messages to specific users in a cost effective way. Personalization can be through simply addressing them by name or incorporating conditional content in the E-mail message based on profile details you have about the user.

Finally, E-mail allows users to respond to you quickly and easily, thereby facilitating two-way communication. Whether by simply clicking the "Respond" button or following incorporated hyperlinks, users can give the school feedback on messages much faster than any print and mail message.

Using E-mail effectively

While there are advantages to using E-mail in the school's communication strategy, there are also issues that must be considered as the school seeks to broaden this channel. Because E-mail is cheap to send, there has been an explosion of "Spam", unsolicited E-mail sent to a huge mailing list in hopes that some percentage of recipients will respond. The explosion of Spam had led to industry and government action to try to reduce its volume.

The CAN SPAM Act of 2003 became effective in January 2004. The intent was to eliminate E-mail sent by Spammers. In general, this legislation should not have an impact on schools or districts. While there are numerous clauses that address how to send E-mail if an organization is advertising or soliciting, the school can meet the requirements and intent of the law by following these guidelines:

- Keep the E-mail subject line and body of the text consistent.

- Make it clear if you are seeking funds or advertising.

- Give people a way out. Do this by including both a physical address and phone number in addition to an electronic means for users to remove themselves from the school's E-mail list.

- Make sure users are aware of the school's privacy policy with regards to their E-mail address and any other information they may provide to the school.

To reduce the incidence of Spam, new E-mail tools have been created to check for clues within the subject line and body of an E-mail and "score" the E-mail based on some of the common Spam characteristics. To keep the school's E-mail from being classed as Spam, make the subject line concise and to the point. Avoid generic terms such as "Join Us". Do not use ALL CAPITAL LETTERS in the subject line or the body of the E-mail. And, do not use extreme punctuation such as exclamation points!!!!.

Another challenge of E-mail is having correct addresses. Some users give a fake address or simply make a mistake when typing. Keep the E-mail list as clean as possible by purging addresses that "bounce" from an invalid address. Provide a way for people to edit their E-mail address and other personal information through the school Web site.

A common issue encountered is the "Aging Inbox". This happens when someone on the school staff is away from the school either temporarily or permanently, but the E-mails keep coming. They may sit in the inbox for days, weeks, even months. It creates a negative view of the school when the parent, volunteer, or community member does not receive a response. You can address this issue either procedurally or by use of a centralized E-mail response management system. An E-mail response management system allows the school to track inbound E-mails so they do not get lost in an individual's inbox.

Building a user list

Unlike a telephone number, an E-mail address is not something you can look up in a book. Building a list of E-mail addresses requires asking users for their address at each different point of communication. Some of the more obvious methods of building a list include:

- Take the opportunity at student registration while parents are providing other types of information to ask for an E-mail address. Go a step further and ask them for what purpose(s) they would like to receive E-mail. For example, medical emergencies, school event announcements, test schedule, or weather alerts.

- If the school has an interactive Web site, ask users for E-mail addresses to provide specific information they may have an interest in such as newsletters, school board meeting briefs, or special event announcements.

- Local PTOs and PTAs are a valuable source of details on parents within the community. Ask them to promote the Web site and solicit E-mail addresses from members.

- Gather E-mail addresses from the messages that are sent to the school. This task is best performed by the district's or school's IT staff members.

Permission based communication

As part of the school's responsibility in collecting E-mails, care should be taken to determine who really wants to hear from the school. Furthermore, the school should ensure that users understand your position on maintaining the integrity of their personal details.

When the school first contacts a stakeholder by E-mail let her know that she has the option of canceling or "opting-out" of future correspondence. This is not difficult if the school has an interactive site that manages the user list.

In addition, the school should develop a written policy for information gathered from the Web site. This policy should contain a section about the type of information (name, E-mail address, E-mail content) the schools obtains through its Web site. The policy should also contain the school's intentions regarding use of the information and with whom the school will or may share it. Have the district's legal counsel review the document. However, do not let the language of the document become too legalistic. Keep it simple and to the point while covering each of the key points already mentioned. Take a look at other Web site's privacy policies as a starting point. Include the privacy policy or a link to it in all E-mails and on the school's Web site.

Designing an E-mail message

E-mail messages face the same obstacles as other communication piece. They have to compete for the time, attention, and interest of the receiver. Use these suggestions to make the school's E-mail messages reader friendly.

Include graphics (sparingly). A picture may be worth a thousand words, but not if it takes too long to display or overwhelms the message. Graphics can be invaluable in an E-mail. Most E-mail systems now have the ability to read messages in an HTML format. Make sure that the graphic is relevant to the message or the school. Also check the layout between graphics and text in the message by sending a version to yourself.

Keep your message short. While E-mail is becoming a larger part of people's daily business and personal life, they still do not expect the body of the text to contain the same amount of information that might be sent via fax or mail. It is better to create a large document in another format and attach it. As an attachment it is more likely to be read than a multi-page E-mail.

Link to the school Web site. Encourage users to click on a link that will take them to the school Web site where you have the space and ability to present them with more information. This also allows the school to track the number of users that come to the Web site from a link in E-mails.

Personalize the message. If possible, use the name of the person to whom you are sending the message within the E-mail text. People have an innate affinity towards communication that is directed to them personally. Conversely, they are more likely to delete the message when it is not personalized. High-end E-mail marketing systems will even allow inclusion of "conditional content" such as a paragraph in the E-mail that changes depending on what grade their child is in or what school he attends.

Test the message before broadcasting it. To confirm that the format of any E-mail the school is planning to send to a broad audience looks acceptable and to ensure that the E-mail will not get "trapped" by Spam filters, test it by sending it to members of the team.

Integrating E-mail with offline communications

An often overlooked advantage of E-mail is as a reinforcement for offline communication. If you are going to send a mail-out to the community, consider first sending an E-mail with an excerpt from the printed piece along with a notice that the printed piece is on the way. If the recipient does not receive the printed piece, he can contact the school to have it resent. Alternatively, put a link in the E-mail to a page or document on the school Web site that describes the printed piece in detail.

FAQs can reduce redundant E-mail

FAQ stands either for Frequently Asked Questions or Frequently Answered Questions. An often quoted statistic is that 80 percent of the questions an organization receives have been asked and answered before. While a FAQ page is not a replacement for phone, E-mail, or face-to-face communication, it can reduce redundant E-mail and telephone inquiries that require staff members' time.

There are two ways to approach FAQs. The school can assume it knows the questions and create a page on the Web site with the questions and answers. Entries might include the school's holiday schedule or fees for extra-curricula activities. This is a good starting point. The disadvantage of this approach is that often once the page is established it is seldom updated. The information becomes out-dated and useless.

A second approach is to implement a knowledgebase system for FAQs. A knowledgebase is a database containing text information that has been "indexed" so that users can search it through keywords, key phrases, category, or other reference indicators. A knowledgebase is most effective if it is tied to the school's E-mail management system so that as questions are answered via E-mail, they are added to the FAQ knowledgebase if appropriate.

Promote interest group subscription

To engage the community in two-way communication, consider offering them the option to join Interest or Notification groups through the school Web site. Participants select the type of information they wish to receive as it becomes available on the Web site. Messages might alert parents that the test schedule for state assessment exams or registration forms for special programs are now available on the school's Web site. The school can keep key communicators apprised of specific issues related to the school. This is also a way to add to the school's E-mail list.

Electronic newsletters

In addition to Notification groups, consider asking users to subscribe to school newsletters through the Web site. Electronic newsletters will save print and postage costs and get to the recipients much quicker. Advertise the newsletter option on the school Web site and via E-mails. Offer an "archive" of newsletters to allow viewing of previous issues.

Online surveys and polls

Surveys and polls have been used by the media, political groups, and industry for some time. However, the application of the Internet for this purpose has become common only within the last few years. The merits of using the Internet for polls and surveys were addressed in the chapter on Marketing Research. It is a quick and inexpensive way to learn what the community thinks on a particular issue or to measure the approval level regarding a school or district initiative.

While online feedback may not have the statistical accuracy of more scientifically constructed "offline" surveys, the advantage of electronic polls and surveys is the immediacy of response and the ability to see the results as they arrive. As an adjunct to offline surveys, this tool can help the district or school get a more accurate picture of how the school is perceived by the community and their opinions on key issues.

There is no doubt that the use of electronic communication can significantly improve two-way communication for schools and districts. Improving two-way communication is essential if schools and districts are to be responsive to their internal and external stakeholders. Like many initiatives, the greatest expenditure of time and money is in the beginning, but the long-term benefits are greater efficiency, better use of resources, and improved communication.

Success Story
Colorado Springs School District 11
Electronic Dialogue: A Means to Greater Community Loyalty

With over 30,000 students, School District 11 is the seventh largest school district in Colorado and the largest school district in the Pikes Peak region. The district includes 38 elementary schools (grades K–5); one K–8 school; nine middle schools (grades 6–8); five high schools (grades 9–12); five alternative schools and/or programs; one digital high school; six charter schools; and adult and family education programs. Nestled at the foot of Pikes Peak and the front range of the Colorado Rockies, Colorado Springs, with a population of about 400,000, would appear to be an idyllic location in which to raise and educate children; and it is.

However, District 11 faces challenges related to the inner city characteristics of the area that it serves, which is the older, more established part of the city. Many of the people in District 11's community are retired or no longer have school-age children, giving them less motivation to vote for additional taxes or mill levies in support of District 11.

Suburban expansion has hit Colorado Springs, like most cities, resulting in many of the more affluent families moving away from the center of the city into school districts which now surround District 11. This has limited the district's ability to expand its service area and reintegrate some of these newer neighborhoods. This keeps the district from being able to expand its taxable base, while the property values have tended to trail the rate of growth of suburban school districts. In addition, as the oldest school district in the Colorado Springs area, District 11 has some of the oldest schools and facilities, which require a lot of maintenance and upkeep and in many instances replacement.

Even with these fiscal constraints, District 11 provides a high quality of educational services to its community and has been recognized for its efforts and results in implementing quality and continuous improvement systems. The challenges faced by the district, however, relate in many ways to how the district and its educational services and staff members are perceived by the parents and taxpayers of the community.

By the Spring of 2002, District 11 had already deployed numerous online programs to help the district administration and individual campuses interact with the community more effectively. These include a library search system (SIRSI) for finding and reserving library resources throughout the district; a school lunch system to allow students and parents to purchase school lunches online; a community education enrollment system; Teacher Connect, Parent Connect and Student Connect, which allowed these stakeholders to monitor, collaborate, and seek answers regarding individual class curriculum and assignments as well as information about individual students.

While many of these applications were part of an overall community relations effort using the Internet, the district was only beginning to look at online tools for marketing and customer service functions at the district level. In early 2002, the communications function was receiving proportionally greater emphasis because of the failure earlier in the decade to pass a bond issue which would have helped the district upgrade many of its older facilities.

District 11 has an active communications and community relations office headed by Ms. Elaine Naleski, and the district Web site contained a broad range of policy and procedural content and went several levels deep with 'sub-webs' for different departments within the district. In addition, the site provided links to many of the operational systems mentioned above.

However, the District 11 Communications and Community Relations Office was only beginning to look at ways to streamline their own communication processes and use the Web more interactively to improve responsiveness to the community. As part of her effort to convince the Board of Education to take action regarding an online community relations system, Ms. Naleski identified several benefits, including faster, more efficient and more convenient delivery of information; customer friendliness (24 hour-a-day availability); quality (e.g., accuracy) of information; the ability to "push out" important information; the ability to track data within the system; and the need to track opinions of the community through online surveying.

Ms. Naleski made a persuasive argument, but there were still concerns about utilizing the Internet for community relations programs, primarily based on a Board of Education perception that it might be seen as less personal than other channels. In the end, Ms. Naleski was able to overcome these concerns because everyone acknowledged the need to take some action to improve the community relations program. From a financial perspective, hiring more staff members to handle these programs was not cost effective; therefore, after almost a year of internal discussion and review, the board gave the D-11 Communications Office the go-ahead to find an Internet-based community relations tool.

One of the first processes identified for improvement was the E-mail system that came through the district's Web site. There were several links on the site where users could click and send an E-mail to the district. The vast majority of these E-mails landed in the inbox of one person in the District 11 Communications Office who then had to track down the answers from a knowledgeable person or department and respond to the users. This process resulted in a relatively long response time, redundant responses to the same questions, and a procedural bottleneck because questions could be processed only as fast as one person could track down the answers.

To address this bottleneck, the District 11 Communications Office decided to develop an online, automated program called "D-11 Answers" that would provide a knowledgebase of frequently asked questions (FAQs) on their Web site. The system would also direct questions to the correct person or department within the district most likely to know the answers, automatically updating the knowledgebase with the answers once staff responded. In addition, the D-11 Communications Office needed a way to track response time and unanswered questions.

When considering options for the system, Ms. Naleski's team had to decide whether to wait on the Information Technology (IT) Department to develop such a program or go outside for assistance. After much internal discussion, it was decided to go with an outside system. Since the D-11 Communications Office did not want the project to depend on availability of IT resources to install a commercial system on the district's own servers, they chose a hosted solution. The hosted system, called "ezCommunicator" had the knowledgebase function and also included several other interactive components. The D-11 Communications Office could have chosen a system which had only knowledgebase functions, but they recognized that they would probably want to expand to use of other online interactive components. Having those components available in a single integrated system made it easier to deploy these other functions on an as-needed basis.

"One of the first and largest challenges we faced was getting buy-in from the rest of the departments within the district office once we had board approval to proceed with the project," says Elaine Naleski. Aside from getting IT commitment to the technical side of the D-11 Answers system, the D-11 Communications Office had to persuade, and in some cases cajole, different departments to take on responsibility for responding to questions in their areas of expertise.

With D-11 Answers deployed, the D-11 Communications Office has been able to track the trend in usage of the system, both for viewing questions and posting questions. They have also, from a quality improvement aspect, been able to track the response time to questions coming through the system and have seen a steady improvement to a level of approximately one business day, which was an original target for quality.

Since November 2003, when the above information was compiled and presented at an international education conference, District 11 has continued to expand their use of the Internet as part of their communications and community relations programs.

In early 2004, the District 11 administration was beginning to search for ways to market particular high schools within the district that were losing students and suffering from poor community perception. As part of the community out-reach and marketing efforts at these high schools, the D-11 Communications Office decided to deploy the same system used at the district level on the school Web sites so that these schools can begin to utilize more interactive, Internet-based tools to strengthen community loyalty.

The D-11 Communications Office has gradually broadened use of the interactive tools within the ezCommunicator system and now distributes electronic newsletters to various subscribers of the system. They use the survey and online poll capabilities to gain quick insights into community interest and positions on certain issues, and they provide users with the opportunity to subscribe to various announcement groups and categories of interest.

In November 2004, District 11 ran another bond election and was successful in getting voter approval for $132 million for capital improvements across the district. While many people were involved and many other methods were used to get out the message about the value of the bond to the community,

District 11 was able to make effective use of their D-11 Answers system to respond to questions submitted by the voters in the community and to take periodic surveys and polls to gauge support.

"We've learned that we could have gained more benefit earlier in using the system if we had planned out how we would apply each of the features to its fullest effect. We also learned that we should have involved more people, including end users, in the process of defining our requirements in order to get their buy-in up-front," says Ms. Naleski. "Using the Internet as part of our communications strategy is a process of continuous advancement. We're always looking for ways to use the Web site and e-mail to refine our message to the community and improve the community's perception of us as a responsive school district committed to the highest level of quality education. Implementing an Internet community relations system has been, and continues to be, a journey for us—not a single event."

6

Media Relations

It has been some time since a school's media experiences were mainly pictures in the local newspaper of a 4-H member proudly holding a prize ribbon in one hand with an arm around the winning animal or a story about the choral group's holiday performance. Today, district administrators often view their dealings with the media with dread and suspicion.

In my experience, people who have children in public schools generally have a more favorable opinion of public education than people who do not. Because people without children in public schools generally have little or no contact with the school, they form their opinions through secondary sources, often the media. The astute administrator is one who recognizes the influence the media has over public perception and makes an effort to work with the media rather than against it.

Most school districts have a media, communication, or public affairs officer who is a professional with experience in interacting with the media. This chapter discusses ways in which schools can help their district's media relations or communication administrator maximize relations with the media by reducing occasions for negative media coverage within their own school environment and by working with neighborhood news services to create an awareness of the school's achievements and activities.

Getting the news out

People want to know what is going on in their local schools. This is especially true when educational issues are gaining national attention. No one knows better what is going on in the schools than the administrators and staff members. Providing positive news-worthy items to the district's media office or to neighborhood papers can play a major role in improving community relations. The school can increase the chances of getting its story told by knowing what constitutes a "good" news item and how to make those items interesting.

Types of stories. There are two reasons why people read or listen to a news item. One is because it contains information they want or need to know. These "hard news" items provide information in a factual, objective, impersonal way. A story about progress on flood damage repairs to the school and how it will affect the beginning of the school year is a hard news story. When submitting this type of news item, provide the most important information, *who, what, when where, why,* and *how* in the first paragraph, then follow with greater detail in subsequent paragraphs. Check all factual material for accuracy, avoid using jargon, and have supporting data for secondary sources.

The factual, objective nature of the hard news story does not mean there is no opportunity to show the school in a positive light. In the above example about flood damage repair, the news item could point out that processes put in place by the school administration resulted in the project being ahead of schedule or that the school has contingency plans in the event of unexpected delays.

Even a negative story can have positive effects if handled properly. A story about bus breakdowns causing children to be repeatedly late for school, may give support to the school district's need to replace old buses.

A second reason people read or listen to news items is because they find them interesting. The feature story provides information, but in a more engaging, attention-grabbing way. Feature stories are an opportunity to create positive awareness of the school. Stories may be of interest because they link to something in the national news, involve an interesting person, describe the school's innovative approach to an issue, or announce an outstanding achievement.

However, the story has to be interesting enough for people to take the time to read or listen to it. How do you get the public interested in reading a news item about the 6th grader in your school who won a regional spelling bee? First, create a headline that will attract interest. A headline that reads, "Could you spell homoeothermic?" is more attention-grabbing than one that reads "Local 6th grader wins regional spelling bee."

Once you have the reader's attention with the headline, keep it by making the news item a dramatic story, adding interesting personal information, and tying it to the interests of the reader. Write about the tension surrounding the spelling bee, provide some interesting information about the winning student, and mention how competition for the spelling bee improved the spelling and vocabulary skills of the school's 6th grade students.

Include an interesting photograph that depicts the drama in the story. For example, the child's face when she realizes she has won or the emotion-filled scene backstage before the finals. The photograph may or may not be included with the story, but it has a better chance if it is interesting and pertinent.

Recently, a documentary film about spelling bees drew audiences to major theatres across the country. How? It told an emotional, dramatic human-interest story. Your articles do not have to be award winning, but they should tell the reader a good story.

Preferably, the person developing and writing news items will be on the marketing team. If there is no one who has the flair for developing stories, appoint a staff member who likes to write, use students from high school English or journalism classes, find a volunteer who has media experience, or check the local college for a journalism student looking for part-time work. The person you select should be willing to make a commitment for the school year. It is also important that the principal and the marketing team should approve all news items that are submitted to any media outlet.

Both hard news and feature stories are opportunities to promote your school. Remember that the media are more likely to run a story if the item is well written and the content has audience appeal

Get to know the neighborhood newspaper

Although the district's media person generally handles the major media contacts, many cities and towns have smaller, weekly papers that cover a specific section of the town. These area papers are a good way to tell local residents about the events and accomplishments at your school.

Neighborhood papers are always looking for stories about what is happening in the area and school news is interesting to many area residents. Generally, neighborhood papers are distributed free through local merchants so people often read them more frequently than major city papers. This makes them a good avenue for disseminating information and promoting school activities.

Personal relationships are important in media relations. Because these papers are small operations, it is easier to develop personal relationships with staff members. Building a relationship with the paper can generate a valuable level of trust that is beneficial to the school and the paper. Begin by setting up an introductory meeting between the paper's staff members and the person who will be working directly with the paper.

The school's principal should be more than just a name or title. Therefore, it is important that the principal be present at the introductory meeting even if he will not be the primary contact with the paper. The principal's presence conveys the importance the school places on the relationship and establishes a personal rapport.

Before the first meeting, look through several recent publications and read articles and editorials to learn something about the paper and the reporters. During the meeting, ask about deadlines, preferences for story length, how articles and press releases should be formatted, photographic requirements, and special interests the paper may have. Follow up the meeting with a thank you note. Put the paper on the school's mailing list. Invite reporters to visit the school and send them invitations to school events.

Once you have established a rapport with your local paper, take care to maintain it. Respect the guidelines that the paper has established, especially those related to deadlines. Do not expect the paper to print everything you submit; although if the stories are well written and timely, they probably will.

Get to know local media that focus their programming or reporting on special ethnic populations within the community. Foreign language newspapers and radio and television stations are outstanding sources for incoming and outgoing information. Because they are in the news business, print and broadcast media are especially aware of major issues in the community. Their language capabilities and credibility within the community make them excellent disseminators of news to ethnic groups within the school's environment. Ask reporters for their assistance in effective outreach to their listeners or readers.

Remember, the relationship is two-way. There are times, for example, at the beginning of the school year, when the media are looking for local school news, Be prepared to meet requests with useful information. By instructing them about educational matters, the school can help reporters better understand the legal, financial, and political issues that schools face and how those issues affect decisions. If there are national or state education matters that the paper wants to address, be available to discuss the issues with them. Try to anticipate what kinds of questions the reporter will want to ask and be prepared. Have backup for any statistics or facts you provide. If the community is concerned about standardized testing, provide the reporter background on the whys and wherefores of testing. Help the reporter develop a holistic view of an issue by providing differing opinions.

The media are in the news business. Do not expect them to overlook negative issues. If negative events involving the school occur, be available to answer questions. It is an opportunity for the school to get its side of the story told.

Always compliment a reporter on a well-crafted story. Thank them when the school's news stories or press releases are used. Conversely, if a reporter's story was unfair or distorted, convey your opinion respectfully, and, if warranted, write a letter to the editor or station manager to state the school's side.

Utilize your district communication office

Even though you may be regularly sending newsletters to the people in your neighborhood, important events and accomplishments should receive district-wide attention. If your school is in a large district with cross enrollment, you may be competing for students with schools within your own district. Getting positive publicity in district-wide publications or major media news sources is a way to promote your school to prospective students outside the school's immediate community.

Do not wait for someone to notice your school. Put together your own stories and photographs in a form that meets the district's requirements and submit them to the press or communication office in a timely manner. Your school's news is more likely to be included in district publications if you create interesting articles that do not require a lot of rework.

Be sure to contact your communication or press office immediately in the event of a crisis at the school. Provide as much information as possible. The media office is limited in its ability to help you if the information you provide is inaccurate or incomplete.

Press releases

Press releases are a way to tell the community about the good things that are happening in the school. Just because you write a press release, however, does not mean the media will use it. Reporters are looking for *interesting* stories. Beyond being interesting, reporters want press releases that require a minimum of work on their part. If a reporter has to spend time making your story fit a specific format, she may not use it. A well-crafted press release will gain the respect of most reporters. Below are suggestions for writing a news release that is "fit to print".

- At the top of the press release provide the following information: Name and address of school, time and date, school contact person with telephone number and email address.

- Have a clear, concise headline that will draw interest.

- Double space the text.

- Include all the most important information in the first paragraph. Answer all the Who, What, When, Where, How, and Why questions. For example:

  Today (when) Riverside High School (who) announced a $200,000 grant (what) from XYZ Corporation (who) to expand its Tomorrow's Scientists Program (why). Riverside High School will use the grant funds to upgrade its present laboratory facilities (where) and provide professional development opportunities for its dedicated science teachers (how).
  This format ensures that if people do not read beyond the first paragraph, they have the most important information.

- Use remaining paragraphs to provide additional information.

- Stick with facts and avoid hyperbole. Provide support for key points, opinions, and claims.

- Do not editorialize. This is not an opinion piece.

- Use interesting and pertinent quotes.

- Do not use jargon.

- Keep it under two pages.

- Check for spelling and grammar errors.

- Submit the press release in a timely manner.

Do not be upset if the item is not used or if only part of it is used. Media staff members other than the reporter may make those decisions. Keep submitting items that you feel are news-worthy and interesting. If your press releases are consistently rejected, ask media representatives how to make them more acceptable.

Use key communicators to dispel unfair press coverage

One of the best ways to mitigate the effects of negative news stories is to maintain a positive impression of the school through the school's key communicators. Think of a time when someone attacked the character of a person you knew and held in high regard. Did you simply accept the negative assertions and think less of your acquaintance? Likely, you defended your acquaintance and challenged the accuser's statements.

Key communicators touch many people in the community through their business and civic activities. If the media have misrepresented the facts in a story about the school or district, act swiftly to inform your key communicators of the specific inaccuracies and provide them with the correct details. If they hear negative stories repeated, they will then have the information to correct them.

Particularly egregious misrepresentations may require that the district hold a press conference to state its case. In such an event, having key communicators publicize and attend the news conference shows community support.

Crisis situations require a plan

Few administrators would view handling a crisis as a marketing opportunity, but having a procedure in place that allows the school to deal with any potential crisis effectively and efficiently should be part of your marketing plan. In part, the community judges the school by its preparedness for and its response to a crisis. How you handle a crisis is a measure of your school's concern for its students, employees, and the community at large. Mismanagement of a crisis can undo the good will and support that the school has worked so hard to build.

In a crisis, the community and the media want information. In addition, parents and staff members want assurance that the school is in control of those things it can control and is doing what it can to address the crisis. How the school handles the situation in the first few minutes and hours is critical. These are moments when high emotions create strong and lasting perceptions, whether justified or not.

The majority of good crisis management takes place before a crisis happens. Having a plan in which everyone understands his or her role will mitigate the chaos that exacerbates a crisis. A school crisis manager and crisis management team, including school counselors, security personnel, and those in charge of school communication, should establish contingency plans. The team should also be responsible for implementing the plan in the event of a crisis. Select individuals you can depend upon to be responsible, rational, and calm under stress.

The team cannot predict every crisis, but it can anticipate those that are likely to occur in a school environment such as violence; drugs; bus accidents; administrator, staff member, or teacher misconduct; fires; weather disasters; medical emergencies; and financial or compliance irregularities.

Issues considered in creating crisis plans should include:

• What crises might occur and what specific actions should the school take in each case?

• What district-wide policies and procedures should be incorporated into the school plan?

• What emergency assistance agencies should the school contact? What specific information should the school provide to them?

• What people such as clergy, psychologists, hazardous material specialists, and others can the school call upon to provide pre- and post-crisis guidance and counseling.

- Who will be the primary source of information to the central administration, staff members, students, parents, and media? What information should the school provide to these groups?

- What channels of communication are available to the school and how can we best use them?

- What translation capabilities are available for community communications?

- Are there sufficient key people, such as coaches, nurses, and teachers, trained in CPR?

- What training and materials are available to ensure that *all* employees are knowledgeable about crisis procedures?

- What are the legal issues concerning liability and confidentiality?

- Do front office staff members, who may receive telephone threats, need training?

- What lessons have been learned from past experiences?

- What can we learn from other schools' or districts' experiences?

- What information is available from external agencies and groups that we can use?

In answering these questions, the planning group should be able to gather enough information to create procedure manuals and develop scenario planning. At least once a year the group should meet to review plans and make required changes.

Effective crises communication is critical

Effective communication is critical when a crisis occurs. Rumors and unsubstantiated reports can exacerbate the crisis and foster panic. Getting information to internal and external groups is a key element in crisis control.

It is the responsibility of the district or school to communicate quickly, completely, and honestly with all internal and external groups. The best way to be prepared is to have a crisis communication plan. The goal is to aim for containment of the situation, not suppression of information.

The principal should be the key spokesperson for the school with an assistant principal or communication specialist as a backup. Advise staff members and students not to give out information to the media, but to refer them to the key spokesperson. Of course, the reality is that in the middle of a crisis and in the immediate aftermath, the media will try to get information from anyone they can whether or not the source is reliable. Nevertheless, it is important to remind staff members and students in crisis procedure training and communication materials of the importance of leaving communication to the appropriate person.

The school's key communicators can help the school disseminate information. It is advisable to include these individuals in creating your communication plan. At the least, they should be aware of what your plan is.

Telephone numbers of parents and guardians should be easily accessible and in multiple forms. An information database housed on a computer system is not accessible if power is lost or the system goes down. Have backup capabilities. Those responsible for calling parents should not engage in long conversations or speculation with them. Use the time only to inform parents of what has happened and what the school is doing. Have people available to communicate with non-English speaking parents.

An emergency information site on the school Web site can help get information out quickly. The community should be made aware of this information site.

Students should hear information from someone they trust. A person trained to deal with various reactions should be present. Give students a place to go. Do not leave them alone. An appropriate person should be available if students want to talk.

Telephone numbers and names of contact persons within the media and other organizations should also be readily available. The key spokesperson should be available to provide to the media some details in response to the following questions:

• What has happened?

• Who was involved?

- Was anyone killed or injured?

- Where did it happen?

- When did it happen?

- How did it happen?

- What is currently being done?

In dealing with the media, the following suggestions will help the spokesperson stay in control of the interview:

- Get the important facts out first.

- Do not speculate or give opinions when answering questions.

- If you do not know something, say so.

- Tell the truth.

- Do not argue with the reporter.

- Remember, nothing is off the record.

- Do not let reporters define the crisis. Correct any misinformation or misinterpretation of information immediately.

- Promptly provide promised follow-up information.

As information comes in, disseminate it to the appropriate people. If possible, someone should document what has happened, what is being done, who has been contacted, and any other useful information that the administration can use at the time or later to assess the situation.

Giving an interview

Generally, the district's communication or press officer deals with the media. However, in some circumstances, it is advantageous for the principal or other administrator to grant an interview. If the school has garnered an outstanding award or has had success with one of its programs, certainly an interview is a good way to communicate that news to the public. However, in circumstances where the news is not good, an interview is a way to neutralize bad press or to show that the school has nothing to hide. If you are scheduled for an interview here are some tips to consider.

Be prepared. Know what you want to say and be prepared to say it in a concise and understandable way. Try to anticipate the kinds of questions the interviewer will ask and have the information to back up your answers. You do not have to commit all facts and figures to memory. When the information is particularly complex, it is acceptable to say. "I am referring to data complied by federal agencies which show…" or "I have here copies of inspection reports which show…." Use mock interviews to practice, preferably with someone like the district communications officer who has experience with the interview process. Make mock interviews as realistic as possible with tough questions, prolonged silences, and aggressive follow-ups from the interviewer.

Tape the interview. Having your own audio or video tape of the interview allows you to rectify any statements taken out of context, misquotes, or inaccuracies. Knowing that a tape of the interview exists, may dissuade the interviewer from putting an inappropriate slant on the final product.

Follow the press release format. Be brief, but get your message across. Begin by giving the most important information first, then elaborating. Otherwise, you may not be able to get in the points that you want to make. Do not use jargon or language that makes you sound condescending. Speak in a way that will appeal to those listening to or reading the interview. Do not exaggerate or use excessive adjectives for effect. "We are proud of our students" is a more powerful statement than," We are really very proud of our students".

Do not let the interviewer put words in your mouth. If an interviewer describes the latest test scores as disastrous, you do not have to accept his assessment. Repeating his assessment by saying "Our scores were not disastrous" only reinforces the statement. Instead say, "Our scores exceeded all schools in the district accept one. Scores for most schools were lower this year because of the new testing requirements".

Beware of the deadly silence. Sometimes an interviewer will not respond to an answer or simply become silent hoping that the interviewee will become flustered and attempt to fill in the void (with some thoughtless remark). If you have said all that you want to say and the interviewer just looks at you, remain calm and wait for the next question.

Be truthful. Be truthful, be honest, do not lie. Do not be tempted to distort the truth even a little bit. Speak the truth even if it hurts. Have you heard the saying, "The cover-up can be worse than the crime"? How many business leaders, politicians, even clergy have made situations worse and prolonged the media's scrutiny by lying. If the media catch someone in a lie, it provides justification for additional and more intense investigation. Generally, people are understanding and even forgiving, unless you lie to them.

Dress appropriately. If you are being interviewed for television, wear conservative clothing in subdued colors. Avoid large patterns and plaids, especially in bright colors. A cream-colored blouse or shirt looks better on camera than a stark white one. A bit of color in a tie or scarf will prevent you from looking too somber.

Do not argue or become emotional. No matter how much the interviewer baits or attacks you, try to remain calm. As with the use of silence, the interviewer hopes that you will become provoked and blurt out an emotional statement. Do not argue. It will make the situation worse. If you do not know the answer to a question, say so and offer to get the information the interviewer wants.

Remember, nothing is off the record. Even if you consider the interviewer a friend, nothing is off the record. Reporters' success depends on getting a story. Few reporters will walk away from a good story because someone said, "Now, this is just between you and me, right?" Do not be lulled into a false sense of security by a smiling reporter who is asking you warm and fuzzy questions. The next question may be a hard-hitting question that takes you by surprise. The best approach is to have a message and stay on message.

Dealing with the media should not and need not be a negative situation. Look upon the media as an avenue for informing the public about the positive aspects of your school or district. Do your part to help reporters do a better job of informing the public. Be prepared for crisis situations. Be honest, informative, and available when events go wrong. If treated unfairly by the media, take measures to disseminate the truth and dissuade future misrepresentation.

7

Building Community Partnerships

In the past, schools' requests for support from external groups were limited to the occasional need for door prizes, sponsorship of events, and raising money for special student trips. Today, greater demands combined with fewer resources require that schools look to external sources for more and different kinds of support. Schools are entering into more defined, long-term partnerships with external partners than in the past.

School administrators recognize that building stronger community relationships can provide much needed resources. Yet, every year districts and the schools in them lose thousands, even hundreds of thousands, of dollars in goods and services and immeasurable amounts of good will from the businesses and organizations in their communities. How? Interviews with businesses and organizations indicate that some of the most common reasons why they choose not to work with a school or district are the following:

• Lack of accountability for goods or services received.

• Lack of planning.

• Lack of professional courtesy.

• Lack of follow through.

• Lack of appreciation.

This chapter provides suggestions for addressing these complaints.

Businesses and organizations can help in a number of ways: mentoring, class speakers, student internships, scholarships, event sponsorship, workplace tours, staff development and providing goods and services. In return, schools can give their partners positive publicity by acknowledging their contributions in several ways: announcements on the school's marquis, articles in the school newsletter, signs or posters that businesses can display, banners, and media coverage of events and special programs. Public awareness benefits both sides of the partnership. The business or organization is recognized as a contributing member of the community and the school is recognized as having community support.

What makes a good partnership?

A partnership is a continuous, mutually beneficial relationship between the school and external organizations. The key words here are *continuous* and *mutually beneficial.*

Have you ever had an acquaintance whom you heard from only when he wanted something? After a while, you dread his calls. Businesses often report that the only time they hear from schools is when they need something. The school can foster a positive relationship with its partners by keeping in contact through newsletters, notes from the students, teachers, and staff members, invitations to school events, meetings, annual reports, and partner appreciation activities.

In one of my workshops, a school administrator complained that a local grocery store that had helped the school in the past was not returning her phone calls. What should she do? Further questioning revealed that the last time the school had any contact with the store was eight or nine months earlier when the store had helped the school with a project. No one from the school had bothered to keep in contact. I suggested she try to rebuild the relationship through interaction that offered a benefit to the store or its employees such as "Partnership Recognition Night" at a school sporting event, tickets to a school sporting event or play for the store employees, or inclusion of the store manager in a community leadership breakfast. After the relationship is reestablished, the school can work with the store in mutually beneficial projects. Companies will be more receptive to school requests if you keep in touch.

Many businesses and organizations are eager and willing to help schools, but they expect something in return, even if it is only confirmation that what they are doing is truly helping the students. Therefore, it is crucial that these relationships be *quid pro quo*, an equal exchange, something for something. If the business sees the school only as an extended empty hand waiting to be filled, the relationship eventually will be unrewarding for both sides. When schools enter into a partnership with an organization, they should be aware of what the partner expects and how they can meet those expectations.

Remember in the marketing communication chapter, I explained the human characteristic of WIFM (What's In It For Me)? Humans comprise organizations, so they experience WIFM also. Companies may need only the acknowledgement that they have made a difference for the students. However, that acknowledgment is important! Part of the school's marketing strategy should include creative ways it can contribute to the relationship and, say "thank you" in a meaningful way.

It is not the responsibility of the school's partners to assess the school's needs and determine how to meet them. Businesses report that they are willing to help schools with their needs, but the schools should to come to them with an understanding of what their needs are, a strategy to address those needs, and specific ideas for how their partners can help and benefit.

The marketing team should look at the school assessment it completed when it was developing the marketing strategy and ask these questions.

- What goals came out of the school's assessment?

- What external resources does the school need to reach those goals?

- Are there groups in the community that can help the school achieve those goals? How?

- Who are the school's past, present, and potential partners?

- What is the school relationship with external organizations?

- What can the school do for its partners?

The school marketing team, with input from staff members, should assess what the school's needs are, then rank them. Start with the top two or three and rewrite them as project goals. Next construct plans for meeting each goal, determine how partners can help, and list the benefits to both the school and the partners. You may need a plan to meet each goal.

Write the plan in the form of a clear and concise proposal that you can present to your partners. (See an example in the case study found in this chapter). Provide support materials to clarify the goal and to describe how the school will use the contributions to attain it. For example, a plan to improve the school's landscaping might include a photograph of the schoolyard as it presently is with an explanation of the improvements the school hopes to make. Any written items submitted to partners, such as proposals and support materials, must be professional in appearance and content.

The school has the responsibility to maximize the benefits of contributions to the school, the students, and the contributors. The team should also consider the school's ability to manage increased support. A school may receive funds or services only to find that the staff members or students are incapable or unwilling to utilize the contribution. Companies report that employees have volunteered to mentor students only to find that the school was too disorganized to take advantage of the contribution, or that a school did not have the internal capabilities to implement a plan thereby wasting monetary contributions.

After the evaluation is complete, divide the potential partners in your community into three action categories: Reaffirm—Reconnect—Reach Out

Reaffirming present partnerships

If partnerships already exist, the school should take action to enhance those relationships. Create a profile for each partner (See an example in the case study found in this chapter). The profile will help the school cultivate the relationship. Each partner profile provides a history of the relationship that will survive staff changes, help to customize communication, and match school requests to the partners' interests and capabilities.

Create a database of all partners or include them in your present database with an indicator that they are partners. At a minimum, the database should include names and titles, phone and fax numbers, and addresses of all contact persons. A database will allow quick retrieval of all contact information. Utilize the database for newsletters, invitations, school announcements, E-mails, and meeting reminders. Use the Internet to search for recent positive news articles about partners and send a brief note to acknowledge the good press coverage. If changes in contact people occur, send the new person information on the school and invite her to visit the school.

Develop a tracking form for partner contributions (See an example in the case study found in this chapter). The tracking form establishes a history that allows the school to provide the partner with an annual report of contributions.

Reconnecting with past partners

Valuable relationships may have ended because the organization found no benefit to the partnership, or they may have withered away from lack of attention. In some cases, economic downturns or turnover within a company causes it to focus on other priorities.

Assess the status and history of the school with the partners. Here is an instance when having a partner profile and contributions tracking system would provide valuable information. Use the assessment to determine why the relationship is not active and what the school can do to rebuild it.

It may require some effort to find out why the partner is no longer involved with the school. Company representatives may be reluctant to justify why the relationship has deteriorated. The usual excuse is that, "Things have changed in the organization" or "We are reassessing our priorities." If you have a good rapport with people in the company who worked with the school, ask them for an honest assessment of what went wrong. Be prepared that in extreme cases it may take time or a change in the company's management before they are willing to resume the partnership.

If it looks as though the school can reestablish the partnership, reconnect with a note, letter, or invitation (See an example in the case study found in this chapter). Do not reconnect by asking for something.

Reaching out to potential partners

New businesses or organizations may have moved into the area, some established businesses may never have been contacted. Research by the marketing team can identify potential partners within the businesses and organizations in the community. List the identified groups and put those with the highest perceived potential at the top of your list. Then take steps to reach out to these groups. Start with the top five in your list.

Do not expect potential partners to come to the school. Although some national companies have established programs for working with schools, many more do not. Many businesses report that they would be open to working with a local school if a school administrator contacted them. Some businesses simply never thought about it. Few companies, however, are willing to spend time trying to determine what a school needs and how to help. That is the school's job.

Find out who in the organization is the best contact person. Most medium to large companies have a public relations or community relations person who handles external relationships. Ask current partners, parents, or community leaders if they are acquainted with any of the potential partners and would be willing to make introductions, provide referrals for you, or supply information about individuals or the business that can make your initial contact more personal.

Send out an introduction letter to businesses and organizations (See an example in the case study found in this chapter). The letter should be an introduction only. The purpose is to start building a rapport. Follow up with a telephone call or, if possible, a brief visit. If an event is occurring at the school, include an invitation.

If the business or organization is new to the area, send a welcome letter (See an example in the case study found in this chapter).

Create a partnership interest survey (See an example in the case study found in this chapter) and send it to businesses that have responded in some way to the school's initial letter. The survey should not be an appeal for contributions, but rather a sincere request for information. Use the information to begin a partner profile. Include the organizations in the school's database and begin sending them your mail-outs.

Making your first meeting a success

Your initial meeting sets the tone of the relationship. Here are a few guidelines to help make your initial meeting a success.

- Find out who the contact person is and make an appointment.

- Before the meeting, find out something about the business or organization. Most companies have a Web site so finding out what you need to know is not difficult. As you look at the Web site, ask these questions:

  - What does the company or organization do?

  - How long has the business or organization been in the area?

  - Who are the key people?

  - What are past community or philanthropic activities?

  - Who comprises their customer or member base?

  - What is the organization's philosophy (usually contained in their mission or vision statement or in their advertisements).

  - Have there been any interesting, positive news stories about the company (usually contained in their "media or press articles" page).

- Call the day before to confirm the meeting and be prepared to reschedule if necessary.

- Be on time for the meeting. Arriving late for meetings is a common complaint from businesses.

- Dress professionally.

- If the organization had a partnership with the school in the past, try to find out as much as you can about the past relationship. Be prepared to address any negative aspects of past partnerships.

- Offer a packet of information about the school. Include in the packet information about present partnerships, copies of any newspaper articles related to partnerships, and a summary of partnership activities.

- Think about the school's goals. How do they align with those of the potential partner? Is there a mutual interest in science, the arts, literacy, the environment, or sports? Develop ways the school can support the partner's interests.

- Do not ask for anything in the initial meeting. The purpose is to introduce yourself and the school and to begin a relationship.

- Invite the person to visit the school or to participate in a partnership breakfast or event.

- Keep the meeting short.

- Send a thank-you note after the meeting.

- Put the organization on the school's mailing list and keep in touch.

Your partners deserve accountability

Businesses are result oriented. To justify initiating or continuing contributions, businesses need to know that their efforts are producing positive results. One of the principal complaints of companies is that often they have no idea whether what they are doing is really helping the students. If a company is allowing employees to volunteer hours in the school, they want to know how the volunteers are helping the students. If the school received a monetary contribution, the organization wants to know how the funds were spent and what benefits were provided. To let partners know how their contributions benefit the students and the school, give them an annual report with clear examples.

The school's ability to provide documentation of contributions may determine whether a company enters into a partnership. Companies may be required to provide documentation of their support to the corporate office. If the company must spend time gathering and compiling documentation material, they may be reluctant to become involved. In some instances, documentation is necessary for tax purposes. Ask your partner in the beginning what level of documentation the company needs.

Time is money

In the private sector, the often repeated saying "Time is money" is true. When business people set aside time to meet with school representatives, they are donating the dollars attached to employee productivity and time.

Missing appointments, chronic tardiness, not returning phone calls promptly, or indifference from the school's administration and staff members indicate a lack of appreciation for your partners' time and money. Businesses report of taking employees away from their duties for a meeting with a school representative who did not come and did not call. Company employees report of showing up for volunteer work only to find that the class had gone on a field trip. This is a waste of the partner's time and money.

It is the responsibility of all school personnel to keep appointments and to be on time. The same rules apply to communication. Your business partners are too busy to call you for no reason; if they call, there is a reason. Administrators should respond to calls and E-mails promptly. Teachers and office staff members should be prepared for volunteers and have meaningful work for them to do.

Can you make a commitment?

People enter into relationships with certain expectations of the each other. Continued inability or unwillingness to meet those expectations by one side will result in reluctance to continue by the other. Businesses and organizations generally want confirmation that their contributions are helping the students, that they will receive positive recognition, and that their efforts will enhance their image in the community.

It is tempting to make promises when the school is eager to get a project going. Those promises must be kept. Before entering into a partnership, the school should have an understanding of the external organization's expectations, the school's ability to meet those expectations, and a commitment to follow through.

Likewise, schools have expectations of what their partners will do and make plans accordingly. Schools should feel confident that their partners will provide the promised support.

The best way to eliminate misunderstandings that come from ambiguity is to write expectations for both sides in a partnership agreement like the example below. Putting the school's and the partner's expectations in writing encourages each side to consider what will be required to follow through on their commitments. Below is an example of a Partnership Agreement

Lincoln Middle School
Partnership Agreement

This agreement is entered into by and between Lincoln Middle School located at 3478 Elm Street, Houston, Texas 77019 and [Name of Partner], located at (Address of Partner) for the purpose of enhancing the educational experience of the students at Lincoln Middle School.

(Name of Partner) agrees to abide by the policies and procedures of the district.

WHEREAS Lincoln Middle School seeks to provide the best possible learning environment for its students through collaborative efforts with community partners, and

WHEREAS (Name of Partner) desires to assist Lincoln Middle School in that effort.

Lincoln Middle School and (Name of Partner) now enter into an agreement in which (Name of Partner) agrees to the following:

(Here list the contribution(s) agreed upon by the organization. Example: XYZ Computer Store will allow any of our employees to donate a maximum of ½ day each semester for the purpose of improving Lincoln Middle School students' computer skills.)

And, Lincoln Middle School agrees to the following:

(Here list activities agreed upon by school. Example: To list XYZ Computer Store as a PAL Patron in all school newsletters, on our school posters, and in our annual report.)

This partnership shall begin on (Date) and be terminated by either party with 14 days notice.

_____   _____
(Signature for Lincoln Middle School)   (Signature for Partner)

Never stop saying "Thank you"

People like to be appreciated. Companies are made up of people. Do not lapse into thinking of companies, organizations, or even groups of people as impersonal entities. There are other schools in your community who will appreciate your partners if you do not.

The school can say "Thank you" in many ways.

- Notes and letters from the school, especially from the students.

- A message on the school marquis.

- An article in the local paper.

- An article in the school newsletter.

- Nomination of partners for local or national awards.

- A recognition luncheon.

- A "Thank You" on the school Web site.

- Invitations to school events.

- A partnerships page in the annual report.

- A banner at school events.

- An hour of holiday music at noon in the partner's office lobby.

- A large poster that can be displayed in the partner's place of business.

- A Partnership Wall at the school (include photographs of events, outings, employee volunteers).

- An Appreciation Rally in which teachers and students express thanks to company representatives through speeches, skits, music, or dance.

- A Partner Recognition Week when students create posters and artwork or write stories. Arrange the students' work in a display that celebrates the efforts of business partners, then give it to the company to exhibit in the company's offices.

Just keeping in touch with partners is a way to let them know that the school appreciates them. Do not forget the people who are volunteering their time. Send birthday cards to volunteers and mentors. Provide them with feedback on their contributions. Company employees often must use personal time to volunteer. If someone donates one hour to the school, she must come an hour earlier, leave an hour later, or use her lunchtime. That kind of dedication deserves to have affirmation of the school's appreciation.

In addition to personal expressions of appreciation from the teachers and students to volunteers, send a note to the contact person at the volunteer's company. Unless the "thank you" letter or note is a follow-up to a major project with numerous participants, do not send form thank you letters. Personally, I find a form thank you letter or note almost as bad as none at all. The volunteer may have given hours of his time, fifteen minutes to write a note is not too much to ask. Below is an example of a brief, but personalized way to recognize the contribution of a volunteer's time:

Ms. Marianne Wilson
Director of Community Relations
Citizen's Bank
123 Main Street
Houston, Texas 77077

Dear Marianne,

We truly enjoyed the opportunity to have Mr. Chen speak to the 6th grade about the Chinese New Year. The children loved seeing his slides and the authentic dragon costume. After Mr. Chen's presentation, many of the children expressed an interest in learning more about China. Some of the students have chosen to write class reports on Chinese architecture and the Great Wall of China. The students and I thank Citizen's Bank for sharing Mr. Chen with us.

Sincerely,

Hal Crockett
Teacher, 6th Grade Social Studies
Lincoln Middle School

Administrators should attend district-sponsored events that acknowledge the contributions of external partners. A school district recently lamented to me that it had gone to considerable effort and expense to host an appreciation luncheon for businesses that had supported the district and its schools throughout the year. Of the 34 schools that had benefited from this support, only 8 of the principals came to the luncheon. The others were "too busy". If school administrators cannot give up two hours to recognize the many hours of labor and thousands of dollars of support, then they should not be surprised when companies move their contributions elsewhere.

Making your partners feel special

A logo is special way to recognize your school's partners. Adapt the present school logo to create a special partnership logo or design an original one specifically for partnerships.

Businesses or organizations can display the partner logo on decals and posters in their place of business or in their advertisements to show their support for your school. Parents can be encouraged to patronize businesses that display the logo.

Use the logo on all communication regarding partnerships and include it in annual reports and newsletters, on banners and the school marquee—wherever partners are recognized for their contributions. Be sure to follow all copyright requirements when designing logos from purchased clip art. (See information on logo design in the Chapter 4, Marketing Communication)

Do not prejudge

"We don't have any businesses in our area." I hear this statement frequently from schools. Generally, what they mean is that the school does not have a *large* business or organization that could become their single benefactor. Schools often ignore small businesses and civic organizations in the community that can make smaller, but significant contributions. Following are potential partners that exist within most communities:

Banks
Car dealerships
Medical and dental clinics
Libraries

Neighborhood newspapers
Copy centers and printers
Restaurants
Shopping centers
Fitness centers
Major chain stores
Grocery stores
Family owned businesses
Professional firms (high-tech, architects, attorneys)
Organizations (civic clubs, garden clubs, non-profit organizations)

These groups can contribute in many ways large and small. A copy center can help with the newsletter. A bank or library can host school exhibits. A fitness center may donate a three-month trial membership as a door prize. Businesses can put up posters for school events or help with fund raising projects. A restaurant can provide food for meetings or an appreciation luncheon.

Build relationships with civic leaders in your community. Regular meetings with community leaders indicate the school's willingness to be an active member in promoting the entire community, not just your school. Include leaders from minority groups in your community.

Meetings with civic leaders, whether as group or one-on-one, are an excellent way to gather information that can help the school be proactive. If your school has meeting rooms, you could make them available to civic groups for meetings after school hours. Display recent student projects and accomplishments for the groups to see.

Developing relationships with the external groups in the community is no longer becoming an optional activity for districts and schools. Building and maintaining these relationships should be a part of the marketing team's strategy.

Administrators should remember that businesses and organizations are not obligated to work with their schools (or any school). The number of organizations and the amount of assistance they can give are finite. Other schools and districts that are willing to work hard to acquire and keep partners may be competing for the same finite resources your school is.

Building partnerships requires a multi-faceted approach. The following case study of Lincoln Middle School illustrates some of the ways to reaffirm, reconnect, and reach out to businesses and organizations in your community.

A Case Study
Lincoln Middle School

Lincoln Middle School has been in the community for over 10 years. Three months ago, Jim Hogan, who had been the principal for nine years, moved to another school and his assistant principal, Amelia Flores, became the new principal. Amelia realizes that many of the changes she would like to make at the school are beyond the school's present resources. Moreover, Amelia recognizes the importance of good community relationships in supporting school initiatives such as attracting students, improving employee morale, and recruiting quality teachers.

Amelia recently formed a marketing team. A goal of the team is to build mutually beneficial partnerships with the businesses and organizations in the community. To move toward this goal, Amelia has appointed her assistant principal, Roland Carter, to serve as the coordinator of all partnership activities. Roland is also a member of the marketing team.

Amelia and Roland call their partnership initiative, The 3 Rs-*Reaffirm, Reconnect, and Reach Out*. Roland, created an association for partners called Lincoln PAL (Partners Allied for Learning). PAL is open to all community businesses and organizations. A sub-group within PAL is PAL Patrons. PAL Patrons are organizations that have donated goods and services to Lincoln Middle School. The school recognizes their support in school communication pieces and other promotional activities. Roland has begun to schedule a monthly breakfast for all PAL members as a way to develop and maintain the partnerships by fostering continuing two-way communication.

To assist Roland in his efforts, the marketing team began by assessing their current partnerships. Lincoln Middle School has two ongoing partnerships that qualify as PAL Patrons. One is a software development company, SeismaTech, and one is a realty company, Reliance Realty. A few other businesses have helped with various needs in the past, but there has been little or no communication with them in a year.

To nuture their present partnerships, Amelia and Roland want the kind of data that is vital to maintaining good relationships. The marketing team has put present PAL members into a database and created a profile for each PAL Patron

Below is a sample of a profile Roland created for SeismaTech. At the top, the profile provides contact information, a brief description of SeismaTech and the length of its partnership with Lincoln Middle School as a quick reference. But, it is the specific details about interests, contributions, reciprocal activities, requirements, and comments contained in the profile that make it particularly valuable to nurturing this partnership.

The school gathers in-depth information of this kind through interaction with SeismaTech. Comments made during an event or meeting, appreciation expressed for a specific action, or specific requirements formally stated in an agreement are noted in the profile.

In this example, comments regarding how much the company president appreciates receiving thank you notes from the children were noted in the profile. Roland uses this information to ensure that notes from the children are a follow-up activity to SeimaTech's contributions. Notation of formal requirements for proposals ensures compliance with company standards.

Lincoln Middle School PAL Profile

Name of company or organization: SeismaTech, Inc.

Address: 123 Elm Street
            Houston, Texas 77019
            P.O. Box 12345
            Houston, Texas 77019-2345

Telephone # 713. 999.9999

Fax # 713.999.9999

Contact Person:
Ms. Kathryn Simpson, Director of Public Relations

Other key people:
Ms. Lynn Jefferson, President
Mr. Steve Brown, Vice President of Marketing

Type of business or organization: Software development firm specializing in products for oil and gas exploration companies

Number of employees: 25

Year partnership initiated: 1998

Special interests:
The company president, Ms. Jefferson, is particularly interested in programs that encourage girls to consider high-tech careers. Ms. Jefferson is also an avid hiker and nature lover. She feels that children should participate more in outdoor activities especially those that involve enjoying and protecting nature.

Past and present activities or contributions:
In 1998, SeismaTech began a tutoring program. The company requests, but does not require, that each employee donate a minimum of 1/2 day each semester to help students improve computer skills. Since 2001, the company has provided an annual 1/2 day outing at the arboretum (transportation, picnic lunch, t-shirt, and a book on nature for each child) for the sixth grade science classes.

Reciprocal activities:
We acknowledge SeismaTech's contributions on our marquee and in the school newsletter. We also receive media coverage of our annual arboretum outing in neighborhood newspapers. SeismaTech is listed in our brochure and on our Web site as one of Lincoln Middle School's PAL Patrons

Formal Requirements:
All requests for contributions must be submitted via written proposals to the Director of Public Relations. All proposals must clearly define the expected benefits to the students.

Send Ms. Simpson a brief annual report on the number of hours donated by employees and the benefit to the children.

Comments:
Always send thank you notes from the children for the Arboretum Day Out. Ms. Simpson has commented on how much Ms. Jefferson appreciates hearing from the children. We always send invitations to school events to SeismaTech employees.

Profiles provide continuity and consistency. If the administration or composition of the marketing team changes, the profile provides new individuals with the information they need for continued success. You cannot rely on people's ability to remember or pass on essential information. I strongly recommend a profile for every school partner. Few schools have so many partners that creating and maintaining profiles would be a labor intensive task. Once a profile is set up, it needs only occasional updating. The benefits far outweigh the effort.

Amelia and Roland want to reconnect with past partners. A past supporter of Lincoln Middle School is American Bank. At one time, the bank was a key supporter of the school. However, the school has had no contact with the bank for over a year. Roland heard from present PAL members that recently the bank underwent some organizational changes and several key people are new. Amelia suggests that Roland find out who the key contact is and send the person an invitation to the next PAL breakfast.

Your first contact with a business or organization should be to get the correct information for your mailing list. You want the name of the person who would be most likely to interact with the school. If it is a small company or organization, the appropriate person is often the owner or president. Larger companies may have a person appointed to handle public or community relations. Get the correct spelling of the person's name, the position title and a mailing address. If possible, get the name of the person's assistant.

This is not the time to ask for something. The purpose is just to get information for future communication. The conversation should be short.

Roland's call to get the information was as follows:

Operator: Good morning American Bank. May I help you?

Roland: Good morning. My name is Roland Carter. I am the assistant-principal of Lincoln Middle School. May I speak to the person in charge of American Bank's community relations?

Operator: That would be Mr. Morrison. I can put you through to his office. Hold please.

Roland:	Thank you
Ms Davis:	Mr. Morrison's office, Alicia Davis speaking.
Roland:	Ms. Davis, I am Roland Carter, the assistant-principal of Lincoln Middle School. Every month we host a breakfast for local business leaders. We would like to send Mr. Morrison an invitation to our next breakfast. Can you give me his full name and mailing address.
Ms Davis:	Yes, it is Stephen Morrison. The mailing address is post office box 4525, Houston, Texas 77019.
Roland:	Does Mr. Morrison spell his first name s t e v e n?
Ms. Davis:	No, it is s t e p h e n. His last name is spelled m o r r i s o n.
Roland:	May I have Mr. Morrison's title.
Ms. Davis:	He is the Vice-president for Community Relations
Roland:	Thank you Ms. Davis. I will send Mr. Morrison an invitation to our breakfast today. I hope that he can attend.

Let us look at what happened in this first telephone contact. In the beginning, Roland identified himself and stated his purpose to facilitate getting to the right person. People in businesses are more likely to help you if you state who you are and why you are calling. It conveys confidence that your call has merit.

Since executives generally do not take calls from people whom they do not know, and Roland can get the information he needs from Mr. Morrison's assistant, he does not try to speak with Mr. Morrison on the first call.

It is wise to remember that secretaries and administrative assistants are the gatekeepers to executives. They are important people to know. I am constantly amazed at the lack of respect some people show for the work of office professionals. If a partnership develops between the school and the bank, Mr. Morrison's assistant will be a key player in getting things done. Roland notes the name of Mr. Morrison's assistant. When Roland calls in the future, he can call Ms. Davis by name. Roland's ability to address Ms. Davis by name whenever he calls or comes for a meeting will create a positive and lasting impression. This may seem like an insignificant gesture; it is not.

I would like to make a comment here about addressing people. Although we live in a culture where most people operate on a first-name basis, do not assume that use of a person's first name is correct in all situations. Unless you live in a town or community where everyone knows everyone and uses first names of address, do not take for granted that it is welcome. Using casual forms of address too soon may offend some people. Roland uses formal terms of address both in referring to Mr. Morrison and addressing his assistant. If the relationship progresses, informal terms of address likely will be used; but, do not assume it is correct to do so in the beginning.

Roland makes sure that he has the correct spelling of Mr. Morrison's name and his title. Not knowing how to spell someone's name is excusable, not finding out the correct spelling is not.

Finally, Roland further engages Mr. Morrison's assistant by thanking her by name and making known his intention to send an invitation. These closing remarks may help Ms. Davis recognize the invitation when it crosses her desk.

Using guidelines for effective communication, the Lincoln Middle School marketing team works on drafting the Reconnect and Reach Out letters to send to organizations from the list they have compiled. Roland asks Amelia to attach her name to all the initial letters. He feels that it is important for Amelia to take this opportunity to introduce herself as the new principal of Lincoln Middle School and to express her desire to take a proactive approach to building better partnerships. Later as Roland builds a rapport with the school's new partners, he begins to take over more of the communication activities.

Amelia's letter to American Bank offers a model for a Reconnect letter. (Sample Reconnect Letter in this chapter) The letter begins with an interesting sentence designed to catch Mr. Morrison's attention and prompt him to keep reading. Avoid staid, overused phrases such as, "The purpose of this letter...", or "I would like to take this opportunity..." Your opening sentences does not have to be one that will be quoted for decades, it just needs to be interesting. In the remaining sentences of the paragraph Amelia sets out the purpose of her letter in a way that recognizes the common interests of the school, businesses, and the community. Amelia emphasizes that partnerships must be mutually beneficial.

In the second paragraph, Amelia confirms her intention to take an active role in working with the community by describing the specific action she has taken already. She introduces Roland Carter so Mr. Morrison will be aware of his role in building partnerships.

In addition to the details of the event, the third paragraph informs Mr. Morrison that he may learn some useful business information about the new housing project. As a businessperson, Mr. Morrison can recognize an opportunity for networking in this gathering.

In the final paragraph, Amelia calls attention to the benefits of working together to provide good schools to the community. She suggests a tour to indicate pride in the school and a desire to have Mr. Morrison see first hand the level of service the school is providing to students.

Amelia enclosed a newsletter to show Mr. Morrison who the other partners are, what their level of activity is, and how the school recognizes them. Companies may be more willing to participate when they see others are involved.

The Lincoln Middle School marketing team has categorized the third, Reach Out, group as those businesses that are new to the community and those that have been in the community for some time but the school has never contacted. New businesses will receive a "welcome to the neighborhood" letter. Established businesses will receive a "get acquainted" letter.

In the "Welcome" letter, (Sample Welcome Letter in this chapter) to Marianne Phillips, Amelia begins with an enthusiastic welcome then immediately gives the name of a school partner, Mira Taylor, as a reference. This is important because as a new business, Ms. Phillips is probably receiving many "welcome" letters. Amelia wants to alert her that this letter is different. Without a reference, Amelia might begin her letter with a statement about the advantage of getting to know the community through involvement with the school. For example, "As a new business, we know you want to get acquainted with the people in the community as quickly as possible. At Lincoln Middle School we try to bring community businesses together through our Lincoln PAL program."

In the following paragraphs, Amelia states the benefits of becoming involved with the school, invites Ms Phillips to a partner breakfast, introduces Roland Carter, and provides information about the school. Amelia includes the school newsletter and other material that contain additional information about school partnerships so Ms. Phillips can see how the school supports it partners.

The "Get Acquainted" letter (Sample Get Acquainted Letter in this chapter) follows the same format except here Amelia acknowledges Mr. Tran's busy schedule and offers an invitation to a school open house where he can meet parents and other businesses partners.

The purpose of these letters is to express the school's desire to work with local organizations for the benefit of all. Some will be interested, some will not. It may require several invitations before a person chooses to or is able to attend. Keep in contact with these groups by continuing to send invitations to events and including them in your regular newsletter mail out.

Mr. Morrison and Ms. Phillips respond that they will be attending the next PAL breakfast. The marketing team has information packets prepared for them. The packet includes the latest copy of the school's annual report, a copy of a newspaper article about PAL sponsorship of an event, a schedule of coming events at the school, names and addresses of PAL members, and a survey (Sample Partner Survey in this chapter) for new members. Roland will use the survey information to identify perceptions about the school, improve the partnership program, and identify those groups that are willing to contribute and the level of contribution.

On the day of the breakfast, the school has designated parking for the PALs with signage indicating the spaces. A sign on an easel at the entrance to the school announces the PAL Breakfast and directs attendees to the school assembly room Roland and Amelia greet the members. Each attendee has a pre-printed name badge with the PAL logo.

Roland introduces the new guests to the other members and ensures that they are included in the breakfast conversation. At the beginning of the meeting, Amelia asks Mr. Morrison and Ms Phillips to take a minute to tell the group something about themselves and their companies. At the conclusion of the meeting, Roland and Amelia ask if their new visitors would like to see the school. Mr. Morrison declines, but Ms. Phillips has a child entering middle school next year and she accepts. Amelia takes her on a tour while Roland escorts Mr. Morrison to the school entrance and encourages him to attend the next PAL breakfast.

Meetings such as the PAL breakfast provide advantages to the school and the businesses. As participants attend the meetings, they see the school first-hand. A clean, orderly facility and a friendly, helpful staff will create a positive impression. The meetings are an opportunity to highlight special school and student projects and accomplishments.

It is important that the topics discussed in the meetings relate to the community, not just the needs of the school. The meetings should provide a forum for exchange of information and a place to network.

Attendees have an opportunity to interact and build relationships among themselves. A member may be interested in talking with Mr. Morrison about a new program the bank has for small businesses. Ms. Phillips may find potential clients for her new public relations firm. Finally, attendees see the school as a supportive and active community participant.

Sample Reconnect Letter

October 27, 2004

Mr. Stephen Morrison
Vice-president, Community Relations
American Bank
P.O. Box 4525
Houston, Texas 77019

Dear Mr. Morrison,

Good relationships like gardens should be nurtured. As the new principal of Lincoln Middle School, I want to engage local organizations and businesses in mutually beneficial activities that make our community an attractive place to live and work. The key words here are *mutually beneficial.*

One of my priorities as principal is to be proactive in our community relations. I have appointed Mr. Roland Carter, the school's assistance principal, to serve as the coordinator of our new Lincoln PAL (Partners Allied for Learning) program. Lincoln Middle School PAL members include local businesses and civic organizations that work together to make our school an asset to the community. PAL activities are also an opportunity to build better relationships among our community organizations.

I have enclosed an invitation to our next PAL breakfast meeting on Tuesday, November 7, at 8:30 a.m. in the school assembly room. Ms. Mira Taylor of Reliance Realty, a Lincoln Middle School PAL, will be speaking about the new residential project under development in our community.

Good schools benefit the entire community. I believe that by working together we can complement each other's objectives. Please join us. It will give you an opportunity to meet some of our PAL members. If you have time, Roland or I can give you a tour of our school.

Sincerely,

Amelia Flores
Principal

P.S. In addition to the invitation, I have enclosed a copy of the latest Lincoln Middle School newsletter. On the cover page is a story about the beginning of school Open House in which several of our PAL members participated.

Sample Welcome Letter

October 27, 2004

Ms. Marianne Phillips
Phillips Public Relations
9735 Sycamore Street
Houston, Texas 77019

Dear Ms. Phillips.

Welcome to our community! Mira Taylor of Reliance Realty suggested I contact you to introduce myself. I am the new principal of Lincoln Middle School.

We at Lincoln Middle School believe that by working with the businesses and organizations as partners in our community we not only improve the learning environment for our children, but also provide our partners with an opportunity for positive interaction with our parents, staff members, and each other. Our goal is to make our community a place where people want to live and work.

I invite you to visit our school and to attend our monthly PAL (Partners Allied for Learning) breakfast. I have enclosed an invitation to our next PAL breakfast on November 7th. Mira will be speaking about the new residential project under development in our community. Also included are our school brochure and one of our newsletters.

I hope to have the opportunity to meet you soon. Please feel free to call me or Mr. Roland Carter, Assistant Principal, who serves as the coordinator of the Lincoln PAL program.

Sincerely,

Amelia Flores
Principal, Lincoln Middle School

Enclosure

Sample Get Acquainted Letter

August 15, 2004

Mr. Tom Tran
Complete Auto Service Center
5656 Washington Avenue
Houston, Texas 77019

Dear Mr. Tran,

Introductions are always better in person, but I know you have a busy schedule so permit me to introduce myself via this letter. I am the new principal of Lincoln Middle School. I served as Assistant Principal of Lincoln Middle School for three years prior to assuming my new duties.

As the new principal of Lincoln Middle School, I believe one of our school goals should be to engage local organizations and businesses in mutually beneficial activities that make our community an attractive place to live and work. The key words here are *mutually beneficial.*

As a first step, I would like to invite you to visit our school during our Winter Holiday Open House on Tuesday, December 3, from 5:30 to 7:30 P.M. In addition to acquainting you with our school, the event will give you an opportunity to meet parents and our school's business partners. I have enclosed an invitation and one of our school brochures.

I hope we will see you at our Open House.

Sincerely,

Amelia Flores
Principal, Lincoln Middle School

Enclosure

Sample Partnership Survey

Lincoln Middle School
Community Partnership Survey

Lincoln Middle School is always interested to learn how we can improve our relationships with our business community. By completing this survey, you can let us know how our school can be a better partner to the businesses and organizations of our community. The enclosed questionnaire was designed to gather information that we can use to achieve the level of service our community partners expect and deserve. The survey will take you approximately 10–15 minutes. Thank you for your participation in this very important effort.

Name: _____

Title: _____

Company/Organization_____

Address:_____

City/State/Zip:_____

Please circle your answers

How often have you visited our school?

Never   1 or 2 times   Several times   Often

If you have visited our school, please answer the following questions

What was the overall impression of the school?

Very good   Good   Fair   Poor

What was the impression of the service provided by the school staff?

Very helpful   Somewhat helpful   Not very helpful

Have you ever contacted the school by telephone or through our Web site?

Never   1 or 2 times   Several times   Frequently

How would you rate the level of response provided by school staff members?

Very good   Good   Fair   Poor

Has your company or organization made any contributions to the school?

Yes   No

If yes, what were the contributions?

Services Goods   Funds

How would you rate the school's involvement with your contributions?

Very good   Good   Fair   Poor

Would your company or organization be agreeable to future participation with our school?

Yes   No

Have you attended any functions that the school holds for it business partners?

Yes   No

If yes, how would you rank the effectiveness of these functions?

Very good   Good   Fair   Poor

Please check any of the following ways your company would like to participate.

Display student work	Donate equipment	Donate supplies
Mentoring	Scholarships	Company tours
Internships	Sponsor field trips	Be a guest speaker
Display school posters	Student incentive programs	
Provide seminars for students, parents, teachers	Purchase school supplies for needy children	

(Use this list to address specific needs of the school, students, and parents. Do not list items or activities that the school is not prepared to utilize)

Please check all of the following ways that Lincoln Middle School may reciprocate your contributions

Recognition on school marquee	Recognition on school Web site
Recognition in the school newsletter	Complimentary tickets to school events
Recognition in community papers	Use of school facilities

Please provide any additional comments, suggestions, or information that can help us improve how we serve our community. We appreciate your time and comments. Thank You!

One of Amelia's priorities is to improve the physical appearance of Lincoln Middle School. Over the years, the school's appearance has deteriorated and some residents in the surrounding area have begun to complain. Amelia also knows that prospective parents and students may judge the quality of education inside by the way the school looks outside.

At the monthly meeting of the marketing team, Amelia tells them that she wants to initiate a project to improve the "curb appeal" of Lincoln Middle

School. Working with Roland, the team defines the goals and works out a plan to implement the project through community support.

The marketing team decides to call the project "Grow With Us". The team establishes a timeline of three months from initiation to completion. A marketing team member contacts the host of a radio garden show for advice on landscaping. The radio host puts the member in contact with a teacher at a local community college who agrees to assign the school's landscaping project as a class assignment. Students agree to work out a landscaping plan that will achieve the school's goals; determine the labor, materials, and funds needed; and supervise the installation.

Next, the marketing team determines how external and internal groups can participate. Working with the college students' estimate of labor, materials, and funds, the marketing team generates a list of potential partners.

The team writes a proposal (Sample Proposal in this chapter) that they will include in their solicitation letters and presentations.

Sample Project Proposal

Lincoln Middle School
Grow With Us Project

Purpose

The purpose of the *Grow With Us* project is to improve the appearance of Lincoln Middle School for the benefit of our students and the community through new landscaping

Goals:

To improve the existing landscaping through plant pruning and removal and soil renovation;
To enhance the existing landscaping with new plants;
To provide screening of unattractive storage areas on school grounds with shrubs; and
To improve the lawn and play area with low maintenance ground cover and stepping stones

Activity

On a selected Saturday in April, Lincoln Middle School will host a Planting Day to landscape our school grounds. Volunteers, with the supervision of plant and landscape experts, will remove dead and diseased plants, prune existing plants, and plant new ones. The PTO will provide refreshments and a box lunch. Volunteers will receive t-shirts with sponsors' names. Lincoln Middle School will provide recognition in several mediums including coverage in local publications.

Benefits

- Provide surrounding residents and businesses with a visually pleasing view

- Create an inviting environment for students, staff, and visitors

- Allow children to learn about horticulture and experience the joy of seeing their work literally grow

- Build an increased pride in our school

- Create a sense of ownership and responsibility among staff and students for maintenance of our school grounds

- Establish a visible expression of what community members working together can do

- Provide an opportunity for positive recognition of our Lincoln PAL (Partners Allied for Learning) Program

Lincoln Middle School contributions:

Coordination of the project
Volunteer labor (students, staff members, parents, and school volunteers)
Water, soft drinks, sandwiches, and other snacks on Planting Day
Design of the event t-shirt
Recognition of project sponsors in a variety of mediums:
    Local media coverage
    Article in school newsletter
    Recognition on marquee
    Signage in front of school

Contributions Needed

Plants (flowers and shrubs) and grass
Planting soil/sand
Mulch
Stepping stones
Event T-shirts with sponsors' name for volunteers
Plant experts to speak to children prior to Planting Day

Volunteers for Planting Day
Gardening equipment

Current Participating Partners

Students from Mr. Simon Randolph's landscape design class at Coastal Community College volunteered to create a landscape design. Students will serve as supervisors on Planting Day.

Northside Voice will publicize the Grow With Us project and Planting Day before and after the event.

The Northside Garden Club volunteered to provide students with information about planting and plant care. Members are contributing plants from their own gardens.

The Northside Homeowners Association has several members who have volunteered to bring their own tools and help on Planting Day.

All of us at Lincoln Middle School sincerely thank you for your consideration of this proposal and we greatly appreciate any contribution you can make. We are proud to have you as a PAL and we want you to be proud of us. Thank you.

The proposal for "Grow With Us" clearly articulates the purpose and goals and defines the contributions of Lincoln Middle School and those needed from partners. The proposal also informs potential partners that work on the project is underway and that some partners are already on board.

One PAL that the school will contact is SeismaTech. Information on the partner profile indicates that the president of SeismaTech is very interested in projects that get children involved in outdoor activities. Amelia sends a personalized letter (Sample Proposal Letter in this chapter) and a proposal to Kathryn Simpson, the designated contact at SeismaTech.

Sample Proposal Letter

February 25, 2004

Ms. Kathryn Simpson
Director of Public Relations
SeismaTech, Corp.
P.O. Box 12345
Houston, Texas 77019-2345

Dear Ms. Simpson,

It is said that, "Beauty is only skin deep," but in our case we need to get to the roots of the problem. Our outward beauty is in need of repair and people are beginning to notice. In an effort to be a good neighbor and to increase community pride in our school, Lincoln Middle School has launched our *Grow With Us* project to beautify our school grounds with new landscaping this spring.

Through the *Grow With Us* project, we will construct a more pleasant learning environment for our students and provide them with the opportunity to experience the joy of creating a garden. Moreover, our neighbors will have a more pleasant view of us.

SeismaTech has been so generous in its efforts to introduce nature to our children we thought you would be interested in our *Grow With Us* project. We are currently developing our promotion materials and would like to include SeismaTech as one of our sponsors. I would appreciate the opportunity to discuss *Grow With Us* with you.

Enclosed is a proposal for *Grow With Us*. Roland Carter or I will call you next week to discuss your level of involvement.

Sincerely,

Amelia Flores
Principal, Lincoln Middle School

Enclosure

Amelia begins her letter to SeismaTech with a sentence that will catch the reader's attention. In the first paragraph, she establishes the need and the school's desire to be a good member of the community by addressing the need. The second paragraph describes the benefits to the students and the community. In the last paragraph, Amelia personalizes the letter to recognize SeismaTech's past involvement and their interest in children and the outdoors. Mention of the promotion materials urges SeismaTech to indicate their intention to participate in order to receive pre-event publicity. In the last sentence, Amelia sets up the next step to include SeismaTech in the project. If Ms. Simpson knows that within five to seven days Amelia will contact her, she is more likely to address the issue promptly.

With modifications, Amelia can use this letter for all groups and individuals the team contacts. A generic variation may be created as a cover for proposals to be distributed at presentations.

After the initial letters are sent, Roland Carter begins calling to confirm participation. Roland also makes presentations to a civic group and a local church that have expressed an interest. A specific date is set for Planting Day. With a specific date, Roland can set up a time-line for activities and delegate responsibilities to marketing team members.

Activities include completion of promotional materials with sponsors names, delivery and storage of donated materials, ordering of event t-shirts, press releases for pre-event coverage, and coordination of PTO participation. Teachers plan classroom activities to generate student enthusiasm. An alternative day is selected in the event of severe weather. Updated information regarding the event is on the school Web site.

In the days before the event, Roland reconfirms with all groups involved including the local media. On Planting Day, everything is in place waiting for volunteers to begin work.

During the Planting Day, Roland and the marketing team constantly monitor the activities to ensure that volunteers have the supplies they need. Students receive special plants and their own planting bed. A marketing team member takes photographs throughout the day. A local television crew shows up during the afternoon to the surprise and delight of the volunteers. At the end of the day, Amelia and Roland gather the volunteers and supporters to express their thanks and unfurl an appreciation banner with the names of all supporters to place in front of the school.

After the event, Amelia and Roland send thank you letters (Sample Thank you Letter in this chapter) to all individuals and groups that participated in the project. Roland secures post-event media coverage with photographs and sends copies of articles to all supporters. The school's subsequent newsletter and Web site provide extensive coverage of the event. A message of appreciation is on the school marquis. The school will include a summary of the project with photographs in the next annual report.

Roland and the marketing team meet to evaluate the event. They outline factors that contributed to its success and discuss improvements for future events.

Sample thank you letter

[DATE]

[NAME]
[TITLE]
[COMPANY]
[ADDRESS]
[CITY, STATE, ZIP]

DEAR [NAME]

Everything is coming up roses and petunias and daisies and lot of other plants and shrubs that make up our beautiful new school landscaping. Without your help, it would not have been a success. Thank you!

The children are so proud of their new school grounds. I heard one student proudly point out the plants, by name, that he had planted. It is amazing how much our new environment has lifted everyone's school spirit.

In case you did not see the pre-event publicity in the paper, I have enclosed a copy of the article for you. Keep an eye out for the post-event article, with pictures, that should appear within the next few days. In addition, we are announcing the names of our sponsors on our school marquee and posting news about the event on our school Web site.

On behalf of Lincoln Middle School students, parents, and employees, I want to say how much we appreciate your support.

Sincerely,

Amelia Flores
Principal, Lincoln Middle School

Enclosure

When looking for external partners, school administrators must consider how much they are willing to contribute toward building relationships. Like any successful relationship, there needs to be an understanding of the nature of the relationship, the obligations attached to it, and a commitment to making it work. As one corporate sponsor told me, "We are not an impersonal organization that simply dispenses funds upon request. We are people who, for whatever reason, have decided to make some level of commitment to public education. Our expectation is that we be recognized and treated as individuals who are working towards the same goal—an improved educational environment."

Success Story
Community Connections for All
Students/Arts Education Matters

In August 2000, a major Houston philanthropic organization, The Robert and Janice McNair Foundation, approached the Houston Heights Association and Houston Independent School District's then North Central District with an offer to establish a partnership designed to improve the quality of life in the historic Heights neighborhood, located five miles northwest of downtown Houston. The resulting agreement, "Community Connections for all Students", began a three-year partnership in which the McNair Foundation pledged $1.5 million to improve school fine arts programs, invest in adult and parent education programs, technology, health education, and to generally improve the quality of life in the community. Through a close collaboration between Joanie Haley, McNair Foundation Executive Director, and Heights resident Jerri Workman of the Greater Heights Education Partnership, "Community Connections", became a model in collaborative initiatives so successful that the McNair Foundation chose to continue its support beyond the original three-year commitment.

A major goal for the school fine arts program component was to create an initiative funded by the McNair Foundation that would have the greatest impact possible on arts education by facilitating partnerships between Houston-area arts organizations and inner city public schools. At the time, the need was great. A variety of factors, mainly financial, had resulted in the elimination of some fine arts teaching positions and reductions in many fine arts program budgets. Six elementary schools, that served approximately 1,500 students, had no fine arts programs at all. Of those elementary schools that did offer fine arts classes, instruction was available only 40–50 minutes once a week. As a result, arts programs on the secondary level were few or non-existent. There was little opportunity for students to experience the fine arts on a meaningful level.

In addition to providing program support, the McNair Foundation also provided matching funds to establish a Coordinator of Fine Arts position to oversee all aspects of the initiative. After an extensive candidate search, R. Neal Wiley was hired as coordinator in August 2000. Mr. Wiley has 25 years of experience as a fine arts educator in public schools, both as an instructor and as an administrator. He serves on the Board of Directors of Chrysalis Dance Company, InterActive Theater, Mercury Baroque Ensemble, is on the Education Committee of Young Audiences of Houston, and serves as a member of Houston Community College-Central's Visual and Performing Arts Committee. Mr. Wiley is also a consultant to several local and state fine arts organizations. These credentials provided the expertise and contacts to establish a successful program within the original allotted time-frame of three years. The program began with five Houston-area arts partner organizations providing programs to schools, and has grown to include fifteen arts and education organizations in all fine arts disciplines.

Mr. Wiley knew with a limited amount of time and money, he had to get the most bang for the bucks he had. It was important early on to convey to teachers, administrators, and parents the many benefits of arts programs. Of utmost importance are recent studies indicating that when students have access to fine arts programs, learning is enhanced and achievement is increased. For students who become active in the arts, the development of patience, persistence, discipline, and a sense of accomplishment are benefits that will serve them throughout their lives.

Mr. Wiley has first-hand knowledge of how exposure to things new and wonderful can affect a child's world. "When we go to Jones Hall (Houston's symphony hall), I always try to run ahead of the children, so I can see the expressions on their faces when they come into the hall's spacious entry," explains Mr. Wiley. "Their looks of wonder and surprise tell you that something exceptional is happening. And our teachers report that learning that one must be very quiet in the symphony hall or during a theatrical performance has resulted in positive behavior modification in the classroom."

Activities in the first phase were also devoted to getting schools and parents more actively involved. To get schools involved, program logistics had to be easy. Mr. Wiley knew that a program involving a complicated process or continual effort would not be well received. At the beginning of each school year, a presentation is made to all principals and each one receives a fine arts packet describing the activities participating arts organizations are willing to provide. One request form lists all activities. Principals simply check off the activities they want for the year. All bookings and communication go through Mr. Wiley's office. In some cases, the schools provide the transportation and the organizations provide the program. In other instances, organizations bring their programs to the school. "I have yet to encounter a principal who did not value fine arts and want the arts in their school", says Mr. Wiley. "Their frustration, and mine, was how to pay for arts programs in the face of declining budgets and in the current atmosphere of high-stakes testing. The approach we have taken, one of collaboration and thinking outside the proverbial box, has taken some time to implement, but the results are undeniable."

Getting the parents' support for the project required overcoming cultural, financial, and logistical challenges to fine arts participation. Mr. Wiley felt the best way to communicate with parents was direct involvement through an arts event. "School events, such as PTA/O programs involving students, are a good way to attract parents to the school," says Mr. Wiley. Parents were also invited to be chaperones on fine arts field trips. In addition to these initiatives, it was decided that an annual community-based signature arts event be held to bring schools and community members together for a special day of fine arts activities.

As a result, an annual Festival of the Arts was established and is held each spring on the John H. Reagan High School campus. Funded by the McNair Foundation, the Houston Heights Association, and several other local businesses and civic groups, the first Festival attracted over 1,000 people. Parents who had never come to the school before were there. The Festival, which showcased hundreds of student visual and performing arts experiences, also included representatives of the local fine arts community, giving the event an added level of significance. Attendance and participation have increased steadily every year thereafter, and plans were made to hold additional Festivals at the other high schools within Houston ISD's Northwest District.

Since the project began in 2000, over 350 campus-based student education and outreach programs have been presented. Over 6,000 students have attended performances at the Alley Theatre and in Jones Hall in downtown Houston. Approximately 30 campus-based artist-in-residence programs have been created for area schools, both during the regular instructional day as well as in after-school programs. The residencies allow artists from the arts partner organizations to work with students on specific projects over a greater period of time, typically several weeks to an entire school year, thereby providing opportunities for students to experience the arts at a depth and complexity previously unavailable to them.

"We're moving away from the 'one-shot' arts experience," explains Mr. Wiley. "We, of course, value individual performances, and we are constantly developing and improving collaboratively-designed integrated lesson plans, pre- and post-performance activities for students, etc., that both enhance the arts experiences as well as tie the experiences to other subject areas. We find that teachers and principals appreciate this a great deal."

Over 150 teachers have been trained in art integration techniques. Foundation donations have been leveraged to bring in approximately $40,000 in additional funds from state and county organizations. By the end of the third year, "Community Connections" was a resounding success, and discussions were initiated to explore ways to expand and replicate the model in other Houston ISD schools.

In a time when diminishing resources are forcing schools to cut back or eliminate their fine arts programs, Joe Nuber, Superintendent of the Northwest Administrative District (NWD) in Houston was determined to maintain an arts presence in the 26 Title I schools in his district, which serve some 19,000 economically disadvantaged inner city children. With plans to expand the original 16 school fine arts initiative to the entire NWD beginning in August 2004, Nuber made the bold step of establishing a Director of Fine Arts position for the Northwest District, and chose Mr. Wiley to continue to implement and expand to scale the established programs. A key factor in expansion was to secure the continued support of the McNair Foundation.

A bilingual parent survey and a campus principal needs assessment were prepared by the NWD Fine Arts Department and administered in December 2003 to determine levels of need and interest. The bilingual parent survey was administered by participating elementary schools and measured the interest in each fine arts discipline-art, dance, music, and theater. The needs assessment done by NWD principals asked them to project their anticipated fine arts course offerings for the coming academic years, as well as to identify areas of weakness or need in fine arts course offerings. Cumulative results of both the parent interest survey and the principal needs assessment indicated overwhelming support and a clear need for arts education programs in NWD schools beyond what the schools alone could provide.

In response to these survey and needs assessment results, not only did the McNair Foundation continue to support the collaborative fine arts model program, it *increased* the level of support for the second phase of the program. This second phase, beginning in August 2004, is called "Arts Education Matters", a ground-breaking and comprehensive program that will incrementally integrate arts education into other core subject areas and daily activities in all of the 26 schools in the NWD over the next five years. Schools will be expected to fund a gradually increasing percentage of the overall cost of programs on their campus. Local businesses will be sought as collaborative partners with NWD schools to financially support fine arts programs at the schools in their neighborhood. Arts Education Matters (AEM) has four major components:

1. Campus-based **performances** for students, faculty and staff

2. Campus-based **artist-in-residence** and/or **workshop** experiences

3. **Field trips** to Arts Partners' venues

4. Comprehensive **curriculum integration staff development** experiences for non-fine arts classroom teachers

All four components are a continuation of the original "Community Connections" initiative. AEM's goal is to expand the components to scale in all 26 Northwest District schools. Additionally, a significant increase in the scope of teacher training through arts curriculum integration staff development opportunities for non-fine arts classroom teachers is a major program component. Without the funds to hire additional fine arts instructors, the goal is to infuse the arts into the schools through non-fine arts teachers. The first step is AEM's "renewal" process in which teachers are renewed by discovering the wealth of ways in which the arts can have a positive impact upon students' lives and learning.

Renewal is an intrinsically motivated approach to self-improvement. Through AEM, educators have the opportunity to learn creative strategies for reaching more students in deep and meaningful ways. Teachers are able to enroll in arts curriculum integration workshops for professional development and gifted and talented credits. One arts partner in particular, the Museum of Fine Arts, Houston (MFAH), has provided the majority of the arts curriculum integration training, and also provides follow-up support in the classroom through an art curriculum integration program, *Learning Through Art*. The program was designed by teachers for teachers to show them how to incorporate art instruction into other subjects. Those who complete the training receive curriculum kits with integrated lesson plans.

To date, more than 150 teachers have gone through the training and renewal process. The response was so great that participation had to be limited. "The MFAH teacher training program, along with their vast Kinder Teacher Resource Center, has been the single strongest component of our overall fine arts initiative", according to Mr. Wiley. "We view *Learning Through Art* as *the* model for arts integration in public schools."

Mr. Wiley is particularly proud of one approach to showcasing students' artwork, the *Art Space* in the Northwest District's administration building, a permanent gallery installation created with help from the Museum of Fine Arts, Houston. Through the use of special framing, lighting, and small plaques with artwork titles and student artist's name, *Art Space* displays selected pieces of children's art as though it were in a museum setting.

Mr. Wiley understands that organizations that donate time and money want to see results. To provide independent assessment, Dr, Cynthia Herbert, based in Austin, Texas, will serve as program evaluator. Formerly Executive Director of the Texas Alliance for Education and the Arts, which was the Texas member of the Kennedy Center Alliance for Arts Education Network, Dr. Herbert has over 30 years of experience in arts education and is considered an expert in her field. The project will be evaluated quantitatively by the number of and type of programs and services delivered to schools, number of children served, number of teachers trained in arts integration techniques, number of schools hosting pilot programs, and the number of hours of programs and services. A random sampling will be made of teachers and students participating in the program to ascertain positive changes in school attendance and test scores, as well as decreased numbers of disciplinary actions and referrals. Qualitative evaluation will involve responses to age- and language-appropriate questionnaires for students; teacher, school administrator, and parent surveys; and observations of program activities by key project personnel.

"I cannot say enough about the generosity and vision of The Robert and Janice McNair Foundation and its Executive Director Joanie Haley," says Mr. Wiley. "Over the years, many well-meaning education initiatives have failed because they were abandoned after a few years for a variety of reasons, lack of sustaining funding being chief among them. The McNair Foundation, Houston ISD's Northwest District administration, and our arts partners know that one must stay the course in order to see measurable results. This is especially true in the arts. Exposure to the arts affects people in evolutionary stages, something that cannot easily be measured as yearly progress on a standardized test. The indirect effect is there. You just have to know how to look for it."

Arts Education Matters is a success story about building partnerships, bringing key stakeholders together, and facilitating discussions to build consensus over time-all with the needs of inner city children in mind. The power of AEM is in the belief that the arts are *essential* to the quality of life, both in and out of school, not a 'frill' or an 'extra'. "At the end of the day," says Mr. Wiley, "we (AEM) must be the advocates for our children and their families for arts education. If we don't speak out for them, who will?"

8

Public Relations, Inside and Out

The role of public relations is to support and enhance the school's marketing activities. Building good will, shaping the way the school is viewed, and creating public awareness of the school's accomplishments are key public relations objectives. However, as with marketing, there are misconceptions about public relations. Often viewed as the "art of manipulation", public relations was frequently associated with the political propaganda, deceptive publicity stunts, and distorted press releases associated with P.T Barnum, speculative land deals, and political campaigns in the early part of the twentieth century. Even today, we still hear the phrase, "That's just PR" to refer to a deceptive or manipulative activity. In truth, public relations has come a long way from earlier bad acts. Public relations professionals have worked hard to gain the public's respect by raising the standards of their profession.

Public relations can add significant value to the school's marketing efforts. In its most literal interpretation, public relations involves enhancing the organization's relationships with external and internal groups or "publics". For public school districts, those groups include virtually everyone. Relationships are enhanced through strategies and activities that seek to improve interaction, understanding, and awareness between the school and its audiences. This chapter provides ways that districts and schools can seek to change not only what they do, but also how they think about the relationships that are so important to achieving their goals.

Got curb appeal?

Remember a time when you went house hunting and the appearance of the prospective house was so unappealing that you did not bother to look inside? You judged the inside without even seeing it. Have you ever picked a new restaurant because it looked elegant, romantic, or fun? Entire industries are built upon the recognition that we often judge people by appearances. Judging by appearances alone may seldom be fair or correct, but the truth is how something looks influences our perception of it. Businesses are very aware of the impression created by their outward appearance and they design their exteriors to appeal to the kinds of customers they wish to attract. Banks do not look like fast-food restaurants and vice versa.

Dirty windows, untrimmed shrubs, graffiti, dead or dying plants, and trash and litter are some of the elements that make a school an eyesore. An unattractive appearance creates a negative perception of the school. Parents of potential students may find the school's appearance so uninviting they do not take the time to find out about the excellent educational environment provided within. Residents in the surrounding area may find the appearance of a school and its grounds an aggravation. A situation that is not good for community relations. Visitors are forming an opinion of the school before they walk through the front door. If the opinion is negative, the job of creating a positive impression is harder.

Because you see your school every day, it may be difficult to judge its appearance honestly. Ask two or three individuals outside your school to give you an honest assessment. Request both a general impression of the school and specific features that affect the overall appearance. You want to know what is appealing about your school so ask for positive as well as negative impressions.

Can you imagine going to a place of business and not being able to find the entrance? What kind of impression would that make? One of the problems I sometimes encounter when visiting schools is finding the entrance. I go to an area that looks like a main entrance only to find it locked with a sign that reads, "Use south entrance". Now I have to figure out where the south side is and it is high noon. Finding the entrance is just half the problem. Next, I have to find the office.

Most schools have a sign that demands, "All visitors must register at the school office." However, the location of the office is not always clear. I have wandered around for 10–15 minutes trying to find the office. One school I visited had its office on the second floor at the back of the building! A school office that is difficult to find gives the impression that administrators are not open to visitors. If for some reason the office cannot be located near the building entrance, display a map stating, "You Are Here" that gives directions.

If making improvements to the school's appearance requires major work, turn it into a school or neighborhood project. For example, if your school needs major landscaping, designate a school landscaping day on a Saturday and include school staff, students, parents and neighborhood volunteers (see the case study in Chapter 7, Building Community Partnerships for an example).

Do not forget the inside. Are the hallways clean and attractive? Are the drinking fountains clean? Does the cafeteria provide an appetizing atmosphere? Are the bathrooms clean? Is there an area in the school office where people can sit? Is the waiting area pleasant? Just a few plants, colorful posters, and a bowl of candy can create a pleasing environment.

Are the classrooms inviting to visitors as well as teachers and students? Are desks facing so that visitors can see children's faces instead of their backs? Is there an adult size chair for visitors?

What about the employee environment? Is the employee lounge comfortable and inviting? Does it have a microwave oven and a place to eat? Is it quiet?

Ask these questions on a regular basis. School appearance says much about school pride and the attitude toward visitors, students, and employees. Keeping the school clean and attractive is everyone's job.

Supportive alumni speak volumes

Alumni are products of your school. Their continued support after they have gone, speaks volumes about their experiences there. Alumni can be great spokespersons for your school especially when they attribute success in later life in part to the instruction they received at the school. Ask them to speak to students about their experiences, accomplishments, or special interests. Alumni who have achieved personal or professional recognition can serve as role models and mentors. We often forget that the renowned artist, brave astronaut, or talented sports figure was once a child sitting in a classroom reading a book or learning multiplication tables. Alumni can give motivation and inspiration that children, especially those in disadvantaged situations, need.

Include alumni in your school's mail outs. If alumni live in the community, invite them to attend school events. If alumni no longer live in the community, encourage them to keep apprised of what is happening at the school through the school's Web site. Communicate with them about major initiatives, news about other alumni, reunions, and school events that occur around holidays when they may be in the area visiting family. Solicit comments about alumni's positive experiences in the school and ask for permission to use these statements in your promotion pieces.

Celebrate cultural diversity

We define culture as the beliefs, practices, values, rituals, and stories that provide an unwritten, even subconscious, influence over our thinking and our behavior. Often we are unaware that we think in a certain way until we encounter someone who thinks in a different way.

Cultural diversity within the school's community is an asset and a challenge. When the school reaches out and includes diverse groups, students have access to a richness of tradition and history that is real and alive. The school is a natural place for people who might not otherwise meet to come to know and learn from each other.

A culturally diverse environment provides students, teachers, and parents with the opportunity to introduce different worldviews into their thinking. Diversity opens students' minds in ways that will serve them well after they leave school. Efforts to include minority or new immigrant parents in school activities give their children a greater feeling of their own sense of belonging. The advantages of diversity are evident in the efforts many private schools employ to achieve it.

Reaching out to a culturally diverse community may pose challenges for some schools that are unsure of how to approach specific groups. Uncertainty often leads to inaction. Inaction leads to greater isolation. Here are some ways to build a welcoming environment.

Break the language barrier. If you have traveled to a foreign country with little or no knowledge of the native language, you probably have experienced the frustration of not being able to communicate. Even if you manage to inquire adequately in the native language, "Can you tell me where to find the train station?" the response may be indecipherable to you.

Now imagine that you are a parent in a foreign country trying to understand about unfamiliar enrollment procedures, homework, immunizations, and school regulations or trying to communicate at parent-teacher conferences and school events. Feelings of frustration and confusion might lead to avoidance.

A principal reason parents with limited English avoid interaction with the school is the language barrier. If your school has a significant number of parents or students of limited English proficiency, having bilingual capabilities is essential not only for good communication, but also for good community relations. The presence of bilingual personnel expresses to parents, students, and other members of the community that their ability to communicate with and participate in the school is important.

Communication channels such as newsletters, the Web site, and bulletins should include information in the major languages of the community. As stated earlier, ensure that translations are of excellent quality.

Do not forget non-verbal communication. Body language, hand gestures, touching, facial expressions, personal space differences, and voice tone are some of the non-verbal communicators that convey different meanings in different cultures. Some cultures look each other in the eye and speak with an intensity, tone of voice, and closeness that make many Westerners uncomfortable. For other cultures, lowering the eyes is a show of respect for the other person's status; to Americans, it may indicate someone is lying or being evasive. Once in the midst of a lively dinner party discussion in Japan, I forgot myself and lightly touched the coat sleeve of the Japanese man sitting next to me. He reacted as if I had stuck him with a pin. My action and his reaction completely changed the mood of the discussion.

As discussed earlier, colors may convey different cultural meanings. While black is the color of mourning is Western culture, in Japan and many Asian countries, white symbolizes mourning. Certain symbols and gestures can have unintended consequences. It would be advantageous to learn something about the meaning of non-verbal communication for groups that have a significant presence in your community. In these days of global trade, considerable information is available.

Become culturally proactive. Provide welcome posters, main telephone messages, and Web site information in the major languages represented in your school or district. Encourage students to share information about special holidays and holiday customs, special foods, and music. Acknowledge holidays, such as the Chinese New Year or Cinco de Mayo with artwork, displays, and entertainment. Develop relationships with specialty media (newspapers, radio and television stations) that focus on specific groups within the community. Invite them to school events and keep them informed on what is happening in the school.

Holding gatherings exclusively for new immigrant groups can increase participation. One district with over two hundred Vietnamese families held a special back-to school event on a Saturday afternoon to help parents get their children ready for school. Large welcome signs in Vietnamese greeted the parents and Vietnamese music played in the background. Vietnamese speakers conducted the program. In addition to school information, the parents received information on community programs and organizations. Coverage of the event by both English and Vietnamese media communicated to the Vietnamese community at large the school's desire to welcome parents. The benefit of the event was evident in the increased participation of parents and the community.

Being culturally proactive also means consideration of the needs and desires of students. In Texas, support for high school football often matches religious fervor. Therefore, it was heretical when a high school principal completely abandoned football in favor of soccer. Gone were the football team and the marching band. The reason for this bold action was the high school's diverse student population that comprises 70 countries and 42 languages. Most of the students are from countries in Africa, Latin America, and Asia where soccer, not football, is the number one sport. A mariachi band now performs while the students play soccer and not one student or parent has complained.

Seek help from cultural or religious leaders. Imagine being displaced from the homeland you have always known and placed in a new cultural situation where you are uncomfortable with the language, unfamiliar with the customs, and unsure of how to get even the most basic things done. The natural thing to do is take refuge within a group or community with people like yourself.

Families that have lived in a community for years may still feel alienated from the community outside their own. Such isolation is detrimental both to the students and to their parents. Knowing how to get through to them is not always easy. Leaders within cultural and religious communities can provide valuable information, support, and credibility for school outreach efforts.

Source credibility is important to persuasive communication. Community and religious leaders can be a voice that lends credibility to school communication. Bilingual community members can serve as the conduit for free-flowing, two-way communication and help the school with language barriers that inhibit communication.

Invite leaders to participate in your key communicators group, include them in your mailing list for newsletters and invitations to school events, notify them of the achievement of students from their ethnic or religious community. Ask them to publicize school events in their own newsletters and bulletins. Seek their advice when reaching out to parents and businesses.

Celebrate diversity in many ways. Look for as many ways as you can to celebrate the diversity of the school internally and externally.

- Incorporate holidays such as Cinco de Mayo and Chinese New Year into class assignments and school activities.

- If the town or community has a parade, participate with a float that exemplifies the school's diversity.

- Create an exhibition of student artwork, family photographs, traditional costumes, and cultural artifacts that represent the various cultural groups in the school and display it in a local bank or library.

- Include ethnic foods, music, and art work at school events.

- Take field trips to cultural museums and special cultural or art exhibits in your area.

- Ask people in the area with special knowledge or experiences in cultural history, art, music, anthropology, or dance to speak to students.

- Ensure that all school publications and other communication channels such as the Web site and videos promote the diversity of the student population through photographs, artwork, cultural event announcements, and language.

Welcome all

The school can get information about new families moving into the community through its relationships with realtors and apartment complexes, or it can get the information from local government agencies. Send preprinted welcome cards to newcomers. Include the school Web site address, names of key administrators, and contact information. Put newcomers' names and addresses in your database.

A beginning of school event is a good way to make newcomers to the neighborhood feel welcome and acquaint them with your school. Do not restrict the invitations just to people with children in your school. Include all newcomers, individuals and businesses. They are potential volunteers and school supporters.

Have someone at the door to greet people and make them feel welcome. Have brochures available to hand out. Also, provide information that newcomers will find helpful such as maps, and information on local services, businesses, and civic organizations (a good way to promote school partners). Have a sign-in sheet so that you can get names and addresses of those who come.

Inviting newcomers also gives the school's external partners such as civic groups and businesses the opportunity to introduce themselves to new neighbors in a positive way.

Reaching out to new parents

Pre-K, kindergarten, and elementary schools can make use of available birth records to reach out to new parents. Send a congratulatory note or letter that includes information about the school and an invitation to visit. Add the new parents to your mailing list for regular communication. Invite them to any open house or events the school is having.

Once a year hold a panel discussion or workshop for mothers of pre-school children to introduce ways they can prepare their babies and toddlers for school by developing their cognitive abilities through activities at home. On the panel include teachers, counselors, and district specialists who can discuss new ideas, offer suggestions, and answer questions. Have information on related books, Web sites, toys, and activities available.

Visitor parking says "Welcome"

Have you ever stopped patronizing a business or restaurant because parking was just too much of a hassle? That is why restaurants and even some businesses provide valet parking.

When conducting marketing workshops, frequently, I am required to circle the school several times before finding a spot a couple of blocks away to park, then lug my presentation booklets, laptop, projector, and other presentation materials down cracked sidewalks, over curbs, through parking lots to reach the school. I have come to prefer 8 a.m. workshops because a 7:30 set-up time means I can probably find a space nearer the school or district office.

Many of the parents who visit your school, especially elementary schools, have toddlers or babies with them. Having to park a block or two away is an irritation and a hardship. Older volunteers may find walking even a couple of blocks in extreme heat or cold taxing and even harmful.

To those of you who have parking spaces designated for visitors, my congratulations! To those of you who do not, consider the impression it makes on visitors. If you truly want to make visitors feel welcome at your school, provide spaces for them to park and have the parking spaces clearly marked.

When a note from the principal's office is a good thing

Too often communication with parents falls solely on teachers. A personal note from the principal to parents and students acknowledging outstanding achievement speaks volumes about the school's appreciation of excellence. Writing a brief note takes only a minute or two, but its effect on the parents and students is lasting. A note to a volunteer or employee for dedication goes a long way toward keeping him motivated. Not only does a note from the principal add special recognition for accomplishment, it also creates a positive communication channel.

To minimize the time required to "think of what to say", create several standard notes then adapt them to the specific situation. If your handwriting is difficult to read, type them, but always sign them personally.

Donuts, coffee, and a "Good morning"

A good way for administrators and staff members to meet parents at the beginning of the school year it to offer donuts and coffee to parents as they drop off their children for school. Even if the principal has time only to introduce herself and say a few words, it shows that the school welcomes them.

It is especially important to have positive interaction with those parents who, for whatever reason, are not active in the school—the working parent who does not have time, the newcomer who feels like an outsider, or the foreign-born parent who feels uncomfortable. A friendly "Good morning", a smile, and a cup of coffee from school staff members is one more way to connect with parents.

By timing this activity with an upcoming event, such as Parent Night, staff members can use the interaction to publicize the event and encourage parents to attend.

Videos for fun and promotion

Videos are a powerful communication medium. Images accompanied by sound attract and hold people's attention. The ability to duplicate and distribute videos simply and cheaply on CDs or DVDs makes them especially appealing.

Large school districts may have departments that provide this service for schools; but new high quality, easy-to-use video equipment and software make creating videos possible for smaller districts and schools. If your budget does not allow for the purchase of new equipment, look for used equipment in the classified ads or run an ad asking for equipment. Check with local colleges, companies, or television stations that may be replacing equipment and are willing to donate their old. Camera stores generally have used equipment from trade-ins at significant discounts.

Videos should have a professional look. A video that looks like someone's bad home movie is counterproductive. If the school or district does not have someone who can produce quality videos, solicit help from local businesses who have expertise in videography, advertising, and public relations. Companies may not be willing to donate all their work, but they may offer a heavily discounted rate if the school recognizes their contribution prominently on the video and in other school communications. Remind them that not only will parents see the video, but also local organizations, other businesses, and the community at large. Allow them to use the video as an example of their work in their own marketing materials.

Check with radio/television departments of local colleges and universities. Professors and students may be willing to work with the school as a class or department project. Do not hesitate to ask for samples of their work. If it is good, they will want you to see it.

Use videos to promote the district or school to parents of potential students, help local civic associations promote the benefits of the community to attract new businesses, solicit support from local organizations, generate school spirit at events, and recruit quality employees. Videos can also recognize academic achievements, articulate the district's vision, recognize community support, provide new student orientation, and acknowledge the dedication of employees. Use the same communication guidelines that you apply to your other promotion material: Keep it short (no more than about 5–7 minutes), keep it relative, keep it viewer-focused, and keep it moving. If you decide to hire a professional video company, use real students and employees, not actors.

Use videos in presentations, include them in information packets to prospective students and their parents, add them to annual reports, and show them at school rallies.

One middle school I visited, made weekly videos in a "morning news" format of students making announcements, recognizing special achievements, and reporting on activities with its community partners. The video was then played on a continuous loop on a television set up in the school's office for visitors.

Videos for absent parents

Missing a recital, special sporting event, or play is always a disappointment to parents and children. The next best thing to having a parent there is being able to enjoy the moment together at home with a video of the event. Parents and students will appreciate the effort the school has made to allow them to share these special times.

Loan the videos for a specified time or ask parents to provide a blank tape to the school for a copy that they can keep. Do not loan the original. Keep originals in a permanent file to provide a visual history of school events. Excerpts from the videos may be used in other promotional videos.

Collaborating to maximize your marketing effort

Collaboration is an organized effort that benefits all participants both individually and as a whole. Through collaboration, schools can maximize their resources, enhance their marketing efforts, and yet remain competitive.

Magnet schools can jointly promote the excellence of magnet programs and the advantages that specialized classes provide to students after graduation, whether in the workplace or in a university. Generally, these schools do not compete for the same students. A magnet school for the fine arts is not likely to lure away a student who is interested in engineering. Collaborating on promotional materials such as brochures, videos, and presentations can maximize their resources.

Elementary, middle, and high schools in the same feeder patterns can market their schools as a continuum of excellence through shared programs and activities. A common logo, slogan, colors, and mission allows for consistency in the look and content of promotional materials.

All the schools in a district can work together to promote the excellence of their schools and the district's benefits to the community. The district may conduct a branding initiative through a collective marketing effort that includes and benefits all schools.

A bookmark can do more than mark a book

Use bookmarks to promote reading, the school, and school supporters (Fig. 8. Hand out the bookmarks at the beginning of school when textbooks are issued. Give a supply of bookmarks to local bookstores and other businesses to hand out to customers. Pass them out at PTO meetings or at presentations to local groups. Distribute bookmarks to parents at the beginning of school.

This promotion vehicle can be virtually cost-free when you collaborate with local businesses to underwrite it. Use one side to promote learning and reading and the other side to acknowledge your sponsor or sponsors.

10 Ways to Help Your Child Learn
Provide a quiet study area for your child
Set aside a certain time each day for study
Look at your child's work and give positive feedback
Provide reference books and other supplies
Show an interest in what your child is learning
Take your child to the library, museum, zoo, etc.
Play games with your child
Meet your child's teacher
Limit television watching
Celebrate your child's accomplishments

10 Reasons to Read to Your Child
Your child will connect reading to a positive experience
You create a physical closeness
It increases your child's vocabulary
You introduce new subjects in an enjoyable way
It is a good way to teach values
It builds your child's imagination
It is a time your child has you to him/herself
It helps your child learn to read
The illustrations encourage creativity
You might learn something

**10 Reasons
to
Read to Your Child**

1. Your child connects reading to a positive experience

2. You create a physical closeness

3. It increases your child's vocabulary

4. You introduce new subjects in an enjoyable way

5. It's a good way to teach values

6. It builds your child's imagination

7. It's a time your child has you to him/herself

8. It helps your child learn to read

9. The illustrations encourage creativity

10. You might learn something

Lincoln Middle School

147 Elm Avenue
Hunter, Texas 78109

These Lincoln Middle School PAL

(Partners Allied for Learning)

Encourage parents to

READ TO YOUR CHILD

Bookworm Books

Young Readers Books

Emily's Used Books

Twice-read Books

Greens Stationery

Best Office Supply

Lincoln MS PTO

Riverview Public Library

Food Basket Supermarket

Reading is to the mind what exercise is to the body.

Joseph Addison

Lincoln Middle School

147 Elm Avenue
Hunter, Texas 78109

Fig. 8

Spend some time at the mall

Set up a table at a local mall on a Saturday afternoon for 2–3 hours or at a local grocery store after work hours, 5:30 p.m. to 7 p.m. to distribute information about your school, meet parents, sign-up volunteers, and find potential business partners. This activity is an effective way to get out of the office and promote your school on a personal level.

Set up a table and staff the table with an administrative person (principal, assistant principal or business manager) and a teacher or volunteer. Put a school banner on the front of the table and set a poster on an easel to identify your school. Have materials such as brochures, newsletters, information about volunteer programs and volunteer forms, announcements about upcoming events, and PTO materials available. Bring business cards.

Use an inexpensive give-away (pencils, coasters, bumper stickers) as a way to make initial contact. Do not get involved in lengthy discussions or complaints about specific students, programs, or issues. Instead, invite the individual to set up a meeting with the appropriate person at the school. Keep your presence upbeat and positive.

Remember that *everyone is in marketing*

Rude or indifferent employees can undermine the best planned and executed marketing strategies. It is important that employees understand that everyone plays a role in making the school's marketing effort a success.

There are a number of ways to make employees aware of their part in the marketing effort.

• Keep them informed via memos or reports at regular meetings about marketing activities, special visitors coming to the school, new partners, or upcoming promotions.

• Enlist their ideas and suggestions.

• Make them ambassadors of the school within their own communities. What they say to family, friends, and neighbors has an impact on how the school is perceived. People will often look to them for the "real story" rather than school administrators.

- Get them involved on some of the "fun" activities involved in marketing, not just the mundane tasks.

- Ensure that they receive credit when a marketing project or initiative is successful.

If the school culture is toxic, detox

As stated earlier, we define culture by the beliefs, values, practices, rituals, and stories that reflect and influence the way we think and behave. Organizations, like individuals have cultures and the people in them conduct themselves within a framework of behavior that reflects the organization's cultural beliefs.

As an organization, a school has a culture. If the culture is positive, the environment is conducive to learning, teaching, and serving the needs of the students, the employees, the parents, and the community. Although there is no one best culture, some of the characteristics that would reflect a positive school culture would be a willingness to improve and grow individually and collectively through change, a commitment to service, a collaborative approach to problem solving and decision making, a respect for and a recognition of achievement, and courtesy toward and respect for others.

Because an organization's culture is so essential to its success or failure, it is important that schools assess their culture and make changes accordingly. If the marketing team has completed an assessment as described in Chapter 2, an examination of the school's strengths and weaknesses can help define its present culture.

Ask each member to write down five adjectives or short phrases that describe the school. The descriptions may be positive or negative. Who are the role models at the school? What criteria define something as "good"? What are the reoccurring ceremonies and rituals at the school? What do they symbolize? How would the team describe them? Obligatory? Fun? Boring? Stressful? Ask employees and students to participate in a similar exercise. Compare the results. What cultural characteristics become evident? If the team feels it needs more assistance in defining the culture, information on culture surveys and books on the subject are available on the Internet.

Next, define the kind of culture the school wants to have and cultivate it. What aspects of the present culture contribute to the desired culture? What aspects detract from the desired culture?

If a desired cultural characteristic is *innovative,* what is the school presently doing to instill, encourage, and celebrate innovation? What aspects in the present culture hinder or discourage innovation? What can be done to change those aspects? Begin to shape the new culture through daily words and actions. Celebrate examples of innovation. Recognize innovative thinking and action through stories in the school newsletter. Put up posters with quotes related to creative or original thinking. Provide books, videos, and training that help staff members develop an innovative perspective.

It is important to remember that cultures do not develop quickly; therefore, they will not transform quickly. Some individuals will resist change. Do not try to change too many aspects of the school's culture at once. Changing a culture, especially one that is deeply embedded, will require persistence, focus, and time.

How's your customer service?

Do you know how you would be treated if you were a visitor or caller to your school? Are you sure? I have called the offices of schools and districts that prided themselves on the quality of their schools only to experience appalling customer service. Remember, few people will call you to complain, but they will complain to others or move on to where they feel more welcome.

Front line staff members, who have the first and most frequent contact with visitors or callers, are critical to how your school is perceived. It is important that all school personnel understand that customer service is an essential part of marketing and that they are key people in delivering customer service.

Make excellence in customer service a priority at your school. Periodically check the level of customer service through surveys or "testers" who call or visit the school to evaluate the level of service. It is vital to set high standards and communicate to all staff members how important they are to meeting those standards.

Do not assume that an employee knows how to provide excellent service because it seems like commonsense to you. Employees may be following examples they have observed in fellow workers. It is difficult for new employees to make changes even when they know the situation in not customer friendly.

You cannot expect employees to meet expectations if they do not know what the expectations are and how to meet them. Create a handbook that clearly states correct procedure for answering the telephone, taking messages, greeting visitors, dealing with parents, and students, and interacting with fellow employees. You may choose to reinforce the importance of customer service by providing employees with training. Training is a non-accusatory approach to setting standards and expectations.

24-hour response time for telephone calls or E-mails

A response policy of 24 hours for administrators and staff members expresses that the school values communication with the community. Without a response policy, a tendency exists for communication avoidance. Ask employees to set aside a couple of times during the day to return calls and E-mails. A response, even if it is only to let the person know that the message was received, is important. A response indicates that the school is making an effort to resolve the issues, find the answers to questions, and provide the requested information. If you know that someone else can respond better to a call, pass on the information with the request for a 24-hour response. Chapter 5 on electronic communication has suggestions for improving the quality and timeliness of communication.

Dealing with difficult people diplomatically

As an undergraduate student, I worked as the front desk supervisor in a hotel that was very proud of its service to guests. As a supervisor, dealing with guest complaints was my responsibility. In my three years at the hotel, I earned the equivalent of a master's degree if not a doctorate in dealing with difficult people. I found the following strategy to be particularly effective when dealing with unhappy or angry people.

- **Do not take it personally.** Generally, the first reaction to an unhappy or angry person is to feel as if we personally are under attack. The person is upset because of a situation—something happened or did not happen. The situation is the issue not you personally. It is surprising how efficient and professional you can be when you disassociate your feelings from the situation. It is difficult at first, but keep reminding yourself throughout the interaction, "This is not about me, unless I let it become about me."

- **Do not make excuses**. People do not want to hear excuses; they want to hear that someone cares about what has happened, appreciates their feelings, and will do what can be done to resolve the issue.

- **Listen**. The first thing an upset person wants is for someone to listen. Listening not only gives you information but also time to understand the situation. Ask questions to determine if there is a single issue or if other issues are involved.

  A parent may say she is upset because her child did not make the debate team. As you listen, watch for non-verbal clues such as body language. Does the person seem angry or worried? By asking questions, you find out that her underlying concern is that her child seems to have lost interest in school and become withdrawn. Her anger is a result of her concern.

  Sometimes a person just wants to express his feelings. He may have placed several calls to the school and received no response. His initial issue may have been minor, but now he is really upset because he perceives the school is unresponsive.

  Take notes to ensure that details are not forgotten or misinterpreted later. Clarify any points that you do not understand or that seem unusual.

- **Express understanding**. I have found that acknowledging a person's feelings and expressing a desire to improve the situation will quickly ease most emotional interactions. People often work themselves into an emotional state, but don't know how to work themselves out of it. You can help tone down a volatile situation by expressing an understanding for the person's feelings. Saying, "I can see that you are concerned about this" or "I understand why this would upset you," validates the person's feelings and acknowledges that an issue exists that needs to be addressed.

- **Allow time for private discussion**. If the person is creating an uncomfortable emotional scene in the school office, invite him into your office. This limits the tirade's effect on others and shows that you consider the situation important enough for your personal attention. Offer coffee, water, or a soft drink. If possible sit in an adjacent chair rather than behind your desk. Ask office staff members not to interrupt you. Then listen.

- **Aim for some initial agreement.** If a person has expressed what action she wants taken, tell her what you are prepared to do and see if you can reach an agreement. If you cannot meet her requests, explain why. The goal is to achieve some kind of agreement at the time, even if it is just agreeing on what the next step should be. Be specific about what you will do. For example, "As a first step, I will speak with the debate coach, Mr. Williams, today about the selection process for the debate team and about Mary's participation. Then either Mr. Williams or I will call you. Is that acceptable?" The parent now knows what will happen and when.

- **Focus on the issue.** People who are angry often use the occasion to bring up other unrelated grievances. Focus on resolving the issue at hand and suggest discussing other matters later.

- **Follow through.** All diplomacy is negated if nothing is done to follow through on assurances. If you have assigned school staff members tasks to resolve the issue, follow up to see that they have completed them. Keep in touch with the aggrieved person until the issue is resolved.

Goodwill begins at school

Public relations is not exclusively external. Successful marketing requires effective relationship management with internal groups too. Sometimes administrators spend so much time building and nurturing relationships with external audiences they forget about one of the greatest assets or liabilities right under their noses—school employees.

Employees talk. They talk to each other, to their neighbors, their families, people in organizations to which they belong, and to people coming to or calling the school. The community may or may not believe all that they hear or read from media sources; but they likely will give credence to what they hear from someone within the school. If employees are unhappy or poorly informed, they can hinder your marketing efforts. Conversely, employees can be goodwill ambassadors who are one of the school's greatest strengths.

To ensure positive interaction with your external groups, it is important to improve the interaction among internal groups of the school. Employees and students are more likely to be friendly and helpful to external groups if a respectful, courteous, and helpful atmosphere exists internally. It is essential that school employees are treated with the same courtesy and respect that is demanded of them. It is the responsibility of the top administrators to establish the proper environment. Require and demonstrate the same principles of courtesy among internal groups as you would with external ones. Below are some suggestion that can help foster good will.

Do not allow staff members to be used as scapegoats. Not only is using staff members as scapegoats demoralizing, but it also allows people to abdicate responsibility by blaming others. When that happens, accountability is lost. If an administrator or teacher is allowed to blame the office staff members because he failed to return a parent's phone call or missed a meeting, the practice will become prevalent and responsibility meaningless.

It becomes difficult for front office employees to work with parents and others if they are constantly seen as incompetent or unhelpful because they have been blamed for others mistakes. Equally important as not blaming people for what they did not do, is recognizing them for what they do.

Recognize employees for their work. Recognizing employees is advice that many people give and not enough follow. Educators above all should be aware of the importance of recognition. Recognition can be a simple "Thank you for your efforts," a formal certificate of appreciation, or "Employee of the Month" with a special perquisite.

Employee of the Month should not become a popularity contest. Use it to recognize real dedication or special efforts. Above all, do not allow individuals to take credit for other people's work. Often people do this under the guise of, "We are all working together for the greater good", usually spouted by the person who is taking the credit. If an accomplishment was a team effort, recognize the entire team, not just the team leader. To foster creativity, innovation, and achievement, give credit where it is due.

Recognize people publicly for their work through announcements at meetings, articles in the school newsletter, an Employee Honor Role poster on an easel at the entrance to the school, or special award pin. Acknowledge the service of long-term employees and recognize their contributions in the annual report or marketing communication as an example of the quality of school personnel. Students can wear ribbons that express their appreciation for efforts of school employees. "Thank you for being here every day", "We ♥ our School Staff Members" or "You R Appreciated". Recognize employees on your school marquis. For outstanding efforts, get district-wide recognition.

Recognize custodians, cafeteria workers, and crossing guards who are sometimes overlooked in the daily routine of the school even though they play an important role in its successful operation. Students should be aware of how these employees make their school a good place to learn. Thank them with a standing ovation at a school assembly. Invite them to all school events. Provide recognition in the newsletter, "Lincoln Middle School is proud of its dedicated employees. Mr. Jones, our custodian, has been with the school for over 10 years. This year during the terrible January snowstorm, Mr. Jones worked long hours to keep our school secure and warm. Thank you Mr. Jones."

The dedication of long-term employees speaks well of your school and its environment. Be visibly proud of what such dedication says about the school.

Have a full staff meeting at least once a year. All employees need to feel that they are a part of the school's past, present, and future success. At least once a year, hold a meeting that includes everyone, office personnel, food service workers, teachers, custodians, and volunteers. Have breakfast or lunch catered. Make it a special occasion.

Review the past year, recognize outstanding work, share plans for the future, and look at the school's opportunities and obstacles. The meeting is an opportunity not only to provide information, but also to listen to employees. Ask for employee input. Employees often see and hear things that those in the central office do not. Encourage them to be the eyes and ears of the school.

If you think that employees may be reluctant to speak, pass out large index cards and ask them to write their comments and questions anonymously. Provide a box, away from the front of the room, where employees can drop their cards.

The objective is to let employees know that they are essential to the organization, and, therefore, contribute to its achievements. This is a good opportunity to remind them that they too are a part of the marketing effort.

Inform employees *first* about issues, changes, or events, that affect them directly. Whether the news is good or bad, all employees deserve to know when things are happening that affect them; and they deserve to know before others outside the organization. It is demoralizing when those outside the organization seem to know more than those inside the organization. This is especially true when the news is not good. The ill will can be devastating to your school internally and externally. Relatively minor issues can become major ones when rumors and hearsay are the main forms of communication. Give employees related details and background information so they can have an understanding of the entire situation.

When news is positive, employees can be your best "cheerleaders". Share good news in a way that makes all employees feel proud. Encourage them to share the good news with their friends, family, and neighbors.

A bulletin, "What is Happening in Our School This Week", that informs about daily happenings and a monthly employee newsletter on larger issues will keep everyone informed.

Employees can be your best supporters in difficult situations. Much good work to build positive perceptions of the school is undone when the need for employees to be informed is not considered.

Extend small expressions of appreciation everyday. Something as simple as using people's names when talking with them can make a difference in how they feel. Make a list of small gestures that express the value you put on employees' efforts and check frequently to ensure that you are matching actions with words. Below are some suggestions.

• Remember staff members' birthdays with a card

• Give each employee a nameplate for her or his desk

• Make copies of articles you find that are related to their jobs

• Provide employee training

• Order in pizza for everyone

• Give staff members a plant for their desks

• Make popcorn one afternoon

• Provide personalized note pads

• Introduce staff members to business partners and VIPs who visit

• Know something about their families and ask about them

The "Butterfly Effect"

In the 1960's, Edward Lorenz, an MIT meteorologist, working on chaos theory, made a stunning announcement. Lorenz proposed that the effects of a group of butterflies flapping their wings in Brazil could spawn tornadoes in Texas. The idea is that small causes can have dramatic, far-reaching effects. The idea of Lorenz's postulation has application in a number of ways. Through observation, we can see the Butterfly Effect at work everyday when small things, positive and negative, trigger much larger events.

Neglecting to say "thank you" or "good job" or failing to recognize that someone put in special effort may seem like a small fault in the big scheme of running the school. However, when these oversights are sufficient in number and occur over a period of time, they can profoundly affect employee morale. The loss of quality employees, poor customer service, and work place errors that result from low employee morale can have dramatic far-reaching effects that extend into the community and influence people's perceptions of the school for some time. Likewise, small gestures that create high employee morale can produce far-reaching dramatic, positive results.

If morale begins to slip or the level of efficiency drops, don't always look for the big issues, it may be something small.

Making a good first impression

A visit may be the first, and only, impression someone has of the school. Providing school tours is an opportunity to make the first impression a good one. Tour guides can be staff members, volunteers, even students, but they need to be prepared to give knowledgeable, well-organized, consistent tours of the school. It is important that a person's interest in the school not be met with insufficient information, well-intentioned hype, or someone's personal issues. Give school guides the information and training to represent themselves and the school favorably.

At a minimum, a tour should include information that visitors are likely to want such as school ranking, test scores, class sizes, special programs, teacher qualifications, etc., a brief history of the school, and the school's plans. You do not want a canned speech so give your guides key talking points and a route, then let them add to it with their own experiences and personalities. Ask each guide to take one member of the marketing team on a practice tour.

Have prepared folders of materials visitors can take with them. Don't forget younger students who accompany their parents on the visit. Have a special packet for them with pages to color or word puzzles that are relative to the school. Include information about extra-curricular activities that may of interest to older students such as sports or arts. Be sure to address student interests during the tour.

To prevent work or class interruptions, have designated days and times for tours from which visitors can choose. Above all the visitors should leave with a feeling that your school is proud of its accomplishments and eager to welcome visitors.

VIPS

Volunteers in schools are important not only because they give labor and expertise to the school, but also because they are beneficial links with the community. Volunteers can be goodwill ambassadors outside the school environment. Too often this valuable resource is lost due to lack of appreciation and disorganization.

School volunteers have told me that they worked in a school for months before office staff members remembered their names. Other volunteers have told of showing up to work with a class only to find out that the class had gone on a field trip. No one had called the volunteers to cancel or reschedule. Who would want to continue to donate time, if no one appreciates it?

Below are some ways that the school and district can show appreciation for the contribution that volunteers make.

- Have an attractive name badge on a neck ribbon for each volunteer.

- Take new volunteers around the school, not only to acquaint them with the school, but also to acquaint the school with them.

- Occasionally have a mid-morning or afternoon meeting with volunteers to chat with them about their experiences, solicit suggestions, or find out what is going on in the community.

- Designate a week for special recognition of volunteers' work.

- Put pictures of volunteers on display in the hallways.

- Invite them to school functions.

- Have something meaningful for them to do.

- Send them thank you notes from the children.

- Have district-wide recognition of volunteer work with a special luncheon. Ask principals to submit candidates for a Volunteer of the Year award and announce the winner at the luncheon.

- Feature the volunteers and their work on the school Web site. Include photographs of them working with the students and teachers.

- Provide volunteer parking spaces if you can.

- Get media coverage of special projects with volunteers.

- Most of all smile and welcome volunteers each time they come to volunteer.

Volunteering is two-way

Volunteering works two ways. When school staff members and students go out into the community as volunteers, they are creating an image of the school as a contributor not just a receiver of services. A group of school volunteers, outfitted in t-shirts with the school logo, helping to clean up a local park or helping to paint the house of an elderly person shows that the school sees itself as a part of the community. Involving students in community service goes a long way towards dispelling any negative perceptions local residents may have of them.

Contact local civic or government organizations for information on volunteer opportunities. Provide a list of volunteer opportunities to individual students and to student organizations. Give the volunteers a group name that connects to the school. Work with a school partner to provide special volunteer t-shirts. Once employees and students are involved keep them motivated with recognition of their efforts through articles in the school newsletter and local media. Include pictures of volunteer activities on the school Web site and in the school's annual report and brochures.

Place mats as promotion

Schools report that often there are small, individually owned businesses in the community that would like to support the school, but their resources limit what they can do. Creating placemats that can be used or sold in local businesses is one way to include these willing partners in a school promotion.

Ask students to create artwork in a uniform size that would make a good place mat. On each piece of artwork, include the name of the student, grade, and the teacher's name. The artwork can relate to particular school achievements or programs, for example, artwork depicting what students learned in the school's new science program or during a summer reading series or a particular event or time. Work with a local print shop to laminate the artwork to use as place mats. Be sure to recognize any contribution of materials and labor on the place mats.

Ask restaurants in the neighborhood to use the place mats for a week or a month. Announce the event and provide a list of participating restaurants in the school newsletter to acknowledge their participation and direct customers to them. Local stores can sell them or the placemats can be sold at school or community events in which the school participates as a fund-raiser.

Making sure everyone gets the picture

Disposable cameras have an expiration date. Ask a local store to donate cameras reaching their expiration date to a class or grade level. Recruit a local photographer or a teacher of photography from a nearby college to make a presentation to the students on how to take good pictures. If having a guest presentation is not possible, get some photography books from the local library and make them available to the students for a week or two before the project starts.

Students then have a specified time to take pictures on a particular theme, e.g. my family, my school, my neighborhood, or a class outing. To hold down costs, students can mat their own photographs.

Exhibit the photographs at multiple locations such as banks, the local library, bookstores, and the school so that each child can have at least one photograph on display. Promote the exhibition through the school newsletter, local newspaper, and communication pieces of the participating organizations. Be sure to recognize the store that donated the cameras.

Making your appreciation public

Good relations with your local newspaper can provide the school with ways to recognize the organizations and businesses that help it. Recognition may be in the form of a letter on the op-ed page with excerpts from students' letters or a special announcement thanking school supporters. Another option is to insert a special page in the end-of-school newsletter with a montage of students' letters thanking supporters. Send extra copies of publications to your supporters so that they may display or distribute them as well.

Be entertaining

Do not limit your student performances to singing Christmas carols in the bank lobby. Use every opportunity to get the talents of your students known in the community. Take inventory of the performance possibilities your students can offer then let local businesses and organizations know about them. Student bands, string quartets, jazz groups, dance ensembles, or choirs can perform at business openings, civic club lunches or dinners, conferences, or community celebrations.

Unless individuals have children in school or volunteer at your school, they probably have little contact with your students. When people have the opportunity to interact with or even observe the students, their involvement becomes more personal. Contact with your students may encourage people to become involved with your school or at the least have a more favorable impression.

Putting hold time to good use

None of us likes to be put on hold; but, it happens. Personally, if I must be put on hold, I would rather listen to classical music, some good jazz, or even new product information than that annoying announcement, "Thank you for waiting. Your call is important to us. Someone will be with you shortly." It is particularly annoying when I have heard it for the fifth or sixth time. If my call is so important, then why isn't someone responding to it.

Try not to make callers to your school wait too long or too often. When it is necessary, utilize the hold time to promote the businesses and organizations that support your school. For example: *Hi, my name is James. I am a student at Lincoln Middle School. All of us in the 6th grade would like to thank SeismaTech Inc. a Lincoln Middle School PAL, for sponsoring our trip to see the new gem and mineral collection at the Museum of Natural Science. Seeing the real thing made our science class even more interesting. Thank you SeismaTech, a Lincoln Middle School PAL.* You can also use hold time to promote school events and recognize student or teacher achievements.

Cost free consulting

Individuals outside your school can provide a different point of view, much needed expertise, and community connections that will maximize your marketing efforts. Even if someone can participate only on an occasional basis, the contribution can be significant.

Look among parents, community partners, and volunteers for people with skills and expertise in marketing, public relations, advertising, graphic design or other services to help with the school's marketing efforts. Individuals with marketing, public relations, advertising, or technical expertise can provide valuable counseling and services. Retired business people have a wealth of knowledge they can share. Members of marketing related organizations may agree to serve as part-time consultants.

As people become involved, they offer access to a larger pool of talent. If an individual cannot help, maybe she knows someone who can. Ask external partners if they know someone from a company or organization who would volunteer some time. If there are universities or art institutes in your area, check with the art, communication, or marketing departments. Graduate students may be willing to accept a project or internship for little or no money. Solicit help through an article about the marketing effort in the school newsletter or even a neighborhood paper.

Set up communication channels so that all external individuals involved in a project know and communicate with each other and the marketing team. Marketing team members should feel that volunteers are there to help them not take over the project. Conversely, volunteers want to feel that they are a part of the team, not just doing assigned tasks.

Including a member from an important demographic or ethnic group within your community can benefit communication and outreach initiatives. If older people make up a significant portion of the community, try to recruit a retired individual who is active in the community as a volunteer consultant.

Be considerate of the volunteers' time. They are there to serve as advisors, not to do the team's work.

Set out the welcome mat for community groups

Making school facilities available for community meetings, evening classes, or sports activities is a way to acquaint local residents with your school and to express a willingness to reach out to all members of the community. It is also a good way to show off the schools achievements.

Allowing classrooms to be used for meetings or classes provides an opportunity to display the school's level of learning and teaching to those who may not otherwise be aware of it. Set up displays of student projects and accomplishments where visitors can see them. Have information about the school readily available.

Check with the district's legal staff to ensure that the school is protected from any liability. Provide groups who wish to use school facilities with district rules and regulations, release of liability forms, and activity restrictions in written form and have them sign any required forms before allowing use of school property.

Good friends to have

Realtors, developers, and apartment complex managers can be some of the best friends a school has. Equally, the school can be a good friend to them. Good schools are one reason why people move into a certain area. Get to know the realtors and builders in your area, have them visit the school, and include them in partner activities.

- Provide realtors and developers with school brochures to include in their sales materials.

- Offer school tours to prospective buyers.

- Put homebuyers names and addresses in the marketing database.

- Ask realty companies, developers, and apartment complexes to put a link to the school's Web site on their Web sites.

- Invite realtors to make presentations such as "Buying Your First Home" or "Selling in a Buyers Market" at the school for parents.

- Ask apartment complexes to include school information in their tenants' move-in packets.

- Send notices of school events to apartments complexes for posting on a community bulletin board.

In addition to student related information, include in the information packet details about volunteer programs, adult classes, and sports and other events that may be of interest to retirees and single tenants.

Recognizing special dates

Special education dates (National Teachers Day and American Education Week) are occasions for community partners to recognize, in a public and supportive way, the contributions of public education and the dedication and accomplishments of teachers. Partners can put posters or exhibits in their businesses, write articles for the local papers in support of public education, and put a "thank you" to teachers on a marquis.

Retail partners (stores, movie theaters, car washes, etc) can give teachers a special discount on National Teachers Day. Promotions of this kind benefit businesses by bringing in new customers and creating loyalty among existing ones.

A daily reminder

Collaborate with business partners to produce a school calendar. Businesses that traditionally give out calendars such as banks, auto dealers, insurance agencies, and printing companies are likely partners. Do not forget local photographic studios, they are a natural partner for this type of promotion.

Sell your partners on the idea by suggesting that calendars with pictures of local school students and activities may be more appealing to customers, especially parents, than the usual pictures of scenery and small animals. The calendar promotes the school within the community and serves as a daily reminder that the business is a school supporter.

The calendar can have a composite of school pictures or a theme such as fine arts activities or new programs in the school. The quality and composition of pictures should be of professional quality. Make sure that photographs taken for inclusion comply with production specifications for high quality images. And, as with all photographs of students, obtain parents' consent.

Night school

Classes at night or on the weekend are a way to reach community residents who do not have children in school. When they come for classes, the people in the community are developing an association with the school.

Parents and community residents of limited English proficiency are often reluctant to participate in or even visit the school because they feel unable to communicate effectively. Offering classes in English is a good way to engage them with the school. Language classes provide a more comfortable environment for parents to interact with teachers and staff members. As parents become more comfortable coming to the school, they may participate more in other activities that include their children.

Individuals within the community may be willing to provide classes on cooking or exercise for a small participant fee if the school provides the classrooms. The school's business partners may offer classes as a way to promote themselves. A local nursery provides a class on gardening tips, a computer store offers tips on buying hardware and software, and a hardware store advises on repair and improvement projects. A local medical center or hospital may provide classes or information seminars on health-related issues. A real estate company can provide a seminar on how to buy or sell a home and the bank can guide participants through the loan process.

Making the most of community events

Community fairs, holiday events, and parades are occasions for the school to interact with many different groups within the community. Events are opportunities to meet people who are not likely to know about the school other than through the media or neighbors. Set up an information booth at community events, march in the Forth of July parade or have a school float for the neighborhood parade.

The school can join with other schools in the area to organize a community-wide fair that showcases the schools and local school supporters. This is also an occasion to highlight how partners' contributions are making a difference at the school. Your partners will love this kind of public recognition.

The ideas in this chapter can go a long way towards establishing good internal and external relations. Good relations with employees, parents, and the community can make your job much easier as an administrator. Incorporate as many as possible into the marketing initiative. Ask other schools what they are doing to improve public relations. Share ideas with them. Look on the Internet for ideas. Many of these ideas require little effort but the rewards can be great.

Summary

The environment is which schools function will continue to change. Demands for higher standards, greater competition from alternative forms of education, increased need for community support, and challenges in recruiting high quality personnel require that schools and districts have the methods, materials, and mindset to be aware of and meet the needs, wants, and expectations of their internal and external stakeholders. An organized marketing effort will help schools accomplish that.

As stated in the beginning of this book, many schools are already marketing, whether they call it that or not. Often what they lack is a strategy to maximize their efforts. I hope this book will assist schools is initiating, implementing, and maintaining an effective marketing plan that will mutually benefit themselves and their communities and thereby enhance the learning experience for all students.

Citations

1. Drucker, peter F. *The Essential Drucker: The Best of Sixty Years of Peter Drucker's Essential Writings on Management*

2. *Whatever Happened to Cabbage Patch Dolls?* Collectdolls.about.com

3. Beckwith, Harry. *Selling the Invisible*: A field guide to modern marketing.

4. Revenues and Expenditures for Public Elementary and Secondary Education: School Year 2001–02, National Center for Education Statistics, www nces.ed.gov.

5. School Enrollment 2000, Population Profile of the United States:2000 (Internet Release), U.S. Census Bureau.

6. *A Nation at Risk*. April 1983. ed.gov/pubs/natatrisk/index.html

7. Farkas, Steve. *What People Really Think About the Education Press, 1997* publicagenda.org

Suggested Books and Web sites

Books

Beckwith, H. *Selling the Invisible*. New York, New York, Warner Books, Inc., 1997.

Parker, R. *Looking Good in Print*. Scottsdale, Arizona, The Coriolis Group, Inc., 1998.

Williams, R. *The Non-Designers Design Book*. Berkley, California, Peachpit Press, 1994.

Anderson, K. and Zemke, R. *Delivering Knock Your Socks Off Service*. New York, New York, American Management Association, 1998.

Web sites

www.nspra.org—National School Public Relations Association is dedicated to improving schools' internal and external communication

www.marketingschools.net—the Centre for Marketing Schools in Australia offers ideas for school marketing that are applicable anywhere

www.knowthis.com—provides articles and information on the basics of marketing for the private sector, but much can be applied to school marketing

www.subscription.corbis.com—offers high quality images and PowerPoint templates www.jupiterimages.com—offers several sources for high quality imagery

www.relatrix.com—provides online systems to improve communication with constituencies.

About the Author

Since I will be guiding you through the marketing process, you may want to know something about me. I have over fifteen years of experience in marketing and pubic relations in a variety of businesses that run the gamut from regional director for a public relations firm that represented resort conference centers to director of marketing for an investment firm that specialized in oil and gas securities. What I came to realize is that no matter what the industry, the underlying marketing principles are the same.

In my present position as Manager of Marketing and Client Relations in the Office of Marketing and Business Development at the Houston Independent School District, I have had the opportunity to apply those principles to our own marketing efforts and to develop marketing workshops for schools. To date I have presented the *Marketing Your School* and the *Building Beneficial Partnerships* workshops to hundreds of school administrators. *How to Market Your School* is a response to requests from workshop participants for a book that would provide a quick, accessible reference for school marketing information.

My academic career includes a Bachelor of Arts in languages and a Master of Arts in communication. As an undergraduate student, I had the opportunity to study in Mexico, Spain, Germany, and England. My experiences in other countries made me acutely aware of the importance of recognizing, understanding, and respecting the differences that exist between groups while utilizing the commonalities to mutual advantage. Through my professional and academic experiences, I have become convinced that knowing your various audiences and being able to communicate with a valid knowledge of *their* expectations is key to successful marketing.

978-0-595-36133-5
0-595-36133-1

27/2 Gift

Printed in the United States
39416LVS00004B/34-51